WW

7+

THE PECULIARITIES OF THE BRITISH ECONOMY

The Peculiarities of the British Economy

Ben Fine
and
Laurence Harris

LAWRENCE AND WISHART
London

Lawrence and Wishart Limited
39 Museum Street
London WC1A 1LQ

First published 1985

Photoset in North Wales by
Derek Doyle & Associates, Mold, Clwyd
Printed in Great Britain by
Oxford University Press

Contents

Preface 7

1 The Peculiarities of the British Economy 9

I Multinational Corporations and Finance

2 The City, the State and Economic Policy 55
3 Multinational Corporations and the British
Economy 81
4 Banks and Industry in the UK: The 'Blocking
Thesis' 122

II State and Industry

5 The Nationalised Industries (*with Kathy O'Donnell*) 147
6 Coal After Nationalisation (*with Kathy O'Donnell
and Martha Prevezer*) 167
7 Nuclear Power 203
8 Arms, the State and the Economy 236

III Specific Sectors

9 The Car Industry 257
10 Electronics 275
11 Coal Before Nationalisation (*with Kathy O'Donnell
and Martha Prevezer*) 285

IV Conclusion

12 Past, Present and Future: The Alternative
Economic Strategy 323

Index 341

Preface

This book represents the results of work done over a number of years, much of it in collaboration in research and writing with others. Those involved are far too numerous to mention except as far as the final writing is concerned. Nevertheless, our debt to all concerned is heavy.

Whilst Ben Fine and Laurence Harris have discussed all of the work, only the introduction and conclusion were written jointly. Ben Fine is responsible for the chapters on multinationals, nuclear power and electronics; Laurence Harris for those on banks, the City, automobiles and the arms industry. The chapter on nationalised industries was written by Ben Fine and Kathy O'Donnell and those on the coal industry by them with Martha Prevezer.

Putting together a book such as this takes time – during which events occur or new materials become available. We have resisted the temptation to revise continually existing chapters. Thus, some are more up to date than others, reflecting both the times of writing and the pace of relevant change, but this should not prove a drawback. For, whilst the book draws heavily on immediate, empirical developments, it does so by setting them within a longer term framework of analysis which, we believe, remains valid.

We are grateful to Iris Manzi, Ann Boomer, Jane Maurice and others for their contributions to the technical side of the book's gestation. The chapters on banks and industry and on the role of the City owe much to Laurence Harris's collaboration with Jerry Coakley and other members of the Open University Financial Studies Research Group, to whom we are grateful for comments. The chapter on the arms industry owes much to discussion with Dave Wield. We have discussed several of this book's ideas and the issues involved with Marjorie Mayo, Elizabeth Wilson and Angela Weir in the context of writing *Class Politics*.

During the course of our work, we have each individually been in receipt of a number of research grants variously funded by the SSRC (now ESRC), Leverhulme Trust, Nuffield Foundation, Central Research Fund of the University of London, and the Open University Research Committee to whom we are grateful.

Chapter 1

The Peculiarities of the British Economy

For more then two centuries the British economy has held a peculiar place in the development of world capitalism. This period has seen it rise to become the 'workshop of the world' on whose Empire the sun never set, and then decline to the position of 'sick man of Europe'. The use of such clichéd images, to represent the British predicament has been powerfully reinforced by the events of the last decade. The crisis of world capitalism in the 1970s, has been followed by a phase of faltering growth, but the British economy has scarcely shared in the limited expansions that have occurred. The economy, particularly industrial production, has stagnated and suffered further relative decline. The 1970s have witnessed a turn-around in the economic ideology surrounding the question of the British economy. Previously, in circumstances of definite if relatively low growth, the problem was perceived predominantly in terms of short-term macro-economic management; it was seen as a question of the right interest rate, exchange rate, level of spending or rate of wage increase. Subsequently the shattered complacency concerning the very possibility of growth has directed attention towards the longer-term characteristics of the British economy and society. This has been especially true of the Thatcher governments whose monetarism encapsulates a strategy to pare the extent and variety of state economic interventions whilst 'reforming' the system of industrial relations.

Discussion of the long-term problems has not completely crowded out the question of immediate economic policy, but a significant shift in public debate has been engineered switching attention away from the failures of politicians, rulers and business, and towards the forces which, working over a century or more, have culminated in the dislocation and decline of recent years – or, at least, the forces which are supposed to have done so. Our thesis in this book is that the widely held view of these forces, shared to a remarkable extent by right and left, is wrong. It is wrong for two reasons. First, the widely-accepted causes of decline (such as the strength of trade unions) do not stand up to careful examination; second, the factors leading up to the present problems have not unfolded as inexorable trends like an automaton, but have been marked by turning points, shifts and changes. Above all, those turning points have meant that political and economic choices have had to be made; those choices and strategies bear as much responsibility for the present as do the more structural historical forces.[1]

Consideration of the British crisis, at least in its economic aspects, therefore has to set the problems and influence of the capitalist world against the factors and strategies that have been special to Britain; Britain's peculiarity. Equally the immediate severity of Britain's problems needs to be seen in relation to longterm influences and their shifts and turning points, internal as well as external factors – both sets of influences are related. The twentieth-century transformation of the world economy has its counterpart in the internal organisation of the British economy. The rise of multinational corporations, the transformation of technology, the interpenetration of trade and finance within the advanced capitalist world, the extension of state economic intervention and the emergence of supernational institutions with economic power, such as the IMF and EEC, imply that the structure of the British economy and society has also been radically transformed. It is relative decline in the light of these transformations that has to be explored in any diagnosis of the British economy.

The alternative type of explanation is all too common. It sees the British economy as a victim of its own success as the first industrial capitalist nation. With this was created a state, an alliance of ruling classes, an unprofessional management system, a rigid trade unionism, or a financial interest that has dictated decline. Paradoxically, it is argued that such debilitating features have become fixed parameters remaining immune to developments that have nevertheless rendered the fabric of capitalism almost unrecognisable over a hundred or two hundred years. In our view the weakness of the British economy was not laid down like an old wine in the seventeeth, eighteenth or nineteenth century with the following years witnessing this weakness being brought to maturity as if the vintage were a bad one and the wine soured. We try to examine the transformations in British capitalism and to discover why these have been relatively unsuccessful for it rather than to deny that they have occurred at all.

In all capitalist economies there is an inherent drive to accumulate, to reinvest profits, expand the capital base and install new technology. It is never a smooth process, for it is pushed forward by competition between capitalists and conflicts embracing capitalist and workers. The outcome is never guaranteed and always implies unevenness in capitalism's development. Competition and class conflict wipe out some firms and can weaken whole industries but strengthen others' profitability and growth. Which sections of the economy suffer relative decline and which grow depends upon which have the most limited potential for reorganisation. Thus, in trying to explain the weakness of British industry in relation to capitalist industry elsewhere (and the decline of some sections relative to others within Britain) we examine the weaknesses and peculiarities of the agencies which have held a special position for promoting or hindering reorganisation. This approach differs from those, whom we shall criticise in detail later, who emphasise the automatic and blanket effects of international competition and class struggle, seeing them as inevitably leading to British industry's decline; there was nothing inevitable about this decline.

Industrial capital itself, financial capital (the City) and the state are the agencies which have, at least potentially, held the power to push reorganisation through. The outcome has been the result of their interaction with each other and with the labour movement in the context of a changing world. The conflict between labour and capital has been the ever-present motor of change, but the character of the changes in Britain has been shaped by the peculiarities of industry, finance, and the state.

The transformations that were at issue at the turning points of the British economy have never been purely economic. The Thatcher governments' attempts to curtail civil liberties, militarise the police, and centralise and stiffen state authority are an example of the political changes that are on the agenda at times of fracturing; another example is provided by Ramsay MacDonald and the National Government in 1931. In addition to political, industrial, and financial strategies, social policies – broadly the construction and dismantling of the welfare state – are always on the agenda at such times. Our central thesis is that the agencies in Britain for reorganisation are distorted and weak in all areas – they were too fragmented in the 1970s, for example, to reconstruct a welfare state appropriate to a rational modern capitalism – but we concentrate on the economic.

The problem has not been a failure of will on the part of entrepreneurs, financiers or the state bureaucracy, although this frequently appears to be the most immediate problem. Rather, the failure is a consequence of the peculiar configuration of relations in which the British labour movement confronts an increasingly internationalised system of production (through multinational corporations) and of finance (through the City). We organise our discussion around the roles played by labour, industry and finance, but we consider the connections between these elements in their totality to be crucial. It is invalid to isolate any one element as the origin of the British predicament, but it is equally inappropriate to list the elements separately and imagine their effects can be added together to provide, cumulatively, an explanation. Instead, we argue that the relationships between the three are complex so that they sometimes contradict and at others reinforce each other, and, in any case, develop historically. Thus, in exploring the anatomy of the British economy, we examine the manner in which the antagonisms and complementarities between labour, industry and finance have developed and have had an impact upon accumulation. Because the state is a crucial factor of cohesion in capitalist society, it is at the centre of these contradictions and its policies form a crystal through which these contradictions can be viewed.

Our general approach of examining relations between labour, industry, finance and the state is of wider relevance than for a study of Britain alone. For example, the modern development of Japanese capitalism is based upon an integrated relation between finance and industry, co-ordinated state policy for industry and a peculiar form of labour relations in giant corporations and small sub-contractors. German capitalism has thrived upon the close relation between finance and industry, but has relied less upon state industrial policy, although the latter has been significant nonetheless.

But, although relations between labour, industry, finance and the state have shaped capitalist development in other countries, we are mainly concerned with British capitalism alone without comparing it to other countries (except for illustration). We avoid using the comparative method because it tends to embrace the notion that there is some ideal model of capitalist development. For example, it is commonly argued that Britain has failed because it is not like Germany (especially lacking the German system of industrial relations), not like Japan (lacking that country's work ethic and management system), or – in the Chicago view of Milton and Rose Friedman – not like Hong Kong. Such ideal models serve a political purpose for the ruling classes, but they have no analytic value. They involve taking an abstract concept of particular features of the 'ideal' country, separating them from the complex historical circumstances in which they have developed and assuming that they could, in principle, have been adopted in similar form in Britain. Our perspective on the peculiarities of the British economy recognises the cultural and social circumstances in which they have developed.

We begin, in this chapter, by reviewing some of the evidence, both theoretical and empirical, concerning the decline of the British economy. The next section concerns the state and its weakness in adopting coherent industrial strategies. From there we examine the symptoms of decline and the special roles played by labour, and finance. In each of these areas we put forward arguments which contrast sharply with those of right-wing economic commentators. But our arguments also differ markedly from the views of many left-wing and Marxist economists. Our main contentions are:

(a) Instead of industry being stifled by an interventionist state, industrial capital has been weakened by governments' continued failure to intervene systematically in production and investment.

(b) Industry's backwardness and the state's industrial timidity both partly result from weaknesses in British trade unionism; too little militancy rather than too much.

(c) They also result from the peculiar character of Britain's financial system, the special role of the City; but it is wrong to see this in terms of the City starving industry of finance or directly controlling the state.

(d) Industry's own unusual characteristic is that multinational corporations have an exceptionally strong presence and this conditions industry's interaction with the state, labour, and finance.

State Economic Intervention

Britain's special weakness in the world economy has often seemed to turn on the question of the state. Margaret Thatcher's government in 1979 opened its first major economic statement with the view that 'public expenditure is at the heart of Britain's economic difficulties'. The explanation given by Sir Keith Joseph spread the blame on wider government activities than just spending: 'governments have over-taxed, over-spent, over-borrowed, over-rescued, over-regulated, and over-manned'.[2] But the New Right is not novel in putting the state at the centre of the question of Britain's economic performance. Since the beginnings of capitalism in Britain, the economic role of the state and its power to strengthen or weaken accumulation has been an object of struggle between the different fractions of the bourgeoisie and their party representatives. The class struggles have concerned issues such as the regulation of the hours of labour (the nineteenth-century Factory Acts), the regulation of foreign trade (the debates over free trade, from the Corn Laws, through imperial preference, to current struggles over import controls), the exchange rate, nationalisation, and government spending on welfare services and elsewhere. Even though the Second World War and the 1944 White Paper on employment policy marked the establishment of a state based upon Keynesian principles of economic management, the state's responsibility for underwriting and guiding accumulation has continued to be the object of struggle since the war. Attlee's government combined nationalisation and the socialisation of welfare services with the dismantling, under Wilson's Board of Trade, of the wartime mechanisms for intervention; the campaign promise on which the Tories were elected in 1951 was to make a bonfire of controls and to weaken the state's role; and Heath's victory in 1970 was again based upon the crude anti-state perspective of *homo oeconomicus*, or in modern English, of Selsdon Man. The New Right may be novel in some respects, but it is engaged in old struggles.

Since the British state in the post-war period has been incomparably more interventionist than in earlier stages, and since it is frequently compared with American and West German states which are taken to be both non-interventionist and at the opposite pole from the British, the British state does not appear to be deficient in the *extent* of its economic intervention but in its *character*. While the state has taken an important role in the economy it is one which has, in important respects, encouraged the preservation of old structures of economic relations instead of guiding the modernisation of capital, or stimulating a type of industrial accumulation that would enable capitalist production in Britain to be founded on a high wage-high productivity basis. In modern capitalist economies states have acted through demand management and its monetary counterparts, intervention in struggles between labour and capital over the distribution of income between profits and wages, and intervention (or participation) in the direction of capitalist accumulation. Since the Second World War, the British state has been deficient in this last activity. Its powers have been directed toward managing aggregate demand and, time and again, to trying to shift the balance of the struggle over distribution towards profit and against the working class (through policies on incomes and taxation) but it has given inadequate attention to the more directive role of intervening in and guiding capitalist accumulation except on a piece-meal basis.[3]

It would be an error to assume that there was one right way that an omniscient technocrat could, decades ago, have laid down for the state to assist British capital, but it is possible to identify the weaknesses that have occurred. Demand management and intervention in distributional struggle have taken place against the background of a secular decline in the rate of profit experienced by British firms and a drastic restructuring of the international division of labour. The real profitability of British industrial and commercial companies (after tax) had fallen as low as 3 per cent by the end of the 1970s,[4] while throughout the post-war years 'economic miracles' were witnessed not only by the bourgeoisies of the old industrial powers like Germany and Japan, but also in the industries of Italy, Spain, Brazil, Taiwan, South Korea and a number of countries still grouped together somewhat uneasily as the 'Third World'. Clearly these were changes that demanded a response from Britain's industrial base; they called for changes in production both in terms of product design and, most importantly, in the *methods* of production. From the point of view of industrial capital in Britain it was necessary that production be restructured in order to create a high-productivity industrial sector that could compete for markets, yield profits and pay for a docile high-wage labour force. However, the state's concentration upon demand management and the holding back of wage demands has, in the neglect of intervention in industrial policy, been at the expense of such a strategy.[5] Both demand management and policies on distribution affect industrial restructuring, but their effects are ambiguous, and without strong state intervention industrial changes are even more precarious than they would otherwise be.

Demand management of a reflationary nature can, if it succeeds in promoting capitalist markets, sustain high employment for substantial periods by bolstering the profitability of inherently outdated industrial processes. It thereby undermines one stimulus to the restructuring of these processes, the classic capitalist stimulus of declining profits and slump. Recognition of this lay at the basis of the 1976 rejection of 'full employment' policies by Callaghan and Healey, and has been carried to an extreme by Thatcher. Equally, though, 'negative' phases of demand management which weaken profitability through deflation (such as the periods of 'stop' which occurred with balance of payments crises in the 1960s) appear to have been an inadequate stimulus to industrial restructuring in the absence of planning and a coherent industrial policy. In their monetarist forms, such as the cuts of 1976, they assisted in achieving the necessary destruction of capital without providing the conditions for its restructuring.

Similarly, the attempts to use incomes policy, taxation, and other measures to boost profitability at the expense of living standards caused British workers to fall behind, for example, their German counterparts from the early 1960s, but it did not facilitate industrial restructuring.[6] On the one hand, it failed actually to increase the rate and mass of profitability that firms needed to underwrite their industrial investment; on the other, the inability of capital and the state to envisage any solution to falling profitability except for wages policies, tax concessions on profits and concomitant reductions in the 'social wage' financed from taxation has meant that the state has been ineffective in guiding the industrial restructuring that could have improved productivity conditions.

The consequence of this combination of policies has been that the British state has been prominent in the workings of the capitalist economy; as implied in the characterisation of our age as 'state monopoly capitalist', the state's actions have ensured that the coercive force of the market has not had free play.[7] However, that has meant that the classic forces behind a dynamic accumulation of productive capital have been weakened and fragmented while the state has not succeeded in filling the space and imposing rationality and direction upon accumulation. This equivocal position is, as much as anything else, 'the British disease'; it is the classic compromise of British liberalism's mixed economy.

Of course, it is not true that the state has simply vacated the field of industrial intervention; new dawns have been pronounced at regular intervals, but in each case they have been reversed or weakened in political conflicts. The institutional structure for intervention has been constructed and reconstructed several times since the war. The post-war nationalisations were the first prominent actions and the struggles over them dominated the question of intervention through the 1950s. The construction of the National Economic Development Office (NEDO) came as a pale imitation of French planning at the end of the Tories' 'thirteen wasted years'. It was followed by the abortive 1965 attempt to construct a 'National Plan' and by the more successful attempt, through the Industrial Reorganisation Corporation (IRC), to fund and guide the creation of monopolies (such as GEC) to rationalise major industries. The early 1970s witnessed new nationalisations, such as those of British Leyland, Rolls Royce and Ferranti, into which the state was forced when its liberal ideology was confronted by industrial bankruptcies, but where it took responsibility for restructuring the enterprises rather than feather-bedding lame ducks. These nationalisations were accompanied by government financing of private rationalisation schemes and were followed by the establishment of the National Enterprise Board (NEB) and the strengthening of training schemes under the Manpower Services Commission.[8]   However, just listing these attempts to construct the mechanisms of state intervention makes clear how circumscribed and problematic they have been. Whereas the 'National Plan' with its promise of almost 4 per cent growth each year from 1964 to 1970 was stillborn, the Industrial Reorganisation Corporation, despite having had some successes in constructing profitable industrial giants after its 1966 establishment, was killed off by the 1970 Tory government's hostility to intervention. The idea of the National Enterprise Board and the institution of compulsory planning agreements held out to the labour movement of the 1970s the prospect for some marginal state intervention. The outcome, however, was that the NEB was established as a financial holding company, weaker than any private investment bank, so that the companies it owned were not nationalised in any substantial sense, and serious compulsory planning agreements were deleted from the agenda. Moreover, the great industries nationalised after the war have been bedevilled by attempts to limit government intervention and to allow production and accumulation to proceed in the manner of private enterprises as far as possible. With this record, the Thatcher governments' huge privatisation programme was hardly a new departure in the 1980s; instead of being a sharp break with the past, marking the success of a new political force, Thatcherism, it was the culmination of the British state's long abdication from the real planning of production and accumulation even in the nationalised industries.

New Technology

Thus the state's role in the economy has not involved the construction of a strong interventionist system for the direction and guidance of industry. This peculiarity is at the centre of Britain's post-war failure to develop a high-wage, high-productivity industrial sector. The effects can be seen in industry after industry; it is reflected not only in the problems of old 'staple' industries such as steel and shipbuilding, but also in the failure to establish a productive base in new industries.[9]

The failure of the state to meet strategic needs of the electronics industries, and particularly the information technology industry, was noted and criticised by the National Economic Development Office (NEDO). Its views, such as the following, have a much wider applicability than to electronics alone:

> The firms ... expect government involvement in drawing up the options and will respond positively to government leadership in making the final choices and coordinating and implementing policies. The EDC believe that successive governments have been inhibited from doing this because the UK, compared to her major competitors, is peculiarly deficient in mechanisms which ensure government and industry are responsive to a common perception of changing markets and technologies.[10]

The NEDO strategy, however, goes even further, since it recognises that the implications of new technology stretch far beyond the privately organised economy. Government, after all, is a major consumer of its products. In the UK, its purchases account for 40 per cent of the information technology subsector and for much of electronic capital for military purposes. Government is also a major provider of research expenditure, spending £312 million in 1978, of which £148 million was designated to private industry (which itself provided £279 million); this accounted for 46 per cent of all government research funding to industry. Despite the relatively large resources devoted to research in electronics in the UK, it is inadequate when compared with other countries once account is taken of the proportion devoted to military uses. There is also provision to be made for the skills of the work-force. Although the number of people in the UK with computer-related skills was 275,000 in 1979/80, this was at least 25,000 too few. In radio communications, the West German-based company Siemens, trains as many engineers as in the UK altogether.

Taken together these factors suggest that a co-ordinated strategy is necessary to provide for the survival, let alone the prosperity, of the UK electronics sector. Integration within production and between production and marketing, research and development, training and financing are all necessary for success. Again, NEDO recognises this and calls for schemes to introduce the new technology into schools and other public and private organisations. The Thatcher government has intervened, but on an insufficient scale; 1982 was Information Technology Year with £1 million provided for publicity and £80 million made available over the following four years to encourage the use and development of new technology. It is sorely inadequate. As NEDO recognises in its guarded recommendations, for education in this instance, the electronics sector in the UK requires a degree of intervention and coordination that has been absent in the UK whether through state or private action:

> Breaking down such deep-rooted beliefs requires a long-term commitment from firms, unions and government. While the state and the industry may have different responsibilities they must be mutually reinforcing and respond rapidly to new market and technological opportunities. Neither the dividing line between responsibilities nor the onus of financial resourcing is entirely clearcut. More appropriate education and training can, however, go a considerable way towards assuring widespread participation in the potential benefits of technical change. It is important that change in the education and training systems occurs in conjunction with positive changes in social welfare provision since both components are necessary to enable the rapid adjustment to new technologies and markets required.[11]

In the absence of such a strategy, the prospects for the sector are already being illustrated by the fate of the British Telecommunications industry. The UK used to supply 20 per cent of the world market, but this has now slipped to 5 per cent; this contraction will limit the potential to diversify into communication and information peripherals. Moreover, the electronics industry does not have a balanced foundation; in Scotland, for example employment in the electronics industry is dominated by the role of satellite affiliates, particularly where non-UK companies are concerned.[12] Little research and development is undertaken and subsidies to the industry cannot be retained within the UK, given the international transfers which take place within MNCs. There is heavy reliance upon subcontracting and low wages which, because of the unequal position of women in the labour market, is achieved through employing large numbers of female workers at low pay.

De-industrialisation

The failure to establish a strong industrial base in the British economy after the Second World War has some clear parallels with the inter-war situation. For example, whereas the American cotton textile industry increased its productivity dramatically in the inter-war years (increasing from 52 per cent to 95 per cent between 1919 and 1939 the proportion of looms that were automated), Lancashire's productivity stagnated. However, the conditions of the post-war world were quite different, so that the explanation of industrial weakness cannot be sought in inevitable long-run senescence. The explanation of the post-war problem has to be sought partly in the factors specific to that era, and especially in the limitations imposed on the British state's economic role.

However, the analysis of that role cannot be a full or adequate study of the problem, for the state's economic position is inseparable from its political dimension, and each has significance only in the context of the class conflicts and the uneven development of capitalism that have shaped Britain's modern history. Before considering the class struggles that hold the front of the stage in the study of Britain, we discuss the relevance of capitalism's uneven development. Britain's position in it is, today, debated under the heading of de-industrialisation; is Britain's current economic travail a harbinger of the society's de-industrialisation, a far-reaching switch from industrial production to unemployment, the production of oil, the receipt of *rentier* income from foreign assets, and the sale of education, medical and a wide variety of consultancy services in a new international division of labour? Such a prospect is welcomed by some, but there is little evidence that this is the direction being taken by the British economy.[13]

The coincidence of the low rate of growth of manufacturing in the post-war UK economy and those industries' decreasing share in world exports of manufactured goods has led many to the conclusion that the industrial base of the country's activity has been shrinking in such a way that the British economy is deteriorating to a state where it will soon meet the rising stars of the underdeveloped world. The figures in the tables do, indeed, give a startling impression. The first is a league table of the advanced capitalist countries' performance in exporting manufactures.

Shares in the Value of World Exports of Manufactures
(percentages)

	1953	1974
Japan	3.8	14.5
West Germany	13.4	21.7
Italy	3.8	6.7
France	9.1	9.3
United States	26.2	17.2
United Kingdom	20.9	8.8

Source: C. Brown and T. Sheriff, 'De-industrialisation in the UK: Background Statistics', National Institute of Economic and Social Research, *Discussion Paper* no. 23.

The table below indicates the low rate of growth of manufacturing output in the UK compared with other advanced economies:

The figures do indicate that through the years of the post-war boom, manufacturing industry located in the UK expanded its output less rapidly than in other advanced capitalist countries and, concomitantly, experienced a dramatic decline in the proportion of international trade that it supplied.

Manufacturing Output 1955-73
Trend Growth Rate (per cent,
per year)

United Kingdom	3.1
United States	4.7
Japan	13.8
France	6.2
West Germany	6.0
Italy	7.3

Source: G. Brown and T. Sheriff, 'De-industrialisation: Background Paper' in F. Blackaby (ed.), *De-industrialisation*, London 1979.

These trends in manufacturing are connected with the relatively poor productivity of British manufacturing industry compared with that located elsewhere. It is dangerous to jump to quick conclusions about productivity performance, for to focus upon low productivity in the British economy does not of itself constitute an explanation of decline nor even necessarily suggest one. Even in its relationship to growth, the direction of causation is ambiguous. Low growth rates can be thought to delay economies of scale, innovation and the replacement of an ageing and obsolescent capital stock, or be caused by it.[14] The evidence for the relatively poor performance of the British economy's rate of growth of productivity is quite extensive, although the making of comparisons is fraught with difficulties. Does the data compare like with like and what methods of aggregation are to be used?[15] In disaggregated studies of particular industries the results are more ambiguous about Britain's relative position. Nevertheless, whether at an aggregate level or otherwise, the fact of the low productivity of British industry is undeniable. The level of productivity is both at a lower level than other advanced capitalist countries and tends to grow at a slower pace.[16] Pratten, on the basis of a survey of labour productivity at the British and overseas factories of international companies in 1972, concluded that on average it was 50 per cent higher in American companies, a third higher in Germany and over a quarter higher in France, although the averages conceal many instances in which UK productivity is as high if not higher than the international average.[17]

In another study, Dunning examines the performance of British and foreign multinational corporations from the point of view of locational and ownership advantages.[18] On the one hand, is the UK an advantageous location for investment? On the other hand, do UK-owned MNCs enjoy specific advantages in, for example, management, technology, etc? The distribution of locational and ownership advantages across countries and MNCs respectively is taken to determine where production is located under which country's MNCs. Whatever the merits of this scheme, it suggests empirically that the British economy is a relatively poor location for investment in manufacturing. Whilst the ratio of the UK outward to inward investment as a whole has fallen over the last twenty years, it has risen for manufacturing alone. UK-owned MNCs supply markets abroad by foreign-based affiliates rather than by exports, but foreign MNCs supply the British market by imports rather than by production located in Britain. In so far as the UK ownership advantages are to be faulted, it is for their specialisation in less technologically intensive industries as opposed to foreign firms in Britain which tend to be concentrated in the more dynamic and technologically advanced sectors.[19]

The distinction between more and less technologically intensive production is taken up by Stout in another way. He reports that

a one-ton 'basket' of German mechanical engineering exports was by 1976 worth about 60 per cent more than a representative ton of British exports, not the 12 per cent more they were worth in 1963 ... A French 'basket' from being 6 per cent dearer had become almost 30 per cent dearer than a British 'basket'.[20]

The conclusion to be drawn is that British exports are of relatively decreasing quality and sophistication.[21] This is a peculiarity of the British economy, as is its deteriorating trade performance, which can be observed in nine out of twelve industrial branches from 1970 to 1977 when import penetration accelerated even though Britain's share of world trade was held up by recession.[22] Stout does not, however, find any peculiarity in the sectoral composition of industrial production which might explain decline by a slow, non-dynamic shift of capital between sectors to those that are expanding and profitable and from those that are not. This is confirmed by Peacock's comparison of British and West German industry.[23]

It is phenomena such as these that have raised the spectre of de-industrialisation over Britain. This is a term that is more used than understood. It was first defined quite modestly by Ajit Singh as the relative shrinking of the manufacturing sector.[24] There is, however, nothing particularly unique about the British economy in this respect, so that within orthodox circles, and for Singh himself, de-industrialisation has to be measured against other indicators of economic performance such as balance of payments equilibrium, full employment and price stability.[25] So, whilst manufacturing employment dropped by 15 per cent between 1965 and 1975, at 31 per cent of total employment in 1975, the UK still had a higher proportion of manufacturing employment than most advanced capitalist countries. Over the same period most countries suffered a fall in the proportion of manufacturing employment, so that the experience of the British economy is more severe than some (although not all) particularly in the 1970s. It is not unique.

The Proportion of Manufacturing Employment in Total Employment

	1965	1975
United Kingdom	35.0	30.9
Japan	24.3	25.8
Italy	28.9	32.6
Belgium	33.9	30.1
France	28.3	27.9
West Germany	36.3	35.9
Netherlands	27.8	24.0
Sweden	32.4	28.0
United States	32.8	29.0

Source: Brown and Sheriff, 'De-industrialisation in the UK: Background Statistics'.

It is obvious that the notion of de-industrialisation does not itself explain the developments encapsulated in these data series; for the explanation we have to look to factors such as the state's role and the forces behind it. But it is also doubtful whether 'de-industrialisation' is satisfactory even as a descriptive label, for what appears to have been happening has not been a demolition of the industrial base and the transfer of manufacturing to the newly industrialising countries. Instead, the gap between the industrial activities of capital located in Britain and that located in countries such as Taiwan, South Korea, Brazil and India remains very large, and in Britain it retains its character as an integrated, structured system in comparison to the distorted industrialisation and social contradictions of the new competitors (a distortion that has often lent credence to the idea that theirs is purely 'dependent' industrialisation).

Britain's manufacturing has declined relative to those of other advanced capitalist countries. That has been the most sharply felt effect of the changing international division of labour, and the idea of de-industrialisation must refer to this for its conceptual content. All advanced capitalist countries have had to face competition in particular industries (such as steel, shipbuilding, textiles and electronics) from newly industrialising countries, but British industry's relative position among the advanced countries themselves has declined. In terms of the proportion of the labour force employed in manufacturing the decline is not unique, being comparable to that experienced in the USA, Netherlands, Belgium and Sweden; in terms of productivity and export performance, however, British industry's position has been unusually weak. These phenomena suggest that 'de-industrialisation' should be understood in the following sense. British industry has, in the post-war years, found a new position in the international division of labour; but rather than involving the demolition of industry it has increasingly taken on the role of a specialist in low-wage, low-productivity industries amongst the ensemble of advanced industrial capitalist economies. To the extent that 'de-industrialisation' implies prognosis and forecasting, the question posed is whether that role is sustainable or whether, on the contrary, industry, finding itself unable to exist profitably in that mode, will be forced to struggle for productivity levels comparable with those of other advanced countries and of the relatively non-unionised newly industrialising countries.

Multinational Corporations

The notion of de-industrialisation, like other categories used to discuss 'the British disease' has to be interpreted with care in order to avoid the false impression that the boundaries of the nation state define the principal object of enquiry. Our discussion has concerned industrial capital producing commodities in Britain, and it is necessary to distinguish that from 'British capital' or 'the British economy'. The reason is that the profits of much 'British capital', capital owned by multinational corporations constituted and controlled in Britain, are generated by productive, commercial or financial operations abroad. Similarly, much capital whose productive operations are located in Britain is owned and controlled by multinational corporations constituted abroad. Indeed, the UK has been second only to the US in the growth of MNCs whose production is on an international basis. In the early 1970s, US and UK nationals controlled more than 60 per cent of all affiliates of MNCs, and almost 75 per cent of the affiliates active in advanced capitalist economies. The growth of MNCs is a manifestation on an international scale of capital's propensity for concentration and centralisation and it goes hand in hand with the development of monopolies at home. In Britain the largest 100 firms now account for almost half of all manufacturing output compared with around 20 per cent between the wars; in many sectors three or four firms account for more than 50 per cent of output, such as cars, petrochemicals and flour-milling.

The British and American experience of its domestic centralisation of capital being accompanied by 'its' MNCs developing production abroad, differs from that of Germany and Japan. In those countries, capitals have grown into monopolies at home without, until recently, expanding foreign plants and affiliates to any significant extent. That differing pattern highlights the difficulties in interpreting statistics and conceptualising the national economy under state monopoly capitalism where production is internationalised by MNCs. Consider, for example, the earlier table's indications that West Germany and Japan have increased their shares of world trade in manufacture while those of the US and UK have declined. What this reflects in part is that while US and UK capital have increased their production facilities abroad, German and Japanese capital have, broadly speaking, expanded their international penetration in a different way, manufacturing at home and selling their commodities abroad. It means that such figures cannot be easily interpreted as 'a weakness of British capital', for British capital is international, but they are pertinent to the problems of productive capital located and operated in Britain. They raise, for example, the question of whether the outward drive of British capital has resulted from factors such as low domestic productivity caused by labour militancy or has, instead, contributed to low productivity by channelling funds abroad. That type of question is considered later in this chapter where we examine the roles of labour and the City respectively.

The internationalisation of British capital also causes difficulty for the conceptualisation of the state and state monopoly capitalism.[26] The considerations we have expressed above on the role of the British state have concentrated upon its position in domestic economic activities, but because of the predominance of British capital's internationalisation that position is combined with the state's activity in respect of the world economy. Policies with respect to the EEC, the International Monetary Fund, tariffs and protection and other international mechanisms have been central to the construction of British capital's modern world role, and these have been pursued while at home governments have attempted to act, to affect the conditions of domestic accumulation. For domestic accumulation occurs within the framework of social reproduction which is primarily organised on a national basis: a national culture, national politics, national structures of education, welfare and family relations, and within all these, as well as domestic accumulation itself, the British state has had to act.

The state's role in social reproduction and its position in domestic accumulation has been deeply conditioned by its international role; it has determined some of the parameters within which the forces of the class struggle have shaped the British state. The commitment given by governments at crucial conjunctures to furthering the internationalisation of capital, adopting the perspective of MNCs and international banking is part of the explanation for the domestic economy's weakness. It accounts in a measure for the fact that the state has taken responsibility for demand management and for intervening in the balance between wages and profits, while failing to secure a strong role in industrial planning and direct intervention in accumulation. Indeed, the notion of a 'British economy' as a unit of analysis, producing, trading and financing with the rest of the world – as if it were an individual on a global High Street – is profoundly erroneous and has been the source of much analytical and strategic mystification. This is particularly so for the traditional methods of macro-economic management. The 'unity' of Britain lies not so much in its constituting an economy as in the more general structure of class relations that it embodies. We investigate these by turning to the issue of labour militancy.

The Question of Labour Militancy

Identifying the role of the state as central to the problem of weak capitalist accumulation in Britain must lead Marxists to question the nature of the class struggle in which this has occurred, considering both its political and economic dimensions. The assessment of that struggle, however, cannot simply be 'read' from the outcome for the state's weakness is compatible with several different 'parallelograms of forces': it could coexist with or even ensue from a chronic instability and crisis in the political balance between labour and capital (as in Italy and in France for the first post-war decade), from the existence of a strong anti-interventionist fraction of capital or from the existence of various labour movement strategies. In Britain, it is, in part, the outcome of the *weakness* of the labour movement, weakness on both the political and narrowly economic fronts. The movement's well-known failure to develop a strong socialist political strategy and the consequent ease with which non-interventionist policies have been won by the right has been accompanied by economic struggles (for higher wages and for influence over the labour process) which have had ambiguous results. They have not succeeded in pushing up real wages, for the worker in British industry is the lowest paid in advanced capitalism, and they have not succeeded in obtaining a sound 'social wage' since Britain's welfare state has failed to maintain the high relative position it held in its early years. If we are to avoid considering the question of the 'weakness of the state' from the point of view of an ideal type – what would a rational, successful, interventionist state in the interests of industrial capital have been and which factors prevented it emerging? – we have to examine the political and economic strategies of the labour movement. We have to analyse the conditions the labour movement has created for the state's growth and changes as well as its direct impact on industry.

Here we concentrate on the direct effect of trade unionism in industry, but, first, let us note the weakness of trade unions at the political level. Fleet Street's highly partisan judgement, which it never tires of repeating, is that trade unions through their block votes in the party conference and electoral college, their money, their sponsored MPs, and their personal friendships, have too much political power in the Labour Party. But in fact there has not been a strong labour movement influence on state economic policy.

While unions in several sectors have argued for a state plan for their sector or planned management of the economy, they have not secured this even under Labour governments. The rail unions have not succeeded in obtaining a planned development of transport. The energy unions have failed to obtain a planned energy strategy; the closest they have come to it has been *Plan for Coal*, relating to coal alone, and, as the 1984-85 strike testified, even the miners' strength has not been sufficient to protect that position. Following the Attlee government's nationalisations the trade unions, at the height of their power, were unable to ensure either that those industries were run as 'commanding heights' or key elements in a plan for development or that trade unions had a role in running them. And, in the 1970s when the Labour Party advertised the value of its collaborative relationship with the unions, the unions were unable to force the Labour government to keep its part of the 'Social Contract': while the unions swallowed an incomes policy the government did not deliver the promised expansion of the welfare state.

If the state's failure to lead a planned development of British industry partly results from the political weakness of trade unions, the backwardness of Britain's industry partly reflects their economic weakness. Unions do have a long history of militancy over wages and production itself, but it has been a fragmented and partial militancy and has not made the gains for workers that an outsider, noting the size of British unionism, would expect. In failing to achieve those gains for workers it has also failed to exert the pressure that would have forced industrial capital to modernise and grow.

Unions' relative weakness in industry during the long post-war boom materialised in their concentration on defensive actions. Actions for wage increases were, time and again, sectional attempts to maintain one group of workers' position relative to others rather than to raise the general level of wages relative to profits. When general wage offensives did occur they were defensive reactions to price increases.

The consequence of this weakness is that British workers, although highly unionised, have not secured high real wages but, instead, are amongst the lowest paid in the developed capitalist world. If unions had been strong they would have obtained high wages which, in turn, would have been accompanied by modernisation and high productivity. Employers would have been forced by high wages to invest in new machinery, plant and methods of production in order to compensate for wage rises with productivity rises.

The idea that union strength is to blame for industrial backwardness is so ingrained that the opposite is worth emphasising. Successful union pressure for high wages would have helped to push industry into modernisation.

Of course, this virtuous circle may have been prevented by a shortage of finance for investment if wage increases had eroded profits. But, as we argue below and in subsequent chapters, industry has not been starved of finance for there was no shortage of credit. It may equally have been prevented by complacency on the part of management. Such a failing could have been overcome by state leadership, but, as we have argued, that was absent. It could also have been overcome by a strong union push for influence over production and investment decisions, but, again, the weakness of the labour movement prevented it from gaining any power over such decisions. Unions were forced into a position where their influence over production could only be defensive and reactive, taking the form, for example, of unofficial strikes over demarcation to protect craft skills from changes in production methods over which they had no say.

Our view that industry's weakness results partly from trade unions' lack of militancy contrasts with the conventional wisdom of both right and left-wing writers. Marxist economists have echoed the right's analysis that high union militancy over wages and production methods have undermined industrial growth and modernisation.

For Glyn and Harrison the major factor in the relative decline of the British economy and in explaining the world recession as a whole is the developing labour shortage arising out of the post-war boom.[27] Britain had very little to draw upon in the way of reserves from agriculture in comparison with the rest of Europe and Japan, and this is reflected, for example, in the drawing of married women into the labour force. This argument is, however, difficult to accept in the light of more disaggregated statistics. In Britain, the absorption of married and part-time women into manufacturing has been a trend over the whole post-war period, even between 1966 and 1976 when 1.34 million jobs were being lost in manufacturing. Typically, however, whilst male full-time employment has been falling in manufacturing, part-time female employment has been rising in the public sector.[28] This is more evidence for a low-wage provision of state services than for a shortage of labour in manufacturing. If Glyn and Harrison are right, a relatively severe shortage of (male or female) labour in Britain would only have pushed down profitability by raising wages above the normal levels elsewhere. Yet the British worker has become not the poor but the poorest of the advanced capitalist world, with industry maintaining competitiveness only by compensating for low productivity by low wages.[29]

Far from the British economy being plagued by high wages, it is perhaps the reverse that is true. Glyn and Harrison's arguments concerning the labour movement's role in the relative decline of the economy ultimately rely upon the assumption that there has been a general labour shortage, and that assumption has been prominent in other analyses of the post-war boom.[30] However, given the depression of real wages, the evidence for such a shortage has yet to be presented and sceptics may point to the flexibility in the labour supply to particular sectors, arising from immigration in the boom years and by changes in women's participation rates, to throw doubt upon the labour shortage thesis.

The question of whether wages have been 'too high', 'too low' or 'just right' is, in some writings, central to the question of whether capital can be successfully restructured. The Cambridge Economic Policy Group, for example, adopted as a major plank the argument that incomes policies could establish a 'correct' level of real wages which, with reflation and trade controls, could facilitate industrial innovation and reorganisation. On the other hand, several Marxist analyses turn on the question of whether the struggles over the labour process have prevented high productivity capitalist accumulation. The argument that the British trade union movement is particularly structured to resist the reorganisation of work practices, and that this lies behind the relative decline of British productivity, is the counterpart to the view that the trade union movement has undermined profits by negotiating wages that are too high. Both arguments are a favourite theme of right-wing commentators. They have also been taken up by writers in the Marxist tradition, both for wages, as we have already seen, and for the reorganisation of the labour process; for the latter, an outstandingly clear account is given by Kilpatrick and Lawson.[31]

For Kilpatrick and Lawson, import controls, whether in conjunction with other forms of economic planning or not would do very little to improve the position of the British economy. The reason is that these policies do not attack what has been the central cause of Britain's economic decline, the long-standing ability of the trade union movement to negotiate, and consequently obstruct, the introduction of new work practices associated with the capitalist reorganisation of production. They argue that trade unionism was established earlier in Britain, prior to the general introduction of machinery, was heavily influenced organisationally by the decentralised, plant-by-plant, control of work practices associated with craft production and has been oriented toward obstructing innovation. Subsequently, the trade union movement has 'evolved' without the ruptures and defeats experienced elsewhere as a result of the rise of fascism or defeat in war. Consequently, it is as if both the nature and the effects of the British trade union movement have stood still over the past one hundred years.[32]

This account is questionable even if we ignore the sharp breaks marked by the 'new unionism' of the late nineteenth century and the heavy defeat of the movement as a whole following the General Strike of 1926.[33] The problem is that the competitive relation between capital and labour is over-simplified and ahistorically conceived. There is supposed to be a simple mechanism of work-place obstruction which is effective irrespective of the existence and weight of alternative pressures.

Suppose, for example, that there had been a highly decentralised trade union system with local control of work practices obstructing the introduction of new techniques, It could not have survived in the manner suggested by Kilpatrick and Lawson. Where, work-place by work-place, the resistance was strongest, those firms would be unprofitable and eliminated by competition. The mobility of capital and the local struggles without solidarity across work-place organisations would ensure that firms or whole industries decline. Trade unionism would tend to see its strength undermined and increasingly ineffective, the more it is based upon work-place organisation and as capital becomes mobile. This is, of course, precisely the sort of argument that is now being used about multinational corporations and their dividing of the work-force of different plants in different countries. But, in principle, it applies equally to different work-places within a country whether they are owned by a single company or not.

A possible response by trade unions, and one that would have to be analysed empirically, is for them to become more nationally organised as, indeed, has happened in the UK. Thus a decentralised system has not predominated in the way Kilpatrick and Lawson assume. To the extent that it has survived it would reflect a great weakness in the obstructive power of the working class rather than its strength at the expense of capital, for local control (as in some form of shop stewards' movement) without national co-ordination is vulnerable to mobile capital. Nor is the existence of national unions adequate to make effective the work-place resistance of the decentralised shop floor to the extent that this does exist. It depends upon the policies of the national union and the unity that it can command.

This means that the arguments put forward by Kilpatrick and Lawson must be treated with some care, and the mechanisms through which the forces which they identify operate should be fully spelt out in order to be able adequately to distinguish their effects. Even if it can be shown to exist, it cannot be presumed that shop-floor resistance alone suffices to explain a slow pace of change in new technology. This is very clearly brought out in an article by Tony Griffin.[34] By comparing the newspaper industries of London, New York and Sydney, he shows that the workers in London have maintained a degree of work-place control (and not simply obstruction) because of the co-existence of the following conditions – perishable commodity (daily newspaper), tied to a specific production location (London as centre of communication), solid union organisation, small number of unions involved, solidarity from other unions involved with the product (distribution). It is the uniqueness of these conditions that stands out relative to other sectors, where the equivalent underlying sources of strength for the immediate producers do not and cannot apply.

This is the light in which the historical material which Kilpatrick and Lawson present should be considered. In this area there is a problem, that general arguments are unconvincing whilst particular cases of workers' resistance holding up new work practices are self-selecting and, of necessity, unrepresentative.[35] They are, in any case, open to opposite interpretations – that workers' resistance is a response to the failure to innovate or to the conditions of accepting innovation rather than to innovation as such. Significantly, the most detailed research that is cited, Lazonick's study of cotton spinning from the mid-nineteenth century onwards,[36] specifically points to the combination of work-place and industry-wide organisation and the dominance of one section of the work-force over another in defending a privileged position. We really do have to question the extent to which this is relevant for or typical of the circumstances in the British economy today, even though its contribution to theoretical and historical questions is invaluable.[37]

The net result of the Kilpatrick and Lawson thesis is to propose a theory of combined and uneven development that has a single, simple property. Country by country, the level of capitalist development is inversely related to the extent of labour movement resistance to the reorganisation of capitalist production and the country-wide resistance is itself formed from its constituent parts at work-places. We have already criticised this approach from the point of view of the theory of competition that it contains, and its conclusions stand in sharp contrast to both the classic Marxist theory that class struggle is a positive force in the progressive development of (capitalist) production and the neo-classical theory that high wages induce increased mechanisation. Following Kilpatrick and Lawson, we would have to conclude that the more the working class struggles over production, the worse off it becomes. If only the British workers had been more compliant, they would now be enjoying work practices, investment per head and wage levels comparable to the West Germans (who would presumably be that little less worse off as unevenness is more evenly distributed to reflect the greater uniformity of class resistance). Empirically this sort of argument on the impact of wage militancy can easily be refuted, since the inverse relations between wage levels and levels of development simply does not exist for British or for other workers. For struggles over work practices there is no such simple empirical refutation of the idea that they are retrogressive, but there are implications of the analysis which do not seem to be borne out.

The first is that if workers' resistance, particularly on a decentralised basis, explained Britain's economic decline, then, where resistance was overcome, productivity should be relatively high. Overall, in so far as competition does not eliminate the capitals weakened by stronger workers' resistance, we would expect to find a wider range of productivity dispersal within sectors of the British economy compared with its competitors, in association with and explaining the lower average level of productivity. There seems to be little evidence on this question, but Stout's analysis seems to suggest that general (and widening) differences exist between British and other country's levels of productivity rather than *within* British industry.[38] Stout searches for potential sources of accelerated productivity growth in Britain in the context of 'catching-up' with elsewhere. In doing so, he brings forward the logical possibility of those who have fallen behind having the greatest potential for productivity increase. For our purposes, this raises a second empirical problem for the Kilpatrick and Lawson thesis. It is not clear why workers' resistance, as they understand it, should lead both to lower levels *and* growth rates of productivity for the British economy. As and when workers' resistance is broken, possibly after a delay, British industry should have been able to attain the productivity performance of other economies. Perhaps the lag structure and stability of productivity innovation would be different, but the trend should be much the same as for other countries (unless it is suggested that an unspecified vicious circle of self-supporting relative decline is entered).

Finally, the ability of the British workforce to defend its work practices is contradicted at the empirical level by the great extent to which it has indeed been subordinated to the forces of the market. The notion of de-industrialisation has forced upon our attention the loss of over two and a quarter million jobs in manufacturing since the mid-1960s, many of these in sectors which are traditionally seen as being the most strongly unionised. This is sharply demonstrated by the coal industry whose most militant union has witnessed low wages, high unemployment and revolutionised methods of production, as we shall see in later chapters.

Kilpatrick and Lawson do not, however, restrict their analysis of the British economy to its industrial relations. They also consider the competitive conditions in which the economy has operated. Here there is an ambiguity in their analysis, one which is repeated elsewhere particularly in popular expositions of the century-long decline of the British economy. It is that, prior to the Second World War, British capital was cushioned from foreign competition by protected markets for goods and finance particularly provided by the Empire. Consequently, there was little coercive pressure to innovate in the domestic economy. Conversely, it is suggested that after 1945 the fierce competition from foreign capital has increasingly undermined these protected as well as the domestic markets. But rather than exerting pressure to innovate, as suggested by the argument for the pre-war period, this time competition has merely served to send the British economy further into decline. If, whether competition is fierce or not, the British economy suffers decline, this suggests that competition is not a causative factor, that it has not been appropriately understood theoretically and that its effects cannot be considered ahistorically.

The City of London

The special problems of British industry, symptomised by de-industrialisation and the weakness of new technology, have to be seen in the context of industry's relation to financial capital as well as its relation to labour. The special position of the British state, making it non-progressive for industrial capital operating in this country, is often explained by its connections with and orientation to the City of London. The left and liberals have, throughout this century, frequently argued that one particular section of capital, the financial interest, has prevented the state from stimulating and furthering industrial growth while at the same time financial capital itself has not filled the gap and has failed industry.[39] That view is undoubtedly correct in a general sense, but many of the arguments and evidence that are brought in its support are wrong. To understand why the relation between state and industry has been so problematic, and why British industry has fared so much worse than elsewhere, a careful assessment of the role and character of the City is crucial.

There are two main planks to the, by now, orthodox left-wing analysis of the City. First, the financial bourgeoisie has formed an alliance with other fractions of the ruling class which ensures the state furthers their interests at the expense of industrial capital. One influential line in Marxist history is the thesis that the old landed classes formed an alliance with the financial bourgeoisie to retain state power in the early stages of capitalism and this alliance has shaped British history ever since. Another version of the alliance thesis emphasises the City's links with imperialism and the overseas investment and trade of sections of British capital; it argues that the two have constituted an 'overseas lobby' or 'sterling lobby' which, particularly in this century, has influenced the state in pursuit of its interests at the expense of British industry. The second plank is that the City has failed industry by failing to supply the finance required to ensure growth and modernisation. The argument is that the City has directed funds toward 'unproductive' uses, thereby creating a shortage of industrial finance, and the finance it has put into industry has been short-term instead of the long-term investment capital that was needed to finance innovation.

Each of the strands in the orthodox left-wing assessment of the City's role is flawed, although they both touch upon important elements of reality. There has not been a permanent alliance between finance and land or finance and internationalised capital squeezing industrial capital at home. And industry has not been, in the modern period, starved of finance for growth and modernisation. The City *has* blocked the development of state policies which are progressive for industrial capital, and it *has* itself failed to stimulate industrial growth, but the source of these vices is more complex than the orthodox line supposes.

The activities of the City fall into two categories, trading and financing,[40] but each has money and monetary assets as its object. Trading in bonds and shares (as stockbrokers do), in foreign exchange (banks and foreign exchange dealers), in insurance risks (Lloyds brokers) and similar financial categories is at the heart of the City's business; the ups and downs of 'the market' – whether it be the stock market, the foreign exchange market or another – dominate the City. And integrally linked to this trading is the City's other function, providing finance. Borrowing and lending, whether to industry, to other finance houses, to individuals or to states is what marks the City off, for trading alone would not distinguish it from other merchants. In the provision of finance, five types of City institutions predominate: banks, building societies, insurance companies, pension funds and investment- and unit-trusts. The differences between types of trading and financing makes it surprising that there could ever be a unified City 'interest', a policy voiced and pursued on behalf of the City as a whole. Yet there have been such policies and the City's interests have been pursued with a clarity that industry has never matched: while the organisations of industrial capital have been chronically fragmented and unable to provide industrial leadership throughout this century,[41] the overall interests of the City have been articulated and struggled for under the leadership of the Bank of England. The unity of the City at this level, despite the diversity and special interests of the institutions within it, results from there being one feature common to all its activities, the making of money out of money.

Profiting from dealing in money, and from borrowing and lending it, defines the City's character. It is the basis of its economic and political power and is at the root of its connection with the state; it explains the manner in which the financial system blocks the state from an active involvement in industry while eschewing any active involvement itself.

The drive toward making money out of money has given rise to a division of functions between the City on the one hand and industry on the other in providing the finance for industrial accumulation. The predominant source of funds for industrial investment has been industry itself; in comparison to other countries British industry has relied to an unusually large extent upon self-financing. In this century the banks have until recently concentrated their loans to industry on short-term financing and, to the extent that insurance companies, pension funds and trusts have related to industry, they have largely invested in stock market securities rather than lending directly to industry. This division of functions has not starved industry of funds but, on the contrary, has secured industry's financial needs in a way that has suited industrial management as well as the City.

The result has been twofold. Industry has not needed to turn to the state for finance (except in particular circumstances which, *in extremis*, have accompanied nationalisation) and there has therefore rarely been a liaison through which the state achieved the ability or need to intervene in management and stimulate accumulation. And the financial institutions themselves have not had to intervene in management; their arm's-length relationship has enabled them to concentrate on reaping profits from money while avoiding involvement with production. The bankers' maxim has been 'We leave industrial management to the people who know about it' and, when it comes to such things as innovation, investment, and the organisation of production, the state has been so uninvolved in industrial finance that even under the most interventionist governments it, too, has left management to the managers.

Origins of the Problem

The division of functions with industry looking after much of its own finance, the financial institutions satisfying industry's residual needs and otherwise concentrating on making money without industrial involvement, and the state being excluded from intervention, has not been paralleled in all advanced capitalist economies. Germany, for example, has been well known since the end of the last century for the degree of involvement of its banks in both the financing and direction of industry. There are three reasons for this division having arisen so strongly in its particular form in Britain: the strength of markets and trading in the City, the size of the state's debt, and the City's international position. Other factors such as the particular character of the concentration and centralisation of banking have worked within the framework of these three.

Markets and trading have always had a major role to play in the City. The stock market for trading in bonds and shares is the oldest stock market and the London markets for trading in other financial assets (including contracts for commodities) have been better developed than in any other country at least since the end of the eighteenth century. One implication, which Ingham has emphasised has been the strength of a specifically merchant-based interest (distinct from a financing interest) in the City's political formation.[42] Another, which is our concern here, is that financiers have escaped the necessity of being involved in the industry they finance.

Always inherent in money and finance under capitalism is a tendency toward maximum flexibility; financial capital always seeks to be independent of constraints and the banks and financiers that control it seek to obtain maximum profit with maximum liquidity. Investment in industry is always a threat to that, for if an industry runs into difficulties – if, for example, its profitable production is threatened by labour militancy – the financier can be locked in. In Britain, however, the strength, size and resilience of the financial market has meant that when industry does issue bonds or shares to finance investment, the lenders lend while not immobilising their capital. They have been able to buy bonds and shares in the knowledge that they can sell them on the market. Avoiding being locked in also means that lenders avoid having to become involved in the management of the firms. By contrast, when Germany's nineteenth-century industrialisation required finance there were not the same well developed markets to provide liquidity and permit the great flexibility that is financial capital's essence. In consequence, financiers there were necessarily involved in a long-term commitment to the firms they financed; in those circumstances finance could only develop on the basis of a strongly interventionist role. Financiers had to intervene in the industries they financed, they had to have an ownership and managerial stake to supervise their investment for there was little room for selling out on the market if the going started to get tough.

Another reason why the strength of markets and trading was so important in the development of British finance is that banks developed an orientation toward providing the short term financial needs of trade, rather than the long term committed money needed for industrial growth. But the banks' concentration on overdraft financing (which is characterised as short-term) in the twentieth century owes much to their own special history, one aspect of which is discussed in Chapter 3.

State debt is the second element that has shaped the City, moving it in different directions from other countries' financial systems. The City turns its face toward the British state just as sun-worshipping civilizations turned theirs toward the golden orb, for lending to the state is more vital to it than lending to industry. Again, the tendency of all finance and money to seek maximum flexibility and liquidity is what gives this factor special importance. Financiers can obtain the greatest flexibility if profits can be made on assets which are not tied up in the business of industry and commerce; the greater the distance from the operation of productive capital the more ideal is financial capital. The interest and redemption value of state debt is backed by the state's power of taxation and, as long as the state itself is stable, is therefore guaranteed in a way that money owed directly by private firms could not be. Lending to the state ranks higher than industrial finance in the calculations of bankers, and financiers everywhere operate in state loans to a high degree.

But the City has, historically, had a stronger orientation toward financing the British state than bankers' elsewhere have towards their respective governments. It is symbolic that the founding of the Bank of England in 1694 was a device for securing a state loan. The growth of the state's outstanding debt to the present has accelerated strongly in particular periods; the Second World War and the immediate post-war years generated an expansion that has had the greatest influence on the character of the 'long boom' and de-industrialisation. The British state financed its great war spending by several means: forced loans from India, other parts of the Empire and other sterling-using Third World countries; lend-lease from the USA; sales of overseas investments (forced upon Britain by American interests); taxation; compulsory loans to the state by ordinary people; and the raising of credit from the City. By the end of the war the City held a mass of government bonds and bills. The post-war nationalisation of coal, railways and other industries increased the volume, for the owners were recompensed with newly-issued government bonds. Thus, whereas the financial system in the United States had low stocks of American government bonds (especially medium and long term) until late in the 1950s, the City was able to operate and deal in a flourishing market in British government bonds while Japanese, West German, and French bankers were involved in the post-war reconstruction of industry.

The predominance of state debt in the City's operations significantly affected its relations with industry. Critics of state spending and socialist programmes argue that state borrowing starves private industry of funds and 'crowds out' its investment financing. There is no evidence that the City's orientation toward the state has had that effect; its importance is that it has enabled the City to carry forward its basic tendency, the distancing itself from involvement in the management and operation of industrial capital. State bonds yield secure profits with the maximum flexibility for they are traded with ease, and their volume and variety in London means that financiers can hold exactly the types they want. Because the City has historically made money from the British state on such terms, their lending to industry, too, has been on terms which give the greatest flexibility and, hence, the least involvement in industry's problems. In the abstract, the City could have reacted differently; the state's debt could have been a secure cushion on the basis of which the City's lending to industry could have been more involved, risky and less arm's-length than otherwise. But, given financial capital's basic tendency toward the greatest flexibility and independence, London's financiers used the availability of such terms on state bonds to impose the same terms on lending to industry; if industrial finance had required involvement in management, money had an alternative bolt-hole. The readiness with which the owners of mines, railways and other industries (except the most highly profitable such as steel) took state bonds for their industrial shares in the post-war nationalisations graphically illustrates the point.

City policies and ideology on state financing, however, have been two-edged and, as a result, have constructed and conformed with the exceptional role of financial capital in Britain. On the one hand, the City has welcomed and thrived on state borrowing because of the flexibility and independence from industrial capital this has given it. On the other, it has fought against the deficit spending that reformist governments would need to carry out in order to plan a rational restructuring of industrial capital. Thus the City has contributed toward blocking coherent state intervention in industry while at the same time itself being oriented toward state financing and avoiding involvement in industrial problems.

International orientation. The third aspect of financial capital in Britain, enabling it to follow the basic tendency of distancing itself from industrial capital in such a way that the role of finance in Britain has been quite different from elsewhere, is its international character. Finance everywhere seeks a world stage to minimise the risks that would arise if its profits stemmed from a narrow or purely local base, but the City has sought and achieved that international role in unique ways.

For much of the nineteenth century, London's bankers and financiers dominated international finance and the latter dominated their business; for example, international finance was the backbone of the London stock market for decades.[43] To some extent this resulted from and reflected the world leadership of Britain's industry, but the City's international importance has continued throughout this century even though Britain's industrial leadership did not.

The conditions the British state secured for financial capital underpinned its modern international role. From the late nineteenth century to the 1960s the Empire was the political framework within which the City's international role developed, maintaining its world predominance despite the relative decline of British industry. In this it marked a new stage in its independence from industry; the City's position as the centre of the investment flows and monetary mechanisms of the Empire and the Sterling Area, which, from the 1930s, was constructed around it, enabled the City to maintain a wider world role around this core.

The political arrangements that maintained the Empire and Sterling Area were the basis; the key to the system was that other countries' foreign exchange reserves were kept in sterling while state intervention to regulate exchange rates gave the stability this needed. When that broke down, the City, particularly London's banks, maintained their international lead with the aid of the state in different ways. From the 1960s the basis of the City's international role switched; instead of its centrality to the Sterling Area and Empire, the City's leading role in Eurodollar operations, multilateral borrowing and lending, became the basis of its world role.[44] The reason London rather than, say, New York became the centre of this new international credit system was that whereas United States banks were hedged round with restrictions and regulations, London banks were, as a matter of policy, less regulated than those in any other advanced capitalist country. In borrowing and re-lending foreign currencies, which was the essence of the new international system, the City had succeeded in ensuring that neither Tory nor Labour governments imposed restrictions.

Thus, the British financial system has consistently had a uniquely favourable framework for its international business and for carrying through the aim which financial capital everywhere seeks to achieve, deriving its profits from world-wide operations rather than tying them to a local basis in national industry. The City is predominantly international in the sense that, because it has taken full advantage of these opportunities, its whole business, including its financing of British industry, is marked by its international business. It is not that the City's overseas lending has starved industry of funds, but that its orientation toward the flexibility and independence from industry that its world role gave it meant that the industrial financing it did do had to be on a similar arm's length basis giving finance the maximum independence. Financial capital in France, Germany, Japan and other countries was not able to achieve such great independence. By comparison its outlets were restricted to industry in those nations, and bankers and financiers had to minimise their risks by involving themselves in the direction and rationalisation of industry rather than distancing themselves from it.

The importance of international business to London's bankers is indicated by their share in it. London accounted for 27 per cent of all international bank loans outstanding in September 1982, whereas its nearest rival, the US, accounted-for only 14.5 per cent (and only 9.3 per cent in 1980). Looking more directly at the significance of foreign business to UK banks, their international loans accounted for 75 per cent of their total lending in 1982.

It is significant that this represents the international business of banks operating in London rather than British owned banks. At the start of the 1980s there were some 400 branches and subsidiaries of foreign banks in London, accounting for a substantial proportion of the City's foreign business and they had made significant inroads into the domestic business of London's banks, especially the United States banks. The strength of foreign-owned banks in London is a measure of the extent to which the City, or financial capital in Britain, is internationalised.

Through its orientation toward markets, toward state credit, and toward international operations, financial capital in Britain has achieved an independence from industrial capital that financiers everywhere seek but rarely achieve as successfully as London's have over the years. As a result, the British financial system has not become involved with industry and has not acted as an external rationalising and disciplining force in the way it has elsewhere. But at the same time it has had a blocking role, preventing the state from playing such a role in its place.

The Peculiarities of the British Economy

The crisis of the 1970s and 80s affected all capitalist economies, Third World countries and even socialist economies. But British capitalism has, rightly, been seen as a special case, the advanced capitalist economy with the greatest contradictions, the most severe problems of accumulation. Its special position has resulted from the peculiarities of the British system. Industrial capital's weakness has related to the limited character of the labour movement (despite the size of trade union membership which has caused it to be seen as the world's strongest); to the role of the City, the multinational corporations and, in relation to all these, the absence of a rationalising impetus from the state.

In the following chapters we go into specific aspects of the British economy, detailing their history and current position to show how the state, City, multinationals and the labour movement have interacted in crucial areas.

In Section I (Chapters 2, 3, and 4) we focus on forces which have had a wide and pervasive influence on the state and industry. In Chapter 2 we examine the relationship between the City and the state which, although severely damaging to industry, cannot be reduced to the terms in which it is often seen. In Chapter 3 we set out the role of multinational corporations in the British economy, locating them in their global context, and in Chapter 4 we examine in depth the relation between finance (or one element, bank finance) and industry.

In Section II (Chapters 5, 6, 7 and 8) we direct attention to specific sectors which illustrate the state's role in production. Chapter 5 demonstrates how public ownership of the nationalised industries has not led to them being a leading sector in a planned industrial expansion although they could have been if different political choices had been made. Chapter 6 deals with the nationalised coal industry as an example of how public ownership of an industry can lead to great improvements in both efficiency and workers' welfare, in contrast to right-wing myths about the inherent backwardness of nationalised industries. Chapters 7 and 8, on nuclear power and the arms industry respectively, illustrate how the state and multinational corporations have interacted in sectors which, while to a large extent privately owned, rely heavily on the state for sales and the conditions of production (such as research and development, and design specifications).

In Section III (Chapters 9, 10 and 11) we detail some aspects of three industries that, while being influenced by the state, have not been as close to it as those in Section II. The car industry's fortunes in the 1970s and 80s illustrate the weakness of the state's intervention in forces loosed by multinational corporations (Chapter 9). The weakness of the electronics industry illustrates the failure of the state to plan adequately the growth of new sectors (Chapter 10). And the history of the coal industry before it was nationalised is one example showing the falsity of the view that workers' obstructiveness has been at the root of industrial weakness (Chapter 11).

In Chapter 12 we draw upon these analyses to argue that if the British economy is to be regenerated it requires strong direction through the state. The Alternative Economic Strategy is a socialist path out of the present dislocation. It envisages the state ensuring that democratic forces determine the economy's direction instead of multinationals and financiers with the free run of unregulated markets. The Alternative Economic Strategy has, however, been criticised from the left as well as the right and in that final chapter we discuss some of those criticisms.

Notes

[1] Significant contributions to understanding the British economy have recently been made amongst others by S. Aaronovitch, et al., *The Political Economy of British Capitalism*, Maidenhead, 1981, A. Glyn and J. Harrison, *The British Economic Disaster*, London, 1980, F. Blackaby (ed.), *De-industrialisation*, London, 1979, R. Caves and L. Krause, *Britain's Economic Performance*, Washington 1980.

[2] For a descriptive account of Thatcher's economic policies and her process of gaining political power, see W. Keegan *Mrs Thatcher's Economic Experiment*, Harmondsworth 1984.

[3] For a comparison of British industrial policy with that of its European rivals, see L. Hesselman, 'Trends in European Industrial Intervention', *Cambridge Journal of Economics*, June 1983, where it is the coherence rather than the extent of intervention in which Britain is seen to be weak.

[4] See *Bank of England Quarterly Bulletin*, June 1979.

[5] For the extent of use of incomes policy in Britain in the post-war period, see, for example, R. Tarling and F. Wilkinson, 'The Social Contract: Post-War Incomes Policies and Their Inflationary Impact', *Cambridge Journal of Economics*, December 1977.

[6] Between 1960 and 1979 from a roughly comparable level, Britain's compensation per employee fell 40 per cent behind that for West Germany and over 25 per cent behind the average for the leading nine European countries. See *National Accounts ESA – Aggregates*, Brussels 1981.

[7] It is important to consider the structure and operation of the welfare state in a full analysis of the British economy because of the relationship between economic and social reproduction. Recent work on the welfare state in Britain would suggest that the backwardness or weakness of the state in

industrial restructuring has gone hand-in-hand with a backwardness in social policy. Britain's early lead in welfare provision has been eclipsed. See I. Gough, *The Political Economy of the Welfare State*, London 1979, N. Ginsberg, *Class, Capital and Social Policy*, London 1980, E. Wilson, 'The Political Economy of Welfare', *New Left Review*, No. 122, and L. Harris, 'The State and the Economy: Some Theoretical Problems', *Socialist Register*, 1980. On the subject of state monopoly capitalism, a category which has developed separately from that of the welfare state, see B. Fine and L. Harris, *Rereading 'Capital'*, London 1979, Chapter 8.

[8] For a discussion of the details of state intervention in this restructuring see B. Fine and L. Harris, 'The British Economy Since March 1974', *Bulletin of the Conference of Socialist Economists*, 12 October 1975, and 'The British Economy: May 1975 to January 1976', ibid., 14 June 1976.

[9] An examination of the protective devices surrounding the colour television industry and its backwardness in the absence of state intervention is to be found in N. Swords-Isherwood and P. Seker (eds.), *Microelectronics and the Engineering Industry*, London 1980, Chapter 12.

[10] Note by Sir Henry Chilver, Chairman of the EDC for the Electronics Industry, NEDC 1981.

[11] NEDO, *Policy for UK Electronics Sector*, London 1982, p.20

[12] See Booz, Allen and Hamilton, 'The Electronics Industry in Scotland: a Proposed Strategy for the Scottish Development Agency', 1979.

[13] P.J. Forsyth and J.A. Kay, 'The Economic Implications of North Sea Oil Revenues', *The Institute of Fiscal Studies*, 1980.

[14] These arguments are particularly associated with Lord Kaldor. For a recent statement in broader and historical context see 'Capitalism and Industrial Development: Some Lessons from Britain's Experience', *Cambridge Journal of Economics*, June 1977.

[15] *New Deal for Steel*, published in 1980 by the Iron and Steel Trades Confederation, as part of a struggle by the union against closures, documents quite well the bias that can be contained in productivity measures particularly when they are designed to demonstrate the inefficiency of workers.

[16] See, for example, G. Brown and T. Sherriff 'De-industrialisation: Background Paper' in Blackaby (ed.), *De-industrialisation*, p.249.

[17] C. Pratten, 'The Efficiency of British Industry', *Lloyds Bank Review*, January 1977, no. 123.

[18] J. Dunning, 'The UK's International Direct Investment Position in the Mid-1970s', *Lloyds Bank Review*, April 1979, No. 132.

[19] For this reason, Dunning suggests that the free flow of investment is beneficial to the British economy, allowing its ownership advantages in low technology to be exploited abroad and the foreign advantage in high technology to be brought to domestic industry. *Laissez-faire* rides again!

[20] D. Stout 'De-industrialisation and Industrial Policy' in Blackaby (ed.), *De-industrialisation*, p.185.

[21] Rather than that they are making, for example, bigger and better vehicles.

[22] Stout, p.172 and Brown and Sheriff, ' ... a Background Paper', pp.241 77.

[23] A. Peacock, *Structural Economic Policies in West Germany and the United Kingdom*, London 1980.

[24] A. Singh, 'UK Industry and the World Economy: a Case of De-industrialisation?' *Cambridge Journal of Economics*, June 1977.

[25] See also A. Cairncross, 'What's De-industrialisation?' in Blackaby (ed.), *De-industrialisation*.

[26] To some extent, state monopoly capitalism has been conceived of as a stage of development within a single country. This severely limits the concept and the understanding of modern capitalism for which state intervention is a generalised tendency across the world economy.

[27] Glyn and Harrison, *British Economic Disaster*. For a more extended treatment of this book, see B. Fine's review article in *Capital and Class*, No. 13, 1981.

[28] See A. Thatcher, 'Labour Supply and Employment Trends' in Blackaby (ed.), *De-industrialisation*.

[29] See 'Comment' by G. Ray, p.74 in Blackaby (ed.), *De-industrialisation*.

[30] A. Glyn and B. Sutcliffe, *British Capitalism, Workers and the Profit Squeeze*, Harmondsworth 1972.

[31] A. Kilpatrick and T. Lawson, 'On the Nature of Industrial Decline in the UK', *Cambridge Journal of Economics*, March 1980.

[32] For a similar emphasis on the lack of 'reconstruction', defeat in war or foreign occupation for the evolution of British trade unionism, see D. Smith, 'Trade Union Growth and Industrial Disputes' in Caves and Krause (eds), *Britain's Economic Performance*. He goes on to argue that 'The system both reflects and reinforces the preference of workers for a secure job and restrictive work rules, at the expense of higher wages.'

[33] As a simple index, between 1920 and 1933 trade union membership fell by almost half.

[34] T. Griffin, 'Technological Change and Craft Control in the Newspaper Industry: An International Comparison', *Cambridge Journal of Economics*, 1984, vol. 8 No. 1.

[35] The same problem exists for the counterpart to the workers' resistance thesis, namely the entrepreneurial failure thesis which holds British management responsible for economic decline. Failures can be identified and even explained but the question remains of how representative these cases are. For a survey of this literature, see P. Payne, 'Industrial Entrepreneurship and Management in Great Britain' in P. Mathias and M. Postan (eds), *Cambridge Economic History of Europe*, Vol. VII, Part I, Cambridge 1978.

[36] The results of Lazonick's work which is in part to explain the slow adoption of ring-spinning in Britain, is published in a number of places. See, for example, 'Industrial Relations and Technical Change: the case of the Self-acting Mules', *Cambridge Journal of Economics*, September 1979. The symposium of which this is a part suffers from the approach criticised in the text here. The competitive relations between and within classes are identified but insufficiently theoretically ordered, so that an unproblematic relation between workers' resistance and its effects in obstructing changing work practices is supposed.

[37] Lazonick, in a later article, argues that the structure of industrial relations in the spinning sector in the nineteenth century has had a continuing influence on the industry more or less to the present day. But he sees it as having created an industrial structure which he emphasises that British

entrepreneurs have failed to break. There is attention to the vertical, horizontal and marketing features of the industry rather than to its industrial relations. See 'Industrial Organisation and Technical Change: The Decline of the British Cotton Industry', Harvard University, mimeo, September 1980.

[38] 'De-industrialisation and Industrial Policy', pp.178-9.

[39] For example, F. Longstreth, 'The City, Industry and the State' in Colin Crouch (ed.), *State and Economy in Contemporary Capitalism*, London 1979, p.183. The Labour Party, 'The City; a Socialist Approach', London 1982; R. Minns, *Take over the City: The Case for Public Ownership of Financial Institutions*, London 1982.

[40] The importance of trading as well as financing is emphasised by J. Coakley and L. Harris, *The City of Capital*, Oxford 1983 and by G. Ingham, 'Divisions within the Dominant Class and British "Exceptionalism" ' in A. Giddens and G. Mackenzie (eds), *Social Class and the Division of Labour*, Cambridge 1982, p.209.

[41] K. Middlemas, *Politics in Industrial Society*, London 1979.

[42] G. Ingham, op. cit.

[43] E.V. Morgan and W.A. Thomas, *The Stock Exchange*, London 1962, Chapter 5.

[44] Coakley and Harris, *The City of Capital*.

I Multinational Corporations and Finance

Chapter 2

The City, the State and Economic Policy

The financing of industry by the City, or its inadequacy, is one plank in many critical analyses of British capitalism; we consider it in Chapter 4. Another is the City's relationship with the British state. The special position of finance in British capitalism has had great significance in circumscribing the ways in which industry has developed and responded and the ways in which the state has intervened or failed to intervene, but the orthodox Marxist and radical explanations of this often misunderstand or oversimplify the nature of this relationship.

The City's effects on industry work through two types of channel, economic and political, and both have their impact partly through their relation to the state. The City's directly economic impact has been at the forefront at several critical points this century. The high exchange rate demanded by the City when the gold-standard was restored in 1925 heightened the problems of the export industries in the inter-war period (although Keynesians who see it as the very cause of the problems are wrong). The City's high interest rates of 1979 and 1980 precipitated the wave of factory closures and redundancies in those years (although they were not the underlying cause). And overseas portfolio investment,the remarkably high export of financial capital since 1979, has been held to have critically shaped the restructuring of industry in the 1980s. The directly political influence of the City was at the forefront in the 1931 crisis when Ramsay MacDonald was re-cast from socialist Prime Minister and installed as the administrator of the bankers' deflation and their policies for restructuring industry. It operated in 1964 to set the terms of Wilson's administration and to bind it (if it needed to be bound) with a commitment to maintain the value of sterling. And in Margaret Thatcher it won its own Prime Minister, typically an outsider with the *arriviste*'s passion for the virtues of finance, who would push through the City's policies.[1]

The economic and political dimensions of the City's impact have interacted throughout this century and so shaded into each other as to be inseparable in practice, but the principles underlying each are distinct. In this chapter,we examine the political role of the City and the direction of its impact on the state's economic policy. In doing so we face the problem of how to characterise the City's 'interests' and its class position, and critically assess some of the Marxian or related orthodoxies on the subject. But we also discuss the more directly economic levers of the City's power, arguing that the neglect of these has caused many to present an over-political view of the City and misunderstand its position as a result.

Whatever the merits of different explanations, the phenomenon to be explained is, in general terms, commonly agreed. It is the City's influence on state policy and on the general conditions of the economy in directions which have weakened industry and hindered industrial accumulation. This influence has been pervasive but has had particular effects at times of crisis and at turning points. The City's influence on the state's economic policy is one aspect of its central role in British economic life. If labour has not been able to force socialist policies through the state and industrial capital has not had a rationalising, forward-looking state machine to lead its development, finance has time and again pursued its perceived interests through the state or in ways which regulate the State's role in constructing the post-war order. In constraining and regulating the state, the City has had a continually blocking role; in the long run this has been more important, although less visible, than its active intervention at times of crisis.

The City and the Post-war Order

The City's role in dramatic crises and turning points this century is well known. Acting through the Bank of England, it was the key to the decision to return to the gold standard at a high exchange rate in 1925 and it was central in using the state's commitment to that system to break the Labour government in 1931. In forcing the Cabinet to consider more and more abhorrent cuts 'to defend the pound' until the Cabinet broke and Ramsey MacDonald became wholly the bankers' own man, the Bank of England was acting as the channel of opinion for the bankers. As so often, its power was presented to the politicians and public in the form of the Bank interpreting financiers' 'confidence' and the bankers themselves found the concept of 'confidence' an irresistible weapon with which to restrict and overturn the Labour government's policies.[2] Similarly financiers, who this time were arbitrarly assumed to be overseas in the form of 'Gnomes of Zurich', figured in the political struggles over Harold Wilson's government's right-wing policies in the mid-1960s; and, in 1976, disturbances in financial markets were the occasion for the adoption of monetarist policies by Callaghan and Healey.

Such crises are the high points of City influence over the state's economic policy, but such events compressed into a few days or hours can be a poor guide to the City's role. Since the Second World War at least, the City has had a longer term perspective in shaping state policy. The 1930s and Second World War marked a fundamental shift in the capitalist world's economic relations. Trade and production were incomparably fractured as was the international financial system over which the City of London had previously been hegemonic. From the early days of the war the question of what kind of world capitalist system would be constructed after the war (and whether it would be capitalist) was on the agenda.[3] After the war this construction and struggles over it took place at the international level (with, for example, the Bretton Woods system, and Marshall Aid) and within each state.

In Britain, the City played a major role in the conflict over the type of economy that was being constructed. The Bank of England, nationalised in 1946 to become formally the arm of the City within the state, articulated and pressed for the policy framework that would serve the interests of finance within post-war British capitalism. The particular policies supported by the Bank have sometimes altered sharply, but its basic objective, has been fixed. For example, although usually deflationist, in 1955 the Bank surprisingly favoured an expansionary budget, and between 1967 and 1972 it switched from a dogmatic favouring of fixed exchange rates ('defending the pound') to supporting flexible exchange rates,[4] but throughout the post-war years it attempted to ensure that the type of system being constructed is one in which capital is regulated principally by the market (especially financial markets) rather than by the state or planning. The City has pursued the construction of such a system from the earliest post-war years until now. Thus, writers who see the long post-war boom as based upon a pact between capital and labour[5] omit one of the crucial factors shaping the economic history of the period, the pursuit of its own interests by a distinct fraction of capital, financial capital which we use here to include both the operations of lending and borrowing and of money-dealing. Similarly, if we examine the City's roles only in the foreign exchange crises such as those of 1976 or mid-1960s we lose sight of the fact that they are only instances within its strategic policies for the whole post war period.

The City's consistent objective of ensuring that markets operate without state intervention has focused on one key market in particular, the market for foreign exchange. In the 1940s and 50s this took the form of a struggle for 'convertibility', or freedom to buy and sell foreign currencies in exchange for sterling, which the City won informally in 1955 and formally in 1958. But convertibility for non-residents did not give British firms and individuals full freedom from exchange controls for all imports of goods and services and, most importantly, for the import and export of capital funds. This became the City's objective from 1958 but it took two decades for it to be achieved. During the 1960s and 70s there continued to exist complex rules over the purposes for which individuals and firms could obtain foreign exchange, and if foreign currency was required in order to invest funds abroad it had to come (at a premium over the normal exchange rate) from a pool of dollars that had arisen from the sale of other foreign assets. The first major economic decision of Margaret Thatcher's incoming government in 1979 was to abolish these controls entirely, which it did in the autumn of that year. The section of the Bank of England which administered the controls was dismantled and its staff of experts in exchange controls (it had 700 staff in all) made a 'gamekeeper to poacher' leap into the arms of the private banks, thereby, argued the City, making it almost impossible for a future Labour government to re-impose exchange controls quickly.

The City's central objective of obtaining freedom for the foreign exchange markets in the post-war order has been followed consistently in pursuing convertibility and the abolition of exchange controls.

With or without such controls, there is a second aspect to freedom for foreign exchange markets. If market forces are to be truly free to operate the state should allow the exchange rate to be at whatever level is determined by demand and supply (i.e. by the dealers buying and selling pounds, dollars and so on for the import-export trade, for foreign investment, or for pure speculation). The Bank of England, as the voice of the City has not had this aspect of market freedom, a freely fluctuating exchange rate for sterling, as an unswerving principle in its aims; on the contrary, until the beginning of the 1970s the Bank was strongly in favour of a fixed exchange rate maintained by the state selling dollars and buying pounds whenever the sterling/dollar exchange rate began to fall (and vice versa when it began to rise). Thus, during the 1960s, for example, the Bank was staunchly opposed to any devaluation of the pound from its par value of $2.80,[6] forced this policy onto Wilson's governments and even adhered to it for a while after Wilson and Jenkins finally devalued the pound in 1967 (an event described by the Govenor of the Bank of England as 'that unhappy occurrence').[7] After 1972 the exchange rate of the pound has been, to varying degrees, allowed to find its own level and change in response to market forces. The City and the Bank of England have been in favour of this system as surely as they were previously in favour of government intervention to fix the rate, although it is significant that the Bank has been more favourable toward some moderation of exchange rate changes by state purchases and sale than has the post-1979 Tory government.

Thus, the foreign exchange market has been central to the City's perspective on constructing the post-1945 economic order, but the City has viewed the two aspects of that market's freedom in different ways; it has been in favour of convertibility and the abolition of controls over the movement of funds, but it has been more favourable (for a long period extremely so) toward market interventions to stabilise exchange rates. This position appears, at first sight, contradictory but in fact it brings out the essence of the City's position. The City and the Bank have worked to ensure that financial markets are free of controls but subject to one qualification, that they operate in a manner which underpins the power of City institutions (in contrast to the power of governments or the directly political arms of the state). In the foreign exchange market, the City's preference for intervention to stabilise the exchange rate at a fixed level (until the 1970s) or to moderate its flucuations (thereafter) has been directed at strengthening the hand of the Bank of England in economic policy compared to the Treasury and government. Day-to-day intervention to support or stabilise the exchange rate is, when it operates, in the hands of the Bank of England and such a system gives the Bank a role in interpreting market forces and, when pressure on the exchange rate mounts, arguing for the macro-economic policies demanded by the speculators. As a result, the City has favoured exchange market freedom in the form of convertibility but freedom qualified by power for the Bank to intervene to stabilise the exchange rate. Nevertheless, the priority has been clear. In the 1950s, when the City and the Tories were first facing the opportunity to 'roll back the state' and show that 'Conservative freedom works', the Bank's overriding objective was to obtain government action to make sterling convertible. At the time it also aimed to have a fixed exchange rate, but so strong was the convertibility aim that the Bank was, at times, willing to agree to let sterling float (be determined by market forces) if that was a necessary condition for achieving convertibility. In 1952, for example, the Bank supported 'Operation Robot', an abortive Treasury plan to withdraw the state from a directive economic role by making sterling convertible on condition that the exchange rate were allowed to float.[8]

If the market for foreign exchange has been one focus of the City's resistance to an interventionist state economic policy, the market for credit has been the other. The exchange rate, determined in the one market, is matched by the interest rate (determined in the other) as a crucial economic variable within the domain of the City over which state control was to be resisted. In the struggle to construct the post-war order, the

City had to re-establish that interest rates lay within the terrain where its market forces were at play and its institutions influenced them rather than under the control of politicians and the Cabinet. In the 1940s, the Labour Chancellor Dalton had subordinated interest rates to a political strategy designed to benefit industrial capital and, in particular, the taking of state control over the nationalised industries. His policy succeeded in pushing interest rates to very low levels.[9] While it was the first financial policy with a long-term political strategy of industrial planning underlying it, the City ensured that it was also the last. Thereafter interest rates were subordinated to the City's foreign exchange policies.

The manner of this subordination changed in the 1970s. While the policy had been to 'defend the pound' and maintain fixed or stable exchange rates, the Bank ensured that rates of interest moved to achieve this. When the exchange rate was falling, for example, a rise in interest rates would be engineered to increase the profitability of funds invested in sterling deposits and bonds relative to investments in other currencies. This policy has never been completely abandoned, even after the Bank relinquished the instrument of an administered 'Bank Rate' which led other rates; but since the late 1970s it has been more relaxed as exchange rate policy has allowed greater fluctuations in the value of the pound. But with the removal of exchange controls in 1979 fluctuations in the demand and supply for sterling credit in the City (which underlie changes in interest rates) have been greatly affected by fluctuations in inflows and outflows into and out of other currencies. The domestic source of demand for credit has been principally the state's need to finance its spending and the main domestic supply of funds has come from the savings of individuals in all classes. Whether the balance of these domestic factors tends to push interest rates up or down has depended on the huge number of foreign exchange transactions that result from movements of international credit and capital.

Since the beginning of the 1950s, therefore, the City has ensured that (in direct contrast to Japan's post-war policy) interest rates are subordinated to the foreign exchange rather than industrial policy and, by the same token, to short-term factors rather than long-term economic strategy. In pursuing this it has had to have a policy on the control of the money supply or banks' lending since the demand and supply for money and credit underlie interest rate movements. Since 1979 the government itself has had control of the money supply at the centre of its strategy with the Thatcher administration arguing that interest rates should be at whatever level is consistent with its money supply targets. Other things being equal, restricted growth of the supply of money would imply high interest rates, for example. The policies of the Bank of England regarding the government's money supply policy illustrate again the City's post-war strategy: it is to obtain freedom for markets as long as it is a freedom from government intervention which allows the City its own power to influence and control those markets. Thus, in the early 1980s the Bank opposed pressures on the Tory government to adopt a new technique for controlling the money supply. This 'monetary base control', would make regulation of the supply of money in the economy effectively automatic and let interest rates fluctuate strongly in response to every change in the demand for money and credit that occured. It was a policy for complete freedom for financial markets within the framework of an automatically controlled monetary base; the Bank's opposition to it was another example of the City's long-term aim of preserving the Bank's right to intervene in financial markets while opposing Whitehall's and, particularly, Westminster's. By opposing monetary base control the Bank was preserving its own right to influence the money supply and to do so by at times acting indirectly upon interest rates rather than being automatically and always excluded from such indirect action.

Class Fractions and Alliances

The City's influence over the British state's economic strategy has long been recognised as a distinctive feature of British capitalism, a key to explaining its particular crisis. In the past two decades, Marxist explanations have been dominated by the thesis promulgated by Anderson and Nairn.[10] In that perspective the British state has been and continues to be dominated by a power bloc in which the City, financial capital, figures large while the interests of industrial capital in Britain and the working class are systematically excluded. Put generally, the thesis has attracted much support, but it is composed of several elements and each of these specific arguments is open to question.

First, it is argued that the role of the City and finance in the power bloc stems from a centuries-old alliance between the old landed classes and financial capital to prevent the industrial bourgeoisie from controlling and transforming the state in the English Revolution and prevented later transformations of the state. Thus, for Nairn the British state has remained 'archaic' and Ingham (who is critical of several other aspects of the Anderson-Nairn thesis) treats the implications of the City/state nexus for today's politics in the same way: 'the dismantling of what is fundamentally a legacy of Britain's *pre-industrial* past would require a far-reaching realignment of British politics in general – so entrenched are the ramifications of the City's hegemony.'[11] This view of the pre-industrial character of the modern British state and the class structure of Britain implies that the origins of unemployment and industrial decline in the 1970s and 80s are to be sought in the seventeenth century, for the hegemony of the City and its allies in the old landowning class was supposedly constructed then and effectively ruled out change since then. It is a curiously monolithic view of British history, all the more surprising because it was originally constructed in an attempt to understand the complexities and anomalies of a society with not just two great classes, the bourgeoise and proletariat, but intermediate classes, fractions of classes and fragmented interests.

In our view that monolithic perspective of pre-determination is misleading. There have been crucial points in British economic and social history when real possibilities of change have been on the agenda; if, at such times, the City and other elements in the ruling bloc have prevented any fundamental shift towards an interventionist capitalist state which promotes industrial strategy the explanation lies in the circumstances of the time rather than the manner in which a seventeenth-century alliance was constructed. One such crucial point was the re-construction of British capitalism after the dislocations of the Second World War (and of the inter-war economic crisis). The election of a Labour government, the strength of socialist and reforming ideas, the resurgence of trade unionism after its low point in the 1930s, and the easily constructed consensus around the idea of re-building production combined to produce a real opportunity for a fundamental shift in the character of the state and its economic role. The shifts that did occur were superficial and in major respects temporary. The explanation for that failure lies in the circumstances of the mid-twentieth century (including the character of working class politics at that time, and the political and economic strategies of the newly dominant United States) and within those circumstances the City fought to shape economic policy in its own interests and to restrict and reduce the state's influence over markets in favour of its own.

Second, the Anderson-Nairn thesis pays no attention to the historical changes in the character of finance itself, except to identify a shift in the international importance of the City of London in the late nineteenth century to provide a new economic base for the ruling bloc which has lasted to the present. Thus, Nairn writes of the period from the 1870s to 1914:

> Less and less able to compete with the new workshops of the world, the ruling élite compensated by extended control of the world's money market – by building up a financial centre in the City of London.

This underpinned the City's hold on state power and 'has carried the old order into the last quarter of the twentieth century'.[12] In fact, the financial conditions (both domestic and international) under which the City has operated have changed at several periods. The international finance centred on London under the pre-1914 gold standard was quite different from that in the inter-war years. Similarly, the City's role in the international financial system was even quite different from the end of the 1960s compared to the first two and a half postwar decades. These differences can be seen by comparing the policies, at first sight similar, of the City toward Labour governments in the 1960s and 70s.

In the first decade foreign exchange crises were a key to forcing Wilson's government to abandon its industrial strategy, and in 1976 foreign exchange crises led Callaghan's government formally to renounce Keynesian employment policies, but the conditions in which the City operated were quite different in each decade. In the first, the City's strategy was to preserve its position at the centre of a network (the old 'Sterling Area') that rested on privileged access to the export of capital from Britain, while by 1976 both the international financial system and London's strength within it was dominated by Eurodollars, a form of international finance that rested on the abolition of such privileged networks.[13] Such changes have radically changed the ways in which the City's influence over the state's economic strategy is exercised; we outline later how the development of Eurodollar finance has affected the rise of monetarism.

Third, the Anderson-Nairn thesis rests on the idea that the City's activities are the provision of finance, channeling funds and credit to borrowers whether they are industry in Britain or firms operating overseas. It is this role that they see as generating the profits with which the City has sustained the old order. This creates a problem which writers within that perspective have had to overcome: since the City's profits are seen as deriving from their loans to industry why should its hold on the state have led to a state bias against that same industrial base thereby weakening the source of the City's profits ? The problem is resolved in this perspective by arguing that the City's finance, especially since the 1870s, has been dominated by lending overseas so that its interests coincide with those of British firms operating internationally rather than with the owners of factories and undertakings in Britain. As Longstreth puts it, there is a historic 'coincidence of interests between imperialists and the City'.

That identification of the City with purely financial capital (in other words as deriving its profits from interest and dividends alone) is, however, mistaken. Ingham correctly argues that the City is dominated by commercial activities similar to those of merchant capital rather than financial, by dealing rather than lending, or, in other words, by fees and commissions in contrast to interest and dividends. Dealing in commodities, money (such as the buying and selling of foreign exchange) and already existing financial securities (such as the bonds and shares dealt on the stock exchange) has historically been a prime activity of the City. Ingham attributes to this the City's practices and its pursuit of state policies which have failed to strengthen the industrial base, for its concern is with the marketability of assets in contrast to the profitability of investments.[14] That argument is more accurate than the Anderson-Nairn thesis, but it makes too sharp a dichotomy between commercial and financial capital. As we argued in the first chapter, financial capital's own essential character is that it is univeral, liquid and easily transformed and transferred, so finance itself requires the development of markets and dealing in financial assets. The commercial and financial activities of the City require each other and the City's interests, policies and effects reflect that interconnection.

But what are the City's interests? A fourth problem with the Anderson-Nairn thesis of the City's political hegemony is that there is no clear conception of what the City should want power for? What interests is it pursuing? And is it legitimate even to assume that there are unified City interests rather than the distinct interests of different City institutions?

City Interests

The economic policies promulgated by the City through its influence on the state in the twentieth century have included cuts in state spending (as in 1931 and 1976), high exchange rates for the pound (as from 1925 to 1931 and from 1951 to 1967), and high interest rates. These have led the City to be rightly categorised as deflationist throughout the twentieth century. But this does not define the City's interests. When deflationary policies have occurred to contribute to crises of production with mass unemployment and the closure of plant and machinery neither these results nor the cuts, high exchange rate or high interest rate themselves constitute the City's basic objectives.

The objective most consistently articulated and pursued by the City's 'politicians' has been the strengthening of the role of London as a financial and commercial centre for the international economy. In this the City's basic interest is, like that of any business, to strengthen its competitive position by attracting, on the best terms, as great a proportion of the world's business in its particular field as will maximise its profits. This fundamental interest explains many of the policies the City has promulgated, and, most notably, its consistent pressure against state controls on the free international movement of capital or on the terms on which it can be borrowed and loaned. The pressure for market freedom has run throughout the City's influence on the construction of the post-1945 economy. It underlay the push for convertibility of sterling in the 1940s and 50s when the shortage of dollars meant that inconvertibility (exchange controls) would have been an absolute prerequisite for any national planning for industry and trade. And it underlay the pressure for the full freedom to export capital from Britain that was granted in 1979 with a resulting upsurge in foreign investment. Those policies concerned the ability to exchange sterling for other currencies, but the most significant success of the City's pursuit of market freedom lay in its ability to persuade all post-war governments to give it almost complete freedom to borrow foreign currencies and re-lend them internationally. While the City's main competitor, New York, was subject to state restrictions on the terms of its credit operations, London's freedom enabled it in the 1960s and 70s to become the world's leading centre for such international intermediation, or Eurodollar credits.

The City's basic interest of strengthening its international position in competition with New York also underlies its specific policies on state spending, exchange rates and interest rates. The exchange rate was maintained at the high level of $2.80 to the pound through the one and a half decades until 1967 when Jenkins devalued the pound. Keynesian liberal economists such as Shonfield and Hirsch and some politicans argued that its level harmed industry in several ways.[15] It directly gave foreign industries a competitive advantage by making British products relatively expensive, while indirectly it harmed industry because to maintain a high exchange rate in the face of speculative pressures British governments had repeatedly to raise interest rates (to attract money into sterling) and cut spending (to reduce imports). The reason the City persisted with this policy was the belief that devaluation would have harmed its success as an international centre.[16] It was argued that the City's success depended on foreign firms and states (particularly those in the Sterling Area) holding their financial reserve in sterling and that a devaluation, by reducing the value of their existing holdings would lead them to lose confidence in the City's probity and to withdraw funds.[17]

The experience of these years reinforced the views that many socialists and liberals had formed in the 1920s, that the City's basic and invariable objective is a high and fixed exchange rate for the pound. Even in the 1980s that view is strongly held. Ingham, for example, writes that the City's basic structure leads it to want 'a currency strong enough to be a basis for international mercantile and banking transactions' thus helping 'to maintain London as an open unrestricted market-place'.[18] But in fact 1967 marked almost the end of the strategy of 'defending the pound'. The following decades have shown that while the City's basic objective is to further the competitive position by successfully resisting state restrictions, it has not needed to defend the pound to do it. London's position as the leading international banking centre became stronger in the 1970s than at any time since before the First World War, and this was achieved while governments eschewed systematic support for the pound and while its exchange rate against the dollar and other major currencies followed a long downward trend. The City's new success lay in its dominance of finance in and dealing in Eurodollars (and other Eurocurrencies) especially after the oil price increases in 1973 and 1979 temporarily concentrated international money in the hands of oil exporting states that invested them in London's banks. And the essential character of this business was that it could involve borrowing and lending denominated in foreign currencies so that the value of the pound was irrelevant to the City's success in this. However, the freedom from controls over such business that the City had won from the British state in the post-1945 new order *was* a necessary precondition.

Thus the City's overriding interest in a leading international position has been manifest in its opposition to controls. In some historical circumstances it has also led to a policy of state support for high exchange rates, but as has been seen since the start of the 1970s, and was even prefigured in the Bank's willingness to 'let the pound go' in return for convertibility when 'Operation Robot' was on the cards in the early 1950s, high exchange rates have not by any means been a permanent component in the City's bid for international leadership.

If the City's basic interest is its own ability to attract international business that is a rather narrow, self-interested and profit-oriented rationale for policies which have effects on all firms and all classes as do exchange rates, interest rates and the restrictions on state spending the City seeks. It is, in a sense, a squalid basis for the struggles of the City; struggles with the grand result evident in its great political effect on the state. It is not, however, the only basis, for the City does have an interest too in the control of the economy as a whole. It is a secondary interest in the hierarchy of aims City leaders articulate and consciously work for, but it is, nevertheless, inescapable, for within capitalism financial capital and money necessarily play a regulatory role.[19] Movements of finance into and out of different lines of industry determine whether factories close here and expand there, and the need to meet high interest payments or to compete with foreign producers whose goods are favoured by a high exchange rate raises the competitive pressures on firms to innovate, rationalise and restructure. The City has an interest in using these levers of control over the economy for ultimately its profits depend on the profitability of the whole economy.[20] But, given the international basis of much of its profits, its concern for regulating British industry and strengthening its profitability is greatly attenuated.

The City's concern with the strength of industry and commerce in Britain has come to the fore both in times of general economic crisis and when financial policies are controversial. That concern takes several forms including the apparently contradictory actions of triggering the bankruptcy of some enterprises while injecting money into others. In the economic crisis of the 1980s, for example, banks with their secure hold on firms' assets as collateral triggered a record number of bankruptcies of firms. At the same time the Bank of England led the setting up of a 'lifeboat' to rescue major industrial and commercial firms in trouble and the commercial banks took an increasing role in sustaining such firms. The unifying feature of all such operations by the City was that it sought to strengthen industry and commerce by imposing some dicispline, or enforcing the discipline of market forces. While triggering bankruptcies eliminates the weakest sections of capital, the 'lifeboat' and similar rescues involve either supporting enterprises that retain a potential for profitable accumulation or restructuring them so that other enterprises gain their profitable parts. Either way, these support operations involve the City in an increasingly controlling role. As a result, banks and funds have come to exercise a greater role in choosing the board and banks have increasingly become actual shareholders in companies.

Now such a disciplinary role for the City over industry is evident, too, in the macro-economic policies the City has imposed on the state, which is our concern here. A high exchange rate which reduces industry's profitability would seem at first sight to be evidence against the City having taken on the role of strengthening industry, but in the financiers' perspective such a policy may harm particular sectors of industrial capital in the short run in order to strengthen industrial capital in general in the long run. Reduced profitability in the short run is seen as a stimulus forcing industry to restructure, rationalise and modernise. And it is viewed as a means of ensuring that industry, in turn, disciplines the working class and resists labour militancy. The City's support for a high exchange rate in the 1960s was defended by the Governor of the Bank of England in such terms. In his Mansion House speech of 1966 he claimed:

> Another favourite taunt in some circles is that we are sacrificing the people to save the pound. On the contrary the pound is being protected for the sake of the people

and the pound

> cannot be treated as a sort of fascinating toy for bright boys to play with. I do not believe in the future of any economy where nothing ever gives way except the exchange rate.[21]

In the next decade, however, the Bank was in favour of an exchange rate flexible enough to 'give way'. In particular it meant that if wage inflation (which they saw as inextricably linked with price inflation) rose faster, falls in the exchange rate could, in principle, compensate for its effects on British industry's foreign competitiveness. Despite this switch in policy, the Bank of England was consistent in its view of finance disciplining industry. If the 'defence of the pound' could no longer have such a role, the new constraint to exert discipline over industry and labour was to be the money supply. If the money supply (or credit expansion) was limited firms and unions would be constrained by a financial squeeze. If, as in 1980 and 1981, this restriction of the money supply itself led to high interest rates and exchange rates they reinforced the competitive pressures on industry's profits and their drive to restructure.[22]

The City's commitment to its interest of disciplining industry, however, has always been subordinate to its interest in promoting itself as the leading centre of finance, and its support for controlling the money supply in order to discipline industry exemplifies this. The Bank of England in the early 1980s has supported control of the money supply as long as the mechanism of control is not so automatic as to undermine its own authority and discretion. And the banks themselves, while supporting the 1976 policy of the IMF and Callaghan regarding the need to control the money supply and credit, were, in the late 1970s, simultaneously expanding credit and their profits by circumventing the restrictions ('the corset') the government placed on them in pursuit of that policy.

The City and State Power

The interests pursued by the City reflect the inescapable roles that finance and money-dealing play in capitalist economies. They are identifiable through both theoretical analysis of the positions those activities have in capitalism and reflections on historical experience. But to identify them does not identify the channels through which they are made effective. What are the agencies and levers through which the City pursued its interests? In British writings this question turns on how the City relates to the state in furthering its interests.

The prevalent Marxist approach to this question most strongly promulgated by Anderson and Nairn sees the City as a well-rooted part of the ruling bloc itself. Its power is political and amounts to having a hold on state power, a shared hold but a dominant hold within the ruling bloc. This thesis, although widely accepted, is extremely weak and we find it unhelpful in analysing the City's power.

The principal weakness of the thesis is that it is not based on an adequate analysis of *how* the City holds its position within the ruling bloc nor the means by which it continues to exert its dominance and wield state power. The limited explanation that is put forward is that there is an undefined and general 'solidarity' between the 'élites'. Thus, Nairn bases his all-embracing thesis on the claim that at least from the establishment of a 'New Imperialism' in the late nineteenth century 'City institutions ... extended virtual hegemony over the state in virtue of the elite social solidarity so strongly rooted in English civil society.'[23] This, translated into another idiom, says no more than 'the old-boy network rules OK'. Conceptually, it is an empty explanation; it claims empirical support from the work of Rubinstein[24] and others, but this concerns the family and other connections between individual capitalists rather than the ways in which political power is held, exercised and maintained. It is based upon the same loose concept of elites and social groups as Nairn's own and upon a concern with the sociological classification of individuals rather than the operation of a class or class fraction.

Ingham picks out and emphasises an aspect of the thesis which does engage more strongly with the question of how state power is exercised. He writes:

> the City's position has been reproduced during the twentieth century after the economic bases for its dominance were eroded – through the weakness of sterling and the economy – by what the *New Left Review* writers have correctly observed as the continued hegemony of a traditional civil élite which has monopolised important *cultural* and *political* assets in the educational system and the Civil Service.[25]

This formulation identifies the specific mechanisms, control of the educational system and Civil Service, through which power is maintained. But this does not solve the problem, for it is surely meaningless to argue that the City controls the educational system since there can be no suggestion that the ideology imparted there, or even that imparted in the public schools which are highlighted by these writers, is specifically and principally one which supports the City's conception of its role. And how can control of the educational system and Civil service be shown? The usual practice of identifying family connections between the personnel of the City and of those estates may establish kinship patterns but cannot establish an identity of interests between the City and other parts of the 'traditional civil élite'.

The remarkable anomaly in the prevalent thesis is that, although the City's interests are economic, although the rationale for its grip on state power is the strengthening of its economic position, the basis of that grip is seen in terms of a (poorly specified) cultural and political dominance. Indeed the thesis is that control is exercised in this way alone because 'the economic bases for its dominance were eroded'.

In reality the City's relationship with the state is based on its economic power, and it is principally through economic levers that it acts upon the state. This explanation differs from the prevalent thesis in two ways. First by emphasising the importance of specific economic levers which act upon ministries and other state agencies rather than an unspecified cultural and kinship homogeneity between the City in general and the state in general. Second, our explanation differs by conceiving the relationship as one where finance and money *act upon* the state instead of deriving their influence from an historical position of the City's representatives and allies *within* the state itself, within the politically constituted ruling bloc. This approach and the prevalent thesis are not mutually exclusive, but our analysis avoids some of the pitfalls of the latter.

The economic levers through which the power of bankers, finance houses and brokers is exerted are crystallised in interest rates and exchange rates. The way these are determined in the money market and foreign exchange market reflect City assessments of the British economy, overseas economies, and the economic impact of state policies. These are the factors that influence the demand and supply of credit and foreign exchange at the margin and those demand and supply positions are the underlying determinants of interest and exchange rates.

Interest and exchange rates have a pervasive influence on the whole economy, but what is most relevant here is that historically they have had a direct impact on the state and the economic policies it adopts. Governments' spending and borrowing plans have been constrained by the cost of the interest at which the City will accept new issues of government bonds. And the ability of social democratic and Keynesian governments (whether Labour or Conservative) to adopt any role for the state that involves high public spending and borrowing has been undermined by speculation against the pound. One clear modern example of the leverage that works through the interest rate and exchange rate was provided by the pressures on the Labour government in 1975 and 1976. The final stages of the long post-war boom put the state in a position where it had large and accelerating needs for credit even to maintain a weak Keynesian policy, and still greater needs if it were to initiate a socialist or non-socialist programme of industrial regeneration. This conjuncture, popularised as 'the fiscal crisis of the state'[26] meant that the state's ability to carry out any such function was dependent upon financiers' willingness to fund it. That, in turn, did not mean that the funds would simply not be made available, for the City itself depends uoon the large base of liquid and relatively riskless assets provided by its holding of state securities, but it meant that the bankers and financiers could dictate high interest terms for the credit and thereby force a reappraisal of the state's Keynesian role. At the same time, the financiers' response to the state's borrowing position led them to move funds out of sterling precipitating, in 1976, another in the series of 'sterling crises' that every Labour government has faced early in its term (and to which every one has responded by consolidating the dominance of policies that weaken the state's economic role). In 1976 these pressures ensured that the government not only renounced socialist measures but also Keynesian objectives and policies.

Class Interests or Market Constraints?

The importance of such economic levers over the state raises some fundamental theoretical problems. The movements in exchange rates and interest rates that have influenced the state have not been engineered by a committee of City patricians to achieve a strategic aim of undermining an independent state power. They are the outcome of market operations by brokers and dealers with very narrow horizons, their own short-term profit. In what sense, then, can the City's effect in preventing the emergence of an industrially oriented state be attributed to the particular interests of the City that we have enumerated? If it is the outcome of the 'blind' actions of thousands of dealers they are fragmented and self-interested.

Thus, there are two conceptions of the unity of the City's actions; a financial community with a unified and essentially political leadership or a set of profit-maximising individuals exerting power through economic operations. A third approach sees the City as made up of institutions of different types, each with their own and often conflicting interests. According to this, the banks with large international operations have an interest in the City's international position which is not shared by, say, the building societies: or the pension funds and insurance companies with large shareholdings have more of an interest in the health of industry than do the discount houses. Indeed, in the intense 1980s debate over the restructuring of the City, such differences are frequently articulated.

Given the existence of these three different approaches and the criticisms we have made of writers such as Anderson and Nairn who adopt the first alone, what is the basis for an analysis of the type we have conducted, a discussion of the role 'the City' as an entity (rather than a fragmented group of individual dealers or of competing institutions) has played with regard to the state and the economy?

The distinct role of the City as a body stems from the distinctive character of the financial capital and merchant capital that are its preserve. In Chapter 1 we identified the contrast between the capital that operates wholly in money, credit and financial contracts and the capital that is involved in industry and its related services. The former is characterised by universality, flexibility and distance from the site of class conflict whereas the latter is specific, relatively tied, and more or less directly involved in class conflict. Moreover, the economic driving force of financial capital is its tendency to become increasingly universal and liquid. This distinct character of the capital with which all parts of the City operate underpins the unitary character of the City's role, even though its economic levers of power result from the actions of individuals and its institutions have conflicts over policy at one level.

The special character of finance and money which springs from its universality and its status as a general, easily transformable form of capital, ensures that whatever the particular immediate interests of any particular City institution, they all share an interest in preserving and extending those characteristics. Moreover, this is reinforced by the layering and interlocking character of the institutions' operations, for they each borrow, lend and deal with each other on more or less unified financial markets. Thus, although the building societies operations' are less internationally oriented than the banks, for example, they share with the banks a fundamental interest in preserving and extending the international competitiveness of the City, for without that the liquidity and extensiveness of the financial markets to which they relate would be limited and jeopardised. The fact that their relationship with the international money markets is indirect compared with the banks' does not alter the fact that they require the liquidity and universality of finance as does any financial institution. To take another example, insurance companies and pension funds that have long term money tied more closely than most to British industry, have no less interest than banks in developing the universal character of finance by strengthening and extending the City's international role (as has been borne out by the alacrity with which they have extended their overseas investment since 1979).

Similarly, the universality and liquidity of the City's capital ensures that the actions of the mass of individual dealers and brokers which push interest and exchange rates up and down with a resulting impact on the state have a unitary character which puts into effect the City's interests. Since money and credit are above and free from the specific and local operations of productive capital, the calculations made by market operators cannot be based upon detailed assessments of specifics. A decision to invest in sterling rather than the dollar cannot be based upon a detailed assessment of the conditions of production in each economy; such an assessment would be relevant only for investments which involve some definite and long-term commitment, while operations in international credit and money markets involve relatively short horizons. Such financial operations require a conventional and simplified way of assessing the 'real economy'; they require indicators which can be easily and quickly assessed as a basis for quick decisions on the money markets. The accuracy of

these indicators as a measure of the health of productive
capital is relatively unimportant compared to the question of
whether financiers agree on their acceptability. As a result they
are subject to fashion, so that in recent decades the City has
used successively different indicators to determine whether to
buy or sell sterling: the balance of payments on current
account, US and UK interest rates, the UK public sector
borrowing requirement and the rate of growth of the money
supply. By buying and selling financial assets in accordance
with such indicators the dealers determine movements in
interest rates and exchange rates which shape and constrain
state policies toward the economy as a whole. The City
people's choice of these indicators reflects the conception of
how economies operate which goes along with the position of
finance in the economy, and the economic levers which are the
effect of such dealing force the state to act on such lines. If, for
example, dealers view high government spending as an
indicator of weakness they protect their profits by selling the
currency and, in much of Britain's post-war experience, the
resulting fall in the exchange rate has led governments to
restrict spending to restore 'confidence'.

The City, then, is both fragmentary and unified. The unitary
character of its interests and their effect stems from the nature
of finance, money and financial securities, the capital in which
it operates. But it also has institutional expression in the Bank
of England. The Bank has, throughout this century, articulated
and represented the interests of the City as a body. Its
representative function has been continued with a full panoply
of leadership roles within the City, including a responsibility
for the City's self-regulation (to protect it from regulation by
Whitehall) and for mediating between competing short-term
interests within the City itself.[27] The Bank's role in articulating
and pursuing the interests of the City as an entity has never
been challenged by the City's individual institutions but has,
instead, been willingly accepted. Its acceptance is not simply
because this role is a precondition for the City's self-regulation
and protection from Whitehall; instead, it stems from the fact
that the special character of finance and money-dealing
produces a common interest which is the basis for acceptance
of a common leadership. In this the City stands in contrast to
British industry, for historically the latter has been unable to

unify behind a strong common body and the Confederation of British Industry and its predecessors have been weak and divided.[28]

Finally, an important characteristic of the City's influence on the British state's economic role is that it does not reflect only the influence of *British* finance and banking. The exercise of power through the financial markets reflects the actions of dealers in money and credit throughout the capitalist world. This is in keeping with the international and universal character of finance and money; it also means that the Bank of England articulates the interests of finance in general in acting as leader of the City. (An illuminating specific example of this general rule was the Bank's role in articulating the views of New York bankers on the Labour government's spending programme in 1931.) Speaking and acting on behalf of international finance and money reinforces rather than contradicts the Bank's role in pursuing the aim of strengthening London's position in competition with other financial centres, for the aim is to build London (and hence the Bank) as the leader of *international* finance and it involves the strengthening of the City rather than the specifically British-owned institutions that operate within it.

Thus, the City has had a major role in ensuring that state power in Britain has not been used to develop and strengthen industrial growth. It has, in effect, 'blocked' the development of a dirigiste, rationalising state. Its ability to do so is based upon the character of the capital it controls and is exercised through its economic position. It is not adequate to analyse it solely in terms of a general political and cultural solidarity that binds a financial and aristocratic élite in an alliance to occupy the key postions in the state. Moreover, the City's strength at the centre of the economy is not immutable nor unchanging. It has had to be reconstructed several times (after the dislocation and growth of state intervention in the Second World War, for example) and it has had to change direction radically at times (as in the switch from an orientation toward the Sterling Area with its imperial legacy to one which was more broadly international from the end of the 1960s). In the 1980s the City's structure and operations are undergoing further changes with the formation of huge international financial monopolies. Periods of change do not themselves undermine the City's fundamental principles and role, but they always carry the risk of instability and they always open the possibility for a government committed to industrial strength to assert its domination over the City.

Notes

[1] Although in several respects the monetarism practised by Thatcher's governments was opposed by City interests. See J. Coakley and L. Harris, *The City of Capital*, Oxford, 1983.

[2] In fact, to divert attention from their own political role (and, hence, reduce the prospect of political action against banks' power) one set of bankers easily points to another group's 'confidence' as the key factor. Thus, in 1931, the Bank of England informed the Cabinet that its expenditure cuts were not enough because they did not win the confidence of New York bankers, while the leading New York banker, in turn, put the responsibility the other way, asking the Bank of England in August 1931: 'Are we right in assuming that the programme under consideration will have the sincere approval and support of the Bank of England and the City generally and thus go a long way towards restoring internal confidence in Great Britian?' (R.S. Sayers, *The Bank of England, 1891-1944*, Cambridge, 1976 and F. Hirsch, *The Pound Sterling, A Polemic*, London, 1965, p.119).

[3] See F. Block, *The Origins of International Economic Disorder*, Berkeley 1977; R.N. Gardner, *Sterling-Dollar Diplomacy in Current Perspectives*, New York 1980; R. Parboni, *The Dollar and its Rivals*, London 1981

[4] See Coakley and Harris, op.cit., Chapters 1-3.

[5] For example, I. Gough, *The Political Economy of the Welfare State*, London 1979.

[6] F. Hirsch, op.cit.

[7] Quoted in J.Coakley and L.Harris, 'Industry, the City and the Foreign Exchanges: Theory and Evidence' *British Review of Economic Issues*, Vol.4, No.10, Spring 1982.

[8] A. Shonfield, *British Economic Policy Since the War*, Harmondsworth 1958, Chapter 8.

[9] J.C.R. Dow, *The Management of the British Economy 1945-60*,Cambridge 1964, Chapters II and IX.

[10] P. Anderson 'Origins of the Present Crisis' *New Left Review*, No. 23; T. Nairn, 'The Decline of the British State', *New Left Review*, Nos 101/2.

[11] G. Ingham, 'Divisions within the dominant class and British exceptionalism' in A. Giddens and G. Mackenzie (eds), *Social Classes and the Division of Labour*,Cambridge 1982, p. 227.

[12] Nairn, op.cit., pp. 12-3.

[13] J. Coakley and L. Harris, The City of Capital, Chapters 1-3.

[14] G. Ingham, op.cit., pp.216-20. The Longstreth quote is from F. Longstreth, 'The City, Industry and the State', in C. Crouch (ed.), *State and Economy in Contemporary Capitalism*, London 1979.

[15] A. Shonfield, op.cit., and F. Hirsch, op.cit.

[16] Coakley and Harris, 'The City, Industry and the Foreign Exchanges', loc. cit.

[17] S. Brittan, *The Treasury Under the Tories 1951-1964*, Harmondsworth 1964, passim.

[18] Ingham, op.cit, p.220

[19] B. Fine and L. Harris, *Rereading 'Capital'*, London 1979.

[20] Coakley and Harris, 'The City, Industry and the Foreign Exchanges', loc.cit., pp.20-1. There the argument is presented in terms of the City representing the interests of capital-in-general.

[21] *Bank of England Quarterly Bulletin*, Vol.6, No.4, December 1966, pp.353-4.

[22] House of Commons Treasury and Civil Service Committee, *Monetary Policy; vol l, Report*, London, 1981, pp.163-1.

[23] Nairn, op.cit., p.12

[24] W.D. Rubinstein, *Men of Property*, London 1981.

[25] Ingham, op.cit., pp.226-7.

[26] Gough, op.cit.

[27] Sayers, op.cit.; M. Moran, *The Politics of Banking*, London 1984, Chapter 3.

[28] K. Middlemas, *Politics and Industrial Society*, London 1979.

Chapter 3

Multinational Corporations and the British Economy

In this chapter we examine the position of multinational corporations (MNCs) in the world economy, bringing together a wide variety of empirical information. This will permit us to analyse more specifically the particular way in which the British economy is affected by the increasing dominance of MNCs over economic life. In general, statistics concerning MNCs exclude the banking and oil sectors, and the analysis here has to conform to this convention since it relies upon the available sources of data. However, the role of financing is considered in other chapters and we devote the first section of this chapter to the oil industry. The industry has been served quite well by academic analyses of it, although these have not always forced themselves into popular consciousness. A most penetrating account of the history and economic structure of the industry is to be found in Kokxhoorn,[1] but those interested should also consult Blair[2] and Sampson[3] for less dense accounts. These accounts will be drawn upon freely without necessarily making further reference. Williamson *et al.* provide detailed historical narratives,[4] and we have used Bina for information on the US domestic production conditions.[5]   In Chapter 2 we examined the significance of Britain's multinational financial system. Here we examine the role of multinationals in commerce and industry itself. Our central argument in this chapter is that multinational corporations have had and continue to have a specially significant role in the British economy. In subsequent chapters we shall examine the ways in which they have influenced particular sectors of the economy (nuclear power, cars and the arms industry) and how they have interacted with the state. Here we set out their overall position and its changes.

To show this in perspective we outline the general character of multinationals and their global history before drawing the implications for Britain. We begin, however, by looking at the specific case of multinational corporations in the oil industry and the implications for British policy toward North Sea Oil.

Oil and the MNCs

The origins of the oil industry date back to the middle of the nineteenth century, when oil began to be used for lighting.[6] The main producer in the last half of the century was the United States, with production rising from 6.5 million barrels per annum in 1873-75 to over 30 million in 1899. The industry was soon to exhibit one of its enduring characteristics, monopolisation, although it was to occur first in the most extreme form of almost complete dominance by a single company, Standard Oil, under Rockefeller's guidance. Through various mechanisms he had gained control of refining capacity and this proved the key to control of the industry as a whole:

> ... the goal Rockefeller set for Standard in 1873 was largely achieved by the end of 1878. Standard either owned or had under lease over 90 per cent of the total refining investments in the United States.[7]

To a large extent, the ability of Standard to monopolise the sector followed from a second and enduring characteristic of the industry, its volatility. Once oil wells are sunk and producing, costs of operation tend to be extremely low and, to some extent, independent of the level of output. If prices are to be high enough to cover fixed costs of drilling, etc., then all operators have an incentive to expand output enormously. This has the effect of driving down the price of oil. In other words, the industry suffers from a chronic problem of excess supply, and unless there is a means to restrict output, competition will drive down its price. The survival of the industry depends upon some form of cartelisation. Through increasing control of transporting and then of refining, Rockefeller was able to offer that stability to individual operators and then to guarantee it through control of the industry as a whole, as those operators were drawn into his orbit of power.

By the end of the century, the control exercised by Standard had already begun to break down. This resulted from increasing competition on two separate fronts. The so-called independents in domestic production were surviving and even thriving by specialising in particular products and this was met by a Standard drive into by-products and marketing. More significantly, Standard was confronting stiff competition on world markets. The main alternative source of output was from Russia. US exports had remained at about 70 per cent of output between 1873 and 1889, but a decade later they had fallen to 60 per cent. Meanwhile, the Russian output of crude had risen from under a third to over a half of the US total and its exports had risen twice as fast.

In 1911, the Standard Oil Trust was forced by a court decree using anti-trust legislation to split up into a number of separate companies. In the next twenty years, with an increasingly diverse set of uses for oil emerging, US output increased more than ten times, revealing the great flexibility of supply and the attendant dangers of overproduction and price collapse. At the same time, control by the non-Standard producers was becoming more significant, the share of the previous Standard producers in refining falling to 63.5 per cent by 1919. By 1938, the industry was still highly concentrated, but now the largest ten companies controlled only 58.6 per cent of refining and the largest twenty 76.6 per cent. The largest twenty companies in crude production only accounted for 52.5 per cent of output and less than a quarter of producing wells. Under the ideology of conservation, the industry set about constructing schemes of output restriction, called pro-rationing, in order to maintain prices and profitability in domestic markets, particularly after the discovery of the prolific Texas reserves:

> While an important objective of pro-rationing, in addition to conservation, was to regulate the supply of crude to the volume which could be produced and distributed without seriously disturbing prices in the domestic market.[8]

Meanwhile, significant changes were occurring in world

supply, following the development of the oilfields in the Middle East. Here, a cartel of the main producers was well-established by the late 1920s involving arrangements amongst the seven companies that were to become called the majors or the 'Seven Sisters'; British Petroleum, Shell, Texaco, Exxon, Gulf, Mobil and Socal, although their names have changed during the course of their histories. Initially, however, and as late as 1929, the US companies had an insignificant share of Middle East oil, but as its relative cheapness became apparent, diplomatic and other leverage was used to obtain a 15.7 per cent share by 1939. This was not for the purpose of serving its own domestic markets, since these were protected from imports in the 1930s, a policy which exposed the nonsense of pro-rationing as a device for conservation. Rather, the US companies needed to serve foreign markets from non-US supplies just as the others of the Sisters did. The one major difference is that the non-US companies served foreign and domestic markets by the use of foreign supplies, whilst the USA served domestic markets through domestic production. Between 1929 and 1939, the US share of world exports had declined from 30.3 to 19.8 per cent.

As a result, at the outbreak of the Second World War, the oil industry had two major divisions in its structure. On the one hand, there was the division between the US market and that for the rest of the capitalist world. Both were subject to cartel arrangements and the latter was protected from the former by tariffs. On the other hand, there was the division between the US majors (five of the Seven Sisters) and the other US producers. This division does not correspond to the previous one, since the US majors served both foreign and domestic markets through foreign and domestic production, respectively.

Following the Second World War, the structure of the industry remained unaltered, but the US used its economic and political hegemony to increase its share of the Middle East reserves. This was essential for the continuing operations of its majors, since between 1945 and 1957 the share of the US in non-communist world reserves fell from 39.8 to 13.9 per cent, whilst those of the Middle East rose from 37 to 71.3 per cent.[9] The rise in importance of non-US oil production increasingly brought the whole structure of the industry into question in the next thirty years because of pressures in the internal US sector as well as in the world markets.

In the domestic industry, the problem was one of rising production costs. Apart from the initial advantage of Middle East oil, costing in the 1950s between ten and fifteen cents per barrel as compared to between one and two dollars in the USA, the better US reserves were becoming exhausted, so that costs of exploration and recovery were becoming more disadvantageous. For example, Bina shows that in the decade covering the late 1960s and the early 1970s, exploration costs per barrel increased by 35 per cent and development costs increased by 195 per cent.[10] In order to sustain the domestic industry until this time, it had been necessary to impose a system of import quotas and to strengthen the cartel arrangements of pro-rationing. By 1959, a voluntary agreement over import restrictions gave way to the Mandatory Import Programme. Nevertheless, imports as a share of total domestic demand crept up in the 1960s, from 19.8 to 22.4 per cent, although these imports were not all from the Middle East. These developments created severe tensions within the domestic industry, since not all sections of it required or desired a high oil price. This was only so for crude producers whereas refiners, for example, would wish for the lowest possible price for their inputs. The effect of the pro-rationing scheme was to increase the cost of production even further for, as Burrows and Domenrich show, between 1946 and 1968 the annual number of shutdown days per annum in Texas exceeded 20 per cent on all but two years and exceeded 50 per cent in all of the last twelve of these years.[11]

In international markets the structure of the industry was also being steadily eroded. Following the Second World War, the non-major US producers had increasingly sought reserves outside the United States. In 1946, 28 US companies were exploring in 78 countries. By 1958, 190 were exploring in 91 countries, although most of these were active in areas such as Latin America rather than in the Middle East. This reflected the tight control that the majors continued to exert over the cheapest sources of oil. Nevertheless, for the non-majors, sources of oil outside the USA, even if not in the Middle East, held out the prospect of cheaper supplies and the possibility of gaining a share of non-US markets. Between 1957 and 1966, the share of the Seven Sisters and the French company, CFP, in non-US and non-communist production fell from 91.7 to 80.8 per cent in crude and from 67.4 to 61.6 per cent in refining.

In response to this situation, the majors began to attack the position of their rivals in the US market. They pressed towards the end of the 1960s for the opening of US markets to imports, a measure of advantage to them given their control over the cheapest sources of oil. At the same time, there was a process of competition to strengthen market position in case cartel arrangements should break down. Since the oil industry involves extraction, refining, distribution and marketing as a vertical process of production and sale, control over any one of these separate processes can carry with it control over the others through power of purchase or sale. For example, if sale outlets are controlled, then where oil is bought from can be controlled. On the other hand, if distribution networks are controlled then who receives oil and at what cost is open to control. Between 1956 and 1968, there was a wave of acquisitions in the US, with the top twenty companies absorbing 226 others.

The non-majors had managed to survive this process and had even been strengthened by it. So much publicity and often animosity attends the activities of the majors that little attention is paid to the other oil companies, particularly outside the US. We have attempted to show that they form a crucial part of the structure of the industry, both for their activities in the US and in the rest of the world. For the former, a high price of oil is necessary in order to maintain US domestic production, as its costs of extraction increase. For the latter, their increasing encroachment upon world markets threatened the stability of oil prices. It is important to recognise that the non-major oil industry is not simply an irritant to the majors, but is itself big business. The eighth largest oil company in the US in 1972, for example, was the sixteenth largest company overall – there being only five US majors, so that these and three other oil companies were amongst the largest sixteen US firms. Amongst a sample of the largest 453 companies in the world, no fewer than 34 were oil companies.

If we now put aside the oil crisis of the early 1970s and examine its results, we can see how the oil industry discovered a solution to the erosion of the world cartel and the pressures on domestic US production. The large increases in the price of oil have sustained the profitability of producers in the USA and have guaranteed sufficient revenue in world production to bind the majors and non-majors together in a cartel that now includes both. The result of this has been to create enormous surpluses on the production of oil from those reserves, nearly all, that are less costly to exploit than those in the USA. What the Organisation of Petroleum Exporting Countries (OPEC) nations and other countries have been able to do is to appropriate some of those surpluses. That they can do so is a result and not a cause of the oil price increase.

To some extent, this might read like a conspiracy theory of the oil price increases in which the latter was a solution to the problems of the industry. Certainly, such a possibility should not be discounted and such theories abound in discussion of the oil crisis.[12] Some argue that the crisis was a US device to improve its competitive position relative to its industrial rivals by forcing a high price of oil upon them, others that it was a device to improve the US balance of payments position through the recycling of petro-dollars. These may or may not have been the effects or the intentions of the actions of the various agencies involved, but the solution to the industry's problems came about through a definite process that can be recognised.

Most important in this was the action of the Libyan government after the coup of 1969 brought General Gadaffi to power. He insisted upon an increase in oil revenues and, since the companies directly involved were not the majors, he was able to obtain better terms, given a lack of alternative cheap supplies to the companies. By doing so and by going on to the nationalisation of companies, Libya was able to demonstrate that the changing economic structure of the industry had also weakened the political position of the oil companies. Previously, and most notably in the overthrow of the progressive régime in Iran in 1953 following a blockade on sale of its oil supplies, the majors had been able to count upon mutual support and political backing in case of progressive measures against them. Now they would have been put in the peculiar position of backing their competitive rivals, if a blockade of Libya were to succeed. With Libya having opened the door to a greater take for the oil-producing countries, its OPEC allies were in a position to march through it, having also demonstrated some ability to control the supply of oil as a result of the political embargo and political cover provided by the OPEC actions, the rise in the price of oil could be justified and the domestic producers in the US guaranteed survival.

But the situation remains extremely precarious, since the high oil price (and the OPEC revenues) are balanced upon an increasingly costly and decreasingly significant production of oil in the USA. Throughout the 1970s, the proportion of oil imported by the USA continued to increase, reaching as high as 47.4 per cent of domestic demand in 1977, when ten years earlier it had only accounted for 20.2 per cent. Meanwhile production of oil in the USA has stagnated. Should the support for domestic production be pulled away, there will be enormous pressure for a collapse in the price of oil until it is held at the level of some newly determined marginal producer. Such a collapse would, however, tend to be self-reinforcing, since the loss of revenue associated with it would tend to induce low cost producers such as OPEC to expand production. In addition, the collaborative arrangements between the majors and non-majors might collapse further intensifying downward pressure on prices as they compete.

This is the context in which to examine North Sea oil and Britain's position within it. Given our previous account, it is not surprising that the major participants in the North Sea are not the majors, as is often supposed, but other companies. For the 37 fields operating or under development in 1973, only sixteen had a more than 50 per cent participation rate by the majors and, for the UK this was true of only nine fields out of twenty.[13] The fate of these fields lies very much in the hands of the non-majors and their fate is to a large extent determined by the majors. Blair has shown how exactly the majors have been able to control the supply of oil.[14] Whilst, for example, the output from each country over the period 1950-70 fluctuated enormously as well as exhibiting different rates of growth, the total for the leading nine producers revealed a simple growth path that could only have been the outcome of collaboration between producers.

It is important to recognise that this collaboration does not simply involve marketing agreements. There are extremely complex relations between all producers covering all aspects of the industry from extraction to sales. Each has different facilities, whether in refining capacity or tankers, and there is considerable co-operation in the use of each others' capacity. This is in order to minimise costs in the complicated process of matching different types of fuel demand to different grades of fuel supply and different types of refining capability. In all of this, the UK must be placed in a highly dependent position in which the belief in an independent depletion or pricing policy can only be an illusion.

This is not to suggest that progressive policies in relation to the North Sea are worthless. Certainly, the state can influence the surplus that it rather than the oil companies takes, but this may be finely balanced in so far as the companies concerned have alternative sources of supply. It must also be recognised that the existence of these surpluses is highly precarious and subject to erosion or collapse should the oil price fall. To obtain the benefits of the production facilities, and to minimise costs, oil should be extracted at the maximum rate but on as few fields as possible, rather than from many fields producing at less than full capacity. Again, it must be recognised that the ability to adopt such policies is currently severely constrained by the cartelised arrangements within the industry. There is little that can be done about this by the UK alone, but both its independence and its negotiating position would be strengthened to the extent that it had its own fully integrated production facilities, from exploration to pump delivery. This is in exactly the opposite direction to which Tory policy is moving.

Multinational Corporations at a World Level

During the course of this century there have been enormous changes in the extent, direction and source of international firms. Between 1900 and 1914 90 per cent of foreign investment had its origins in the UK, France and Germany, with over 56 per cent originating from the UK. By the 1930s, the UK and USA had become equal in supplying foreign investment and were responsible together for over 80 per cent.[15] Half of this investment was located in the underdeveloped economies.[16] It was also primarily concerned with

primary production and portfolio investment or with the
financing of infrastructure such as transportation.

Immediately after the Second World War, the field of
international investment was dominated by the United States:

> In 1960, the US accounted for about three-fifths of the
> accumulated foreign direct investment stake of market economies.
> The UK was responsible for one-sixth, and the rest was fairly
> widely dispersed among the other OECD countries. Of the new
> investment (including reinvested profits) between 1945 and 1960,
> the US share was nearer three-quarters – and of that directed to
> manufacturing industry, more than four-fifths.[17]

In this period, the direction of this investment was
predominantly to Canada and Latin America, 'no less than 70
per cent of US investment was made in Canada and Latin
America in 1950 and 64 per cent in 1959' according to
Dunning.[18] The 1960s were to see a dramatic change in
direction as US investment flooded into Europe. Dunning
reports that

> In 1959, 18 per cent of the US direct capital stake was in Europe,
> 34 per cent in Canada and 30 per cent in Latin America and the
> Caribbean. By 1972, the respective proportions were 33 per cent,
> 27 per cent and 18 per cent[19]

At the same time, investments became increasingly oriented
towards manufacturing with its share of US foreign investment
rising from 30 to 40 per cent during the 1960s.[20]

Whilst the direction of US investment to Europe has
continued in the 1970s, this decade has also been marked by
the relative decline of the US as the source of foreign
investment. From the late 1960s (and from earlier), the US
share of stock of direct investment abroad has declined from
just under 50 per cent to a little over 45 per cent by 1978. Over
the same period the British share has fallen from over 15 per
cent to little over 11 per cent.[21] Whilst these proportions
remain large the increasing shares of West Germany (from 2.6
to 8.6 per cent) and of Japan (from 1.3 to 7.3 per cent) in this
period have been dramatic, although West Germany's
investment has predominantly been in developed countries,

while Japan's has been concentrated in less developed countries.

The relative decline of US MNCs is brought out to some extent in the data for the rate of establishing or acquiring new affiliates abroad (see Table 1). This has declined sharply from a peak in the late 1960s. At the same time, as Table 2 illustrates, the US and UK were losing their share of the world's largest enterprises.

Table 1

New Foreign Affiliates of the largest 180 US MNCs
Annual Average

	1951-60	1961-65	1968	1974	1975
Total	295	645	1006	619	376
Developed economies	181	444	720	385	235
Developing economies	114	201	286	234	141

Source: United Nations, *Transnational Corporations in World Development: a Re-examination*, New York 1978.

Table 2

Origin of World's Largest 483 Industrial Companies

	1962	1977
US	292	240
UK	51	40
Other European	91	104
Japan	29	64

Source: J.H. Dunning and R.O. Pearce, *The World's Largest Industrial Enterprises*, Farnborough 1981.

From Table 3, it can be seen that there are over 10,000 MNCs with over 80,000 foreign affiliates. The fact that the UK is the country of origin of almost as many affiliates as the USA, even though its investment share is less than a quarter of the USA's makes clear that affiliates are of varying size and the same is true of the companies that own them.

Table 3

Distribution of Parent Companies Based in Developed Capitalist Economies and Their Foreign Affiliates, by Country and Country Groups, 1977 with Percentage shares in 1980 shown in brackets.

Home country	Parent companies		Foreign affiliates of development market economy-based firms in:					
			Total affiliates		Developed market economies		Developing countries	
	Number	Percentage of total	Number	Percentage of total	Number	Percentage of total	Number	Percentage of total
United States	2,826	26.3	26,884	32.6 (34.3)	19,255	31.4 (31.2)	7,629	36.3 (42.4)
United Kingdom	1,706	15.9	21,803	26.5 (25.4)	16,277	26.6 (26.8)	5,526	26.3 (21.9)
West Germany	1,450	13.5	6,812	8.3 (7.5)	5,582	9.1 (8.6)	1,230	5.8 (4.7)
Switzerland	871	8.1	3,698	4.5 (4.2)	3,168	5.2 (5.0)	530	2.5 (2.0)
Netherlands	622	5.8	3,951	4.8 (4.5)	3,111	5.1 (5.1)	840	4.0 (2.8)
France	599	5.6	4,103	5.0 (4.8)	2,736	4.5 (4.6)	1,367	6.5 (5.2)
Canada	452	4.2	2,450	3.0 (3.1)	1,966	3.2 (3.5)	484	2.3 (1.9)
Japan	382	3.6	2,407	3.0 (3.1)	1,161	1.9 (1.8)	1,246	5.9 (6.4)
Others	1,819	17.0	10,158	12.5 (13.1)	7,969	13.0 (18.4)	2,189	10.4 (12.7)
Total	10,727	100.0	82,266	100.0	61,225	100.0	21,041	100.0

Source: United Nations, Transnational Corporations in World Development, New York 1978 and 1983. In 1983, there were 98,000 affiliates of which approximately a quarter were located in developing countries.

According to the Commission of the European Communities, 60.7 per cent of 9,481 MNCs in 1973 had affiliates in 1 or 2 countries, and 79.7 per cent in five or fewer countries. Only 324 MNCs had affiliates in more than twenty countries.

The activities of some 430 of the world's largest industrial MNCs in 1978 ... less than 5 per cent of all MNCs – account for, at least, three-quarters of all foreign affiliates and about the same percentages of foreign investment.[22]

We have to examine the data with caution, however, since a foreign affiliate may involve little more than a subsidiary organising foreign sales of exports.

Quite clearly, a relatively small number of firms dominate the world capitalist economy. This is reflected in concentration ratios shown in Table 4. Despite the rise of the largest MNCs, these ratios have remained remarkably stable over a long period and have even declined in some instances. This is not because of the expansion of MNCs through diversification, since an average value of output outside main industry for the largest MNCs appears to be about 20 per cent.[23] Nor is it explained by an emerging host of smaller MNCs as competitors for these alone account for only 20 per cent of MNC activity. What has been happening is that the large MNCs have all been expanding across many countries, establishing new affiliates and thereby stabilising overall concentration ratios by interpenetrating each others markets. The global spread of the largest MNCs is indicated in the following table for a sample based on the Harvard Multinational Enterprise Project.[24]

Table 4

Largest firm concentration rations,[1] *1962, 1967, 1972, 1977, by industry*

Per cent

	1962	1967	1972	1977
Aerospace[2]	42.7	40.7	37.3	41.6
Office equipment (including computers)[3]	65.4	70.8	70.2	70.3
Petroleum	46.8	43.2	41.4	36.9
Electronics and electrical appliances	39.4	36.2	33.5	33.7
Chemicals and pharmaceuticals	29.8	27.3	25.5	25.2
Industrial and farm equipment	33.6	31.9	32.9	34.8
Shipbuilding, railway and transportation equipment[4]	74.0	65.1	52.8	53.8
Rubber[3]	52.3	55.8	57.9	55.9
Motor vehicles	67.5	64.6	58.1	54.3
Metal manufacturing and products	31.7	29.1	27.2	26.7
Building materials[5]	44.1	46.3	50.3	52.9
Tobacco[3]	61.1	59.8	58.0	61.8
Beverages[3]	53.9	52.8	56.2	57.1
Food	38.8	36.3	34.6	34.9
Paper and wood products[6]	29.5	26.8	26.6	28.4
Textiles, apparel, leather goods	28.6	28.5	30.0	28.7

[1] Except where otherwise specified the sales of the 3 largest firms in the world as a percentage of the sales of the 20 largest firms in the world.

[2] Sales of 3 largest firms in the world as a percentage of 15 largest firms in the world.

[3] Sales of 3 largest firms in the world as a percentage of 8 largest firms in the world.

[4] Sales of 3 largest firms in the world as a percentage of 7 largest firms in the world.

[5] Sales of 3 largest firms in the world as a percentage of 11 largest firms in the world.

[6] Sales of 3 largest firms in the world as a percentage of 19 largest firms in the world.

Source: Dunning and Pearce, *The World's Largest Industrial Enterprises.*

Table 5

Networks of Foreign Manufacturing Subsidiaries of 315 Multinational Companies 1950 and 1970s

Number of enterprises with networks including	180 US-based MNCs		135 MNCs based in UK and Europe	
	1950	1975	1950	1976
Fewer than 6 countries	138	9	116	31
6 to 20 countries	43	128	16	75
More than 20 countries	0	44	3	29

Source: Harvard Multinational Enterprise Project, in Vernon, op.cit.

The extent of the international spread of MNCs is also indicated by the ratios of overseas production to total company production and to parent company exports. On average, MNCs appear to produce approximately one third of their output abroad but to provide for foreign markets more by foreign production than by exports, but there are differences between countries as is indicated in Table 6. Whilst the established foreign investors (US and UK) have high levels of 'multinational production' which have stagnated over the past five years, the newer internationalisation of production (Japan and West Germany) have lower but rising ratios. Given recession conditions over much of the period, it is perhaps to be expected that domestic production might be maintained at the expense of foreign. (Figures for 1972 and 1977 for a different sample of 523 firms show rising ratios for all countries. For a sample of 219 firms in 1977, 138 expected 'multinationality of production to increase' in the next five years, 62 expected it to remain the same with only 19 expecting it to decrease.)[25]

Much international expansion of MNCs is based upon exports 'internal' to the firms, that is of exports of parts and components to overseas affiliates without the intervention of the market. For a sample of 329 firms, the ratio of internal to total exports is 32.8 per cent and this is more or less the same for all countries except for USA (45.5 per cent) and Japan (17 per cent) at the two opposite extremes.[26] What does emerge from the statistics, however, is that the more a MNC relies

Table 6

Overseas Operations of MNCs

	Overseas Production Ratio[1] Percentage		Overseas Market Ratio[2] Percentage	
	1974	1978	1974	1978
USA	32.8	32.6	91.6	91.5
Europe	40.7	42.2	71.3	71.3
Japan	4.9	8.2	17.1	24.3
West Germany	21.5	24.6	46.4	50.2
UK	43.2	45.2	80.4	79.2
Total	33.3	33.6	77.3	76.1

[1] Ratio of sales of foreign affiliates to total company world wide sales.
[2] Ratio of sales of overseas affiliates to sales of overseas affiliates plus parent company exports.

Source: Dunning, Haberich and Stopford, *The World Directory of Multinational Enterprises*, from a sample of the world's 430 largest MNCs.

upon overseas affiliate production, the more it relies upon internal exports. On average, when overseas production exceeds 15 per cent of total production, internal exports account for over 40 per cent of total exports and this figure rises to over 60 per cent when the proportion of overseas production exceeds half of total production. For individual countries, approximately half of trade for the USA in the 1970s was within the MNC system, whereas for exports it was 29 per cent for Sweden in 1975, 30 per cent for the UK in 1973 and 59 per cent for Canada in 1971.[27]

Whilst in part the swing of foreign investment has been away from primary production and towards manufacturing, the sort of manufacturing undertaken by MNCs differs according to its country of origin. The USA and West Germany, for example, are primarily involved in what are described as the more technology-intensive sectors, whilst Japan and the UK are oriented towards the less technology-intensive sectors, as is shown in Table 7. Consequently it can be seen that there is no simple relation between the sectoral, regional and chronological structure of MNC investment.

Table 7

Percentage Outward Direct Investment Stake of Four Countries in 1975

	More Technology-Intensive*	Less Technology-Intensive*
US	67	33
UK	44	56
Japan	39	61
West Germany	69	31

Source: Dunning, Haberich and Stopford, *The World Directory of Multinational Enterprises.*

* The more technology-intensive industries are taken to be chemicals, mechanical and electrical engineering, motor vehicles and rubber, with the other manufacturing sectors taking up the less technology-intensive industries.

Finally we turn to the methods by which the MNCs have established and reorganised their international activites. For US MNCs, the predominant means of establishing affiliates in developed countries has been through acquisition, rather than through formation of new facilities, whereas the opposite is the case for their affiliates in the less developed countries and this has become more so over time except for the period 1973-75 (see Table 8.) For non-US MNCs, acquisition as the path of entry seems to have been well established from the outset (Table 9). This is in part also reflected perhaps by the changing methods of ownership of affiliates:

> the proportion of foreign affiliates established in developed countries between 1961 and 1975 with a 100 per cent ownership was 25.3 per cent compared with 41.1 per cent of those set up before 1960 ... In 1975, minority ownership accounted for 43.9 per cent of Japanese overseas ventures compared with 8 per cent of US based multinationals.[28]

MNCs from all countries of origin appear to be utilising more 'liberal' methods of ownership even as those that are already more liberal increase in relative importance. Nor do MNCs appear to provide large quantities of finance for investment.

Table 8

Method of Entry of Affiliates of 180 US MNCs 1951-1975

	1951-1966		1967-1969		1970-1972		1973-1975	
	New	Acquired	New	Acquired	New	Acquired	New	Acquired
Developed[1]	1761	1861	687	1130	540	952	427	528
Less Developed[2]	1473	708	539	313	532	249	479	173

[1] Canada, Europe, Australia, New Zealand, Rhodesia, South Africa.
[2] Rest of the world.

Source: J.P. Curhan et al., Tracing the Multinationals, Lynn Mass. 1977.

Table 9

Method of Entry of Non-US MNCs in Manufacturing Prior to 1971

	New	Acquired
Developed	1,271	2,535
Underdeveloped	1,036	688

Source: J.W. Vaupel and J.P. Curhan, *The World's Multinational Enterprises*, Cambridge Mass. 1973.

On average, by the mid-1970s, over 80 per cent of their investment funds were financed other than by direct flow from parent company. For US MNCs, only 11 per cent of funds was provided by direct flow investment.[29]

The rise of the MNCs has not, however, been a smooth expansion. Table 10 illustrates the 'exit' of US affiliates, whether 'exit' be by sale, liquidation or merger. From 1951 to 1975, these were 4,793 such exits compared with an entry of 13,795. But the pace of exit as compared to entry has increased sharply as entries have themselves declined absolutely in the more recent years. For non-US MNCs, exits from the developed countries appear to have run at a rate of just over 20 per cent for the period up to 1971 and for just under 20 per cent from the less developed countries over the same period.[30] Elsewhere the significance of disinvestment has been demonstrated in volume terms, with almost 30 per cent of gross investment in the six EEC countries being swept away by a disinvestment flow back towards the original investing countries in the period 1967-75.[31]

Theoretical Reconsiderations

The previous section has demonstrated the complexity of the MNC sytstem and has done so only by touching upon a small proportion of the data concerning their operations.

The weight of accumulated investment in the past by US (and UK) corporations has to be set against the emerging international operations in production of West German and Japanese MNCs. But even though these two countries emerge

Table 10

Exit and Entry of Affliates of US MNCs

| | 1951-1966 Total | | 1967-1969 Total | | 1970-1972 Total | | 1973-1975 Total | |
	Exits	Entries	Exits	Entries	Exits	Entries	Exits	Entries
Developed	799	4,249	757	1,956	880	1,579	820	1,002
Less Developed	453	2,546	364	907	343	825	365	686

Source: Curhan et al., Tracing the Multinationals.

together in this respect, they do so in very different ways. West Germany leads an export-based drive into Europe for the purposes of high technology production abroad. Japan seeks low-wage sources of labour in the newly industrialising countries of South East Asia. The USA and the UK are driven by both motives in their expansion of foreign investment (see below). What is characteristic of the MNC system is that these different phenomena co-exist and cut across each other. Rapid change is both possible and likely and the mechanisms exist for it to occur as the data on the processes of reorganisation by 'exit' and 'entry' have demonstrated.

In the case of the USA and the UK we can perhaps study the process of formation and development of MNCs at the leisurely pace of a hundred years, just as Marx studied the formation of capitalism itself as it came into being in Britain over a period of hundreds of years. But the developments of this century are now being compressed as the system of MNCs is extended, in part because the mechanisms for it to do so have already been established, and in part because of the coercion of competition. Accordingly generalisations about the sectoral composition, regional origin or regional location of MNCs are over simplistic. These characteristics are the products of a previously developed international division of labour even as a new one is created with it as its basis.

These observations are perhaps borne out by considering the orthodox economic analysis of MNCs.[32] Initially, in the post-war period, foreign investment was dominated by the USA and this was explained in one of two ways. Either USA firms had specific *ownership* advantages over the firms of other countries and these could be anything from market power to technological know-how, or other countries had specific *locational* advantages over the USA, these ranging from wage levels through all aspects of government economic policy to cultural characteristics. A calculus of ownership and locational advantages cannot, however, explain either the timing of foreign investment or why it should occur rather than production by indigenous firms which have purchased licences or patents. Vernon extended the theory of the product cycle to international trade and investment. US firms with a lead in new products or technology export to some markets abroad until these are large enough to justify production facilities to follow.

These are set up as affiliates rather than through licensing because of market imperfections in licensing. The costs in creating and policing a market for patents, etc. may be greater than those associated with setting up a production affiliate.

The three elements of location advantage, ownership advantage and market imperfections have been brought together by Dunning to form the self-styled 'eclectic theory' of international trade, production and investment. The eclectic theory has been used to chart the progress of MNCs and forms the basis on which most data have been collected in the search for country-specific advantages of location and ownership, as well as ownership advantage by sector (for example, to be associated with higher research intensity or capital expenditure).

This theoretical analysis is in the accepted tradition of ortho-dox micro-economics. It builds up a view of the capitalist system from the aggregated behaviour of individual firms with their given characteristics. These determine trade, production and investment according to the given characteristics of countries. The result is a theory of 'trade' in comparative (ownership and location) advantages supplemented by a theory of market imperfections. As a result, there can be no notion of the movement of the system as a whole, independent of and as a coercion upon its individual MNCs. Rather, the operations of MNCs are reduced to a calculus of differing country and ownership characteristics which can necessarily run to an indefinite list (Dunning names at least thirty ranging from government intervention to 'psychic distance' – see chart opposite.

What is absent from the theory is a causal link between the various characteristics. This would lead to a questioning of the validity of the distinction between ownership and location advantages. Are advantages of US MNCs to be distinguished from the policies and practices and system of US imperialism? Interestingly, the product cycle theory is one that cuts across the calculus of advantage. A product advantage involves both a firm to exploit it and a domestic market for it to serve prior to international expansion. The post-war expansion of US capitalism is explained in the crudest and most economistic terms by using the product cycle as a proxy for US imperialism. For Vernon there is a tendency, not perfectly realised or realisable, for firms to become nationless with the formation of a global spread or network of affiliates. Innovation would

CHART

The Eclectic Theory of International Production

1. *Ownership Specific Advantages* (of enterprises of one nationality (or affiliates of same) over those of another)

   (a) *Which need not arise due to multinationality* – Those due mainly to size and established position, product or process diversification, ability to take advantage of division of labour and specialization; monopoly power, better resource capacity and usage.
   Proprietary technology, trade marks (protected by parent *et al* legislation).
   Production management, organisational, marketing systems; R and D capacity; 'bank' of human capital and experience.
   Exclusive or favoured access to inputs, e.g. labour, natural resources, finance, information.
   Ability to obtain inputs on favoured terms (due e.g. to size or monopsonistic influence).
   Exclusive or favoured access to product markets.
   Government protection (e.g. control on market entry).

   (b) *Which those branch plants of established enterprises may enjoy over de novo firms.*
   Access to capacity (administrative managerial, R and D, marketing, etc.) of parent company at favoured prices.
   Economies of joint supply (not only in production, but in purchasing, marketing, finance, etc. arrangements).

   (c) *Which specifically arise because of multinationality.*
   Multinationality enhances above advantages by offering wider opportunities.
   More favoured access to and or better knowledge about information, inputs, markets.
   Ability to take advantage of international differences in factor endowments, markets. Ability to diversify risks e.g. in different currency areas.

2. *Internalisation Incentive Advantages* (i.e. to protect against or exploit market failure).
   Avoidance of transaction and negotiating costs.
   To avoid costs of enforcing property rights.
   Buyer uncertainty (about nature & value of inputs (e.g. technology) being sold).
   Where market does not permit price discrimination.
   Need of seller to protect quality of products.
   To capture economies of interdependent activities (see 1(b) above).
   To compensate for absence of futures markets.
   To avoid or exploit Government intervention (e.g. quotas, tariffs, price controls, tax differences etc.).

To control supplies and conditions of sale of inputs (including technology).

To control market outlets (including those which might be used by competitors).

To be able to engage in practices e.g. cross-subsidization, predatory pricing etc. as a competitive (or anti-competitive) strategy.

3. *Location Specific Variables*
(These may favour home or host countries).

Spatial distribution of inputs and markets.

Input prices, quality and productivity e.g. labour, energy, materials, components, semi finished goods.

Transport and communications costs.

Government intervention.

Control on imports (including tariff barriers), tax rates, incentives, climate for investment, political stability etc.

Infrastructure (commercial, legal, transportation).

Psychic distance (language, cultural, business, customs etc. differences).

Economies of R and D production and marketing (e.g. extent to which scale economies make for centralization of production).

Source: Dunning, 'Explaining Changing Patterns of International Production: In Defence of Eclectic Theory', *Oxford Bulletin of Economics*, 1979, No.41.

take place as and where it is required and therefore the product cycle could no longer explain the timing of trade and investment. This is the response implicitly to the rising challenge to US MNCs even as these spread, for whatever the theoretical deficiencies of these analyses they have always contained the best available empirical observation and description:

The evidence is fairly persuasive that the product cycle hypothesis had strong predictive power in the first two or three decades after the Second World War, especially in explaining the composition of US trade and in projecting the likely patterns of foreign direct investment by US firms. But certain conditions of that period are gone. For one thing, the leading MNCs have now developed global networks of subsidiaries; for another, the US market is no longer unique among national markets either in size or factor cost configuration. It seems plausible to assume that the product cycle will be less useful in explaining the relationship of the US economy to other advanced industrialized countries, and will lose some of its power in explaining the relationship of advanced industrialized countries to developing countries. But strong traces of the sequence are likely to remain.[33]

Significantly Dunning also recognises the interdependence between ownership and location advantages even if it is situated within a process of evolutionary change as one brings the other and vice versa:

> a difficulty in testing these hypotheses is that today's ownership advantages of enterprises may be the inheritance of yesterday's country-specific endowments.[34]

In this context, government policy and its associated determinants such as class struggle become one among many advantages (or disadvantages) rather than a means by which to break from or to promote the power of the MNC system. But just as Vernon begins to abandon the product cycle theory, so Dunning finds it necessary to write 'In Defence of the Eclectic Theory' and does so by introducing a dynamic element of advantage change over time generated by the economic decisions of the past. What each writer is charting, within an unsuitable analytical framework, is the decline of US MNCs, the spread of MNCs from other countries, the increasing internationalisation of production but the continuing weight of the existing pattern of foreign investment upon these processes.

One effect of these orthodox theories is to defend the system of MNCs. In Dunning's case, it is a system in which location advantages of nations and ownership advantages of firms are traded to the mutual benefit of each, except in so far as MNCs exploit market imperfections. Otherwise, firms bring their expertise to bear upon a nation's resources through a system of trading that takes place within the firm itself. For Vernon, the product cycle at an international level is the means by which new technology and products are spread across the world creating new centres of innovative production.

The experience of underdeveloped countries suggests this picture is far from reality. Not surprisingly, it has given birth to a radical tradition of criticism of the role of MNCs in exploiting and consolidating the conditions of underdevelopment, hardly described adequately in terms of 'market imperfections'. This is not our direct concern here. In the next section, however, we interpret the role of the MNCs in the UK economy in a similar light. We examine the extent in the UK to which they draw upon and reproduce its condition of relative decline within the advanced capitalist economies. Before doing so, it is worthwhile examining how apologetic orthodox economists can be for the system of MNCs. We do so for their effect on employment.

There are now a number of studies of the employment effects of MNCs and also their effects for other targets of macro-economic policy (inflation, exports, balance of payments, etc.)[35] We shall focus our attention on Stopford.[36] He concludes, as do more studies, that MNCs are beneficial both to the countries from which they originate and to the countries where they establish affiliates. Inward investment, for example, is seen as providing employment and a base for exports whereas outward investment also provides for exports (as inputs). In each case there is a transference of locational and ownership advantages which are beneficial both from the allocative point of view as well as from the diffusion of innovation. The role of market imperfections tends to be neglected despite the preference of MNCs for affiliates in sectors in which domestic concentration of production is high.

These conclusions drawn one by one for each country (even the underdeveloped) are quite remarkable. Taken together they imply that the MNC system is employment-creating even as we have been faced in the 1970s with unprecedented levels of unemployment for the post-war period. How is it that these conclusions are drawn and in what way are they erroneous? The method of analysis is by *comparison* between the performance of MNCs and domestic based producers. It is not surprising that it can be shown by most indicators that the MNC affiliates perform better. This follows from the fact that they are in the vanguard of capitalist production and therefore best able to expand during boom and survive recession. But to conclude that the MNCs are thereby, for example, employment-creating involves two fallacious assumptions. One is that the operations of the MNCs and of the domestic producers are independent and thereby a legitimate basis for comparison. But, it is more plausible either by oligopolistic power within a sector or by employment effects across sectors that MNCs will determine the place of domestic producers and pass on the employment effects of their own operations. More generally, the second fallacy is that the relative expansion of the MNC system *relative* to domestic producers is a measure of the *absolute* success of that system. It could only be so if full employment were guaranteed and this is precisely what the MNC system has not provided, particularly in the case of Britain. Moreover, the apparent provision by *individual* foreign MNCs of high technology employment in the UK is itself only the counterpart of the system as a whole failing to provide such employment for the British economy as a whole.

MNCs and the UK Economy

The best way to describe the relationship between MNCs and the British economy is to see it as representative of the role of MNCs at a world level but in more extreme form. Apart from Canada, Britain has been the major recipient of US direct foreign investment, and this accounts for an overwhelming proportion of the foreign industrial investment in Britain. But, as Table 11 indicates in a number of ways, the position of US capital in Britain has been in relative decline in the 1970s even as MNC capital has increased in importance. As Table 10 previously illustrated in terms of exit and entry of affiliates, since the end of the 1960s, US MNCs have been on a relative and even absolute decline within the world economy. Britain is in the position of relying heavily upon foreign-owned, particularly US-owned, MNC affiliates.

Table 11

Foreign Participation in UK Industry

	Establishments		Employment		Net Output	
	1971	1981	1971	1981	1971	1981
Foreign Owned as Percentage of Total of which	1.9	2.6	10.7	14.9	14.1	18.6
US	68.8	53.4	74.9	66.2	76.4	69.6
EEC	14.6	20.3	12.7	14.8	11.8	13.1
Other	16.6	26.3	12.4	19.0	11.8	17.3

Source: Business Monitor, 1971 and 1981

What appears to be happening is that as the share of US foreign capital is declining at a world level, it is increasingly focussing its effort in Europe. But even this is inadequate to maintain the share of US capital in Britain (see Table 12). This would conform with an interpretation that sees European-operated American capital as being increasingly centred outside Britain, with the latter being used for lower productivity and wage employment such as assembly. Table 13 demonstrates the changing shares of foreign investment in the UK.

Table 12

Shares of US Foreign Direct Manufacturing Investment

	In Europe as a percentage of world investment	In UK as a percentage of European investment
1961	38.1	54.7
1965	39.9	42.9
1970	42.5	36.3
1974	46.7	30.3
1979	49.4	29.2
1982	54.2	27.8

Source: Survey of Current Business (various issues).

Table 13

Foreign Direct Capital in the UK in all Industries, excluding Oil Banking and Insurance, Percentage Shares of Book Value

	1962	1968	1974	1978	1981
US	64.1	66.8	55.8	58.3	56.3
Western Europe	20.0	21.8	28.7	29.4	26.7
Rest of the world	15.0	12.4	15.5	12.3	17.0

Source: Business Monitor, MA4, 1981 Supplement.

For foreign investment abroad by UK companies, Table 14 demonstrates the enormous switch away from investment in

Commonwealth countries (from both developed and under-developed nations, but more from the latter) and the increasing importance of UK investment in both Europe and the United States. British MNCs tend to exist for much smaller companies than for other countries, with a large number of capitals each operating a small number of affiliates. These co-exist with large MNCs operating as many as a hundred or more affiliates. According to a 1981 survey of British MNCs, there were in 1978 14,193 affiliates (average of seven and a half); the largest 147 (7.8 per cent) MNCs accounted for 7511 (52.9 per cent) of these affiliates and for 84.5 per cent of all assets of overseas affiliates.[37]

Table 14

UK Outward Direct Investment Excluding Oil, Banks and Insurance
Percentage Shares of Book Value

	1962	1968	1974	1978	1981
US	8.8	10.7	12.7	18.6	28.0
Western Europe	13.4	17.6	27.4	31.2	23.2
Commonwealth	60.2	53.9	44.7	34.9	36.5
Rest of the world	17.6	17.8	15.2	15.3	12.3

Source: Business Monitor, MA4, 1981 Supplement.

In the UK, US MNC affiliate behaviour seems particularly volatile and more dependent upon acquisition than establishment of new production facilities. The extent of exit of USA affiliates is also large and rising even as the total number of entries falls. For non-US based MNC affiliates, from a sample of 354 affiliates existing up to 1971, 18 per cent existed in that period, and of 337 entering 63 per cent did so through acquisition.

For foreign trade, Panic and Joyce have reported that 87 enterprises alone were responsible for half of UK exports in 1976.[38] The top 260 enterprises accounted for two thirds of exports. In 1976, 29 per cent of exports went to overseas affiliates of the exporting company and this figure reached 31 per cent for 1979.[39] For US MNCs more than half their exports from the UK are internal to the company. Dunning finds in

110

Table 15

Entry of US MNC Affiliates 1951-1975

	1951-1966		1967-1969		1970-1972		1973-1975	
	New	Acquired	New	Acquired	New	Acquired	New	Acquired
Entries	185	289	80	212	59	206	56	127

Source: Curhan et al., Tracing the Multinationals.

Table 16

UK Exits and Total entry of US MNC Affiliates 1951-1975

	Up to 1950	1951-1966	1967-1969	1971-1973	1973-1975
Entries	276	608	326	272	186
Exits	—	155	127	147	155

Source: Curhan *et al., Tracing the Multinationals.*

1973 that for a sample of the largest 500 US MNCs in the UK, a mere 79 accounted for 79 per cent of their exports and 57.6 per cent of these exports went to their overseas affiliates.[40] By 1979, we find that the largest 56 exporters amongst US MNCs account for three-quarters of all US MNC exports and that 66 per cent of these exports are internal to these firms.[41] For other foreign MNCs exporting from Britain, the largest 29 amongst these export 76 per cent of foreign MNC exports from the UK and 40 per cent of these are internal to these firms. The 70 largest UK MNCs account for 69 per cent of UK MNC exports and of these 30 per cent are internal to these firms, perhaps suggesting that their foreign production is more independent than that of foreign MNCs rather than less internationally developed. MNCs as a whole account for over 90 per cent of UK exports with approximately 30 per cent coming from foreign subsidiaries located in the UK.

The sectoral distribution of foreign investment within the UK differs sharply from the overseas investment of UK MNCs. Inward investment is made up of about 70 per cent within the more technology-intensive industries whereas outward invest-ment is approximately 55 per cent within the less technology-intensive industries. These divisions are rather crude but they suffice to demonstrate that UK MNCs are more active in the less skill and capital-intensive industries both at home and abroad. Stopford demonstrates that the picture is not quite so clear.[42] He divides the British MNCs into two types. The first, a minority, constitute global MNCs that operate in the advanced sectors and the competitive markets of advanced capitalism. These contrast with the majority which has avoided international competition by exporting to, and then producing within, the less competitive and at times protected Commonwealth markets.

Our interpretation is slightly different. Although it has been traditional to see the Empire as a source of privileged *markets* for UK exports, this tends to neglect the role of Empire as *producer*. This role is clearly raised by the development of production by UK MNCs in the Empire. There the role of British imperialism becomes one of guaranteeing more or less exclusive control of production relations as well as of market relations, to exclude other export *and* investment. This may well have become increasingly problematical with the dismantling of trade restrictions in the post-war period and the gaining of independence by colonies. Nevertheless, British MNCs have been and, to a lesser extent, continue to be heavily involved in 'colonial' production. Within the underdeveloped world, this production may be relatively advanced, although it depends upon low wages and exploitative working conditions as compared to the advanced capitalist world. Within the MNC, this production is integrated back to Britain. It brings more advanced production to the UK relative to its origins in the underdeveloped world, but relative to other advanced capitalist countries the effect is to direct the British economy towards more labour intensive low-wage production. This is particularly so given the weaknesses of the British economy. For where more capital intensive production is involved and has been utilised by British MNCs, the MNCs have been in a position to locate such production in advanced countries other than Britain.

In short, British MNCs may well divide into two types as suggested by Stopford. One type, with long colonial traditions, is involved in low-intensity production. It thrives upon conditions of low wages whether in the underdeveloped world or in Britain, and has evolved out of the peculiarities of Britain's imperial past and economic weaknesses. In terms of the eclectic theory, this type of MNC has acquired and utilises a low-intensity advantage abroad and at home. By doing so, it reproduces these disadvantageous conditions. The second type of UK MNCs are those that are fully and successfully internationalised, possibly with a colonial tradition, but whose connection with Britain as such is only in name and as a matter of convenience. They have no particular commitment to establish production facilities in the UK and therefore make no special contribution to the capital-intensive development of the British economy.

The situation with regard to US and European, particularly West German, MNCs locating in the UK is rather different. Historically, the US MNCs have had a technological advantage, and whilst it has been exploited in Britain, it is now subject to erosion and reorganisation with Europe rather than the UK as its base. On the other hand, West German MNCs are expanding from an export-led basis and would appear to continue to have their domestic economy as the centre of operations, even as technologically-intensive assembly or whatever is located elsewhere.

To sum up, the prospects for the British economy remain extremely bleak since the complex of MNC operations appear almost uniquely designed to exploit as well as to create a relatively declining industrial base characterised by low-wage and low-intensity production.

The quantitative importance of MNCs, whether of British or foreign origin, also stands out. This, together with the international penetration and interdependence of their operations, raises enormous problems for socialist strategy in Britain as elsewhere. These are problems which have been invariably neglected or ignored, only surfacing occasionally when the power of one or more MNCs has been challenged and been found to be formidable. It is inadequate to shrug off these problems by reference to a strategy of planning agreements or nationalisation as economic and political expediency permits. In the following sections, we consider policies that have been adopted towards MNCs. In the final chapter, we comment upon the strategies that remain open.

Nationalisation of MNC Foreign Affiliates

The purpose of this section is to examine the extent to which foreign affiliates of MNCs have been subject to nationalisation. There is more data available on this for the expropriations undertaken by developing countries although this is far from extensive. Hawkins, Mintz and Provissiero have examined the government takeover of US foreign affiliates over the period 1946 to 1973 and collected information on 170 instances.[43] The vast majority of these (93) are to be found in Latin America, followed by Africa, (51), and in part this reflects the direction of US investment. Of these nationalisations 81 per cent are considered to have resulted from a leftward change in government and compensation was paid in 90 per cent of cases. The proportion of affiliates nationalised is extremely small (less than 1 per cent) but had increased from 13 during 1946-61, 22 during 1962-1966, 78 during 1967-71 to 57 in 1972-73. The nationalisations, however, do seem to be of the largest affiliates, four times the average size, unless over-compensation had been paid. The sectoral composition of the takeover includes 69 from extraction, 32 from finance, 51 from manufacturing and distribution, and 18 from transportation, communication and utilities. These findings are confirmed by Bradley who finds that a high proportion of the takeovers are explained by the action of a very few countries.[44] Williams provides the only comprehensive information on the value of takeovers and of compensation paid, in this case for foreign investments from all countries.[45] Over the period 1956-1972, 40 developing countries have nationalised foreign capital involving assets worth $10 billion at the end of 1972. Compensation paid was in the region of $4 billion, just over 40 per cent of the value of assets. Of the 121 nationalisations covered, 54 were totally uncompensated.

The most comprehensive and more recent information on takeovers of foreign affiliate by numbers is to be found in UN reports.[46] Between 1960 and 1976 71 countries have been involved in 1,369 takeovers. Most countries were involved in fewer than five takeovers, 34, but six expropriated between 31 and 50 affiliates and nine over 50 affiliates. What stands out is the accelerating pace of takeovers for the more recent period, one that is reproduced across all sectors of the economy. The vast majority of takeoves have been of US and of UK firms, with UK companies in the majority. But again the more recent figures reveal an acceleration in the takeover of US firms, particularly in the early 1970s, and a spreading of nationalisation across all countries of origin of foreign investment. All analyses of takeovers comment upon the tendency of nationalisations to proceed in waves whether this wave is transmitted by sector (as for copper, bauxite, or oil) or by region (as for Latin America).

about the possibility of agreement emerging over the nature of a code, and to be equally pessimistic that such a code could be implemented at the expense of the system of MNCs. The reason for this is that whilst the code may appear under the guise of international control *over* MNCs, it is better seen as a code of conduct *amongst* the MNCs themselves. For example, bribery and corruption are indeed a product of the system of MNCs but are not of its essence, and in general the system could operate as well if not better without the deleterious publicity associated with it. More generally, the international code that could emerge would be a reproduction at a world level of corporate laws and practices that emerged in the nineteenth century to promote capitalist accumulation at a national level. Given the different stages of development of MNCs of different countries, it is extremely unlikely that capitalists themselves could agree on a code that would suitably represent fragmented interests. The absence of any world state to implement such a code would make it a dead letter even if it could be written. This is not an argument for abandoning pressures for control over MNCs but rather to see them as originating predominantly from individual national regulations.

Here there is more evidence of what can be done. Nevertheless

> conspicuously absent in developed market economies are explicit policies on international industrial location or division of labour ... Their absence reflects the predominant role assigned to market forces in respect of international industrial allocation.[50]

As for nationalisation, the less developed countries have been far more active. There have developed a host of policies ranging from differential taxation and tax havens (for 1968 one-eighth of foreign income of the leading US-based transnational corporations appeared under tax haven jurisdictions) to government grants and loans, with contracts ranging from joint venture to simple product sharing. It is not our purpose to review these different schemes here nor to assess the extent to which they appropriate control from the MNCs individually or as a whole. We merely note that such schemes are varied, extensive and of increasing importance.

Much the same is true of the relationships between socialist countries and MNCs. The United Nations gives a selection of co-operative agreements of different sorts that had been agreed between the USSR and the MNCs of seven countries, all involving primary production, and reports a growth of industrial co-operation schemes from 600 in 1973 to over 1,800 at the end of 1976.[51] These arrangements now involve many industries and many countries.

Control of MNCs through trade union activity is as likely as such control coming from an international code of practice. There is not even much noise let alone much activity. Here the need for international organisation and solidarity is axiomatic but no more in existence because of this. Opposition by MNCs to international trade union links are to be fully expected. This is because evidence suggests that MNCs tend to adapt themselves to national levels of wages and systems of industrial relations, although there are notable exceptions. In other words, an important aspect of their operations is to exploit the differences between countries.

As already observed, the regulation of MNCs by developed countries contrasts sharply with that of underdeveloped countries by virtue of its relative absence. In general, there do not exist institutions specifically established to monitor the operations of inward or outward investment of MNCs. Exceptions are measures such as those introduced by Canada, fearful rather late in the day of losing its sovereignty to the USA. Regulation, where it has occurred, tends to be the result of the action from institutions pursuing policies which are not specifically directed towards the operations of MNCs. This could involve taxation policy, import controls, balance of payment regulation or monopoly policy. For Britain, it is symptomatic that perhaps the most important intervention against a MNC before the Chrysler rescue was the initiative of the National Health Service in its action in response to Hoffman-La Roche's pricing policy. The weakness of the industrial policy then and since is becoming legendary, but it and other policies have had little or no specific orientation towards MNCs. As Hodges observes

> in most important respects the Labour government did not seek to differentiate between foreign-owned and domestic business enterprises in the formulation and execution of its economic policies. When it is recalled that the value of foreign investment in the UK almost doubled between 1964 and 1970 ... this lack of differentiation is surprising.[52]

We might observe that it is more criminal than surprising!

Moreover the recent abolition of exchange controls has merely freed MNC operations even more in (and out of) the UK. Nevertheless, state intervention against MNCs has been substantial from time to time in various advanced capitalist countries other than Britain, particularly Italy and France. Indeed, over twenty of the world's largest 430 world MNCs embody substantial state-ownership (12 of these with a majority share). More generally, large MNCs are often the most favoured beneficiaries of the various forms of state aid, whether to pre-empt closure or to encourage investment. For example, Stopford reports that in 1978 36.8 per cent of UK government assistance to create and safeguard jobs was accounted for by foreign-owned enterprises.[52]

This brief review of government policy indicates, particularly for underdeveloped countries, that a wide variety of, and at times extensive, interventions have been made into the operations of MNCs. The results have done little to change the balance of power against the MNCs and to guarantee progressive economic development. This has always been most marked in the case of the underdeveloped world; for the advanced capitalist countries, it is a conclusion, following the recession of the 1970s, that cannot be avoided. Nevertheless, government policy, and often the discussion of socialist alternatives, proceeds as if oblivious to the realities of the world of MNCs. Contributions such as Servan-Schreiber's or Stuart Holland's, whatever their analytical and practical merit, stand out as exceptions. In the current period, we are witnessing not only the continuing expansion and interpenetration of the world's MNCs, they are also involved in a dramatic reorganisation of the world's division of labour within and between sectors of the economy, nations and between the developed and underdeveloped worlds. This reorganisation has profound implications for inter-imperialist rivalry, as Japan and West Germany expand production internationally, and for the continuing stability of the world financial system. To recognise these developments is not to remain abreast with them because of the veil of ignorance that surrounds the activities of MNCs both individually and collectively.

The (secretive) power with which multinationals have been and are reshaping the international division of labour and British workers' place in it has been maintained with the support of successive British governments. The failure to develop any effective planning or state intervention in production and investment has meant that what is produced, how it is produced, and what the implications are for living standards and the quality of life in Britain have to a large extent resulted from the unfettered world-wide strategies of multinationals. Multinational corporations have had much greater significance for the British economy than for West Germany, Japan and comparable countries. Their power and the legacy of weak policies toward them increase the difficulties for future socialist strategies, but the Alternative Economic Strategy we discuss in Chapter 12 is a way forward which confronts them.

Notes

[1] N. Koxhoorn, *Oil and Politics: The Domestic Roots of US Expansionism in the Middle East*, Frankfurt 1977.

[2] J. Blair, *The Control of Oil*, London 1977.

[3] A. Sampson, *The Seven Sisters*, London 1975.

[4] H.F. Williamson and A.R. Daum, *The American Age of Illumination, 1859-1899*, Evanston 1959, and H.F. Williamson, R.L. Andrews, A.R. Daum and G.C. Klore, *The American Petroleum Industry: The Age of Energy, 1899-1959*, Evanston 1963.

[5] C. Bina, *The Economics of the Oil Crisis*, London 1985.

[6] See Williamson and Daum, op. cit.

[7] Ibid., p.429.

[8] Ibid., p.713.

[9] See D. Gisselquist, *Oil Prices and Trade Deficits*, New York 1980.

[10] Bina, op. cit.

[11] See J.C. Burrows and T.A. Domenrich, *An Analysis of the United States Oil Import Quota*, Lexington 1970, and D.R. Bolic and M. Russell, *Limiting Oil Imports: An Economic History and Analysis*, Baltimore 1978.

[12] See Gisselquist, op. cit., and R. Vernon (ed.), *The Oil Crisis*, New York 1976.

[13] See *Petroleum Economist*, April and June 1983.

[14] Blair, op. cit.

[15] See H. Souza, 'Notes on World Capital' in C. Furtado *et al.*, *The Internationalisation of Capital*, Toronto 1978.

[16] See B. Fine, 'World Economic Crisis and Inflation' in F. Green and P. Nore (eds), *Issues in Political Economy*, London 1979, reproduced in B. Fine, *Economic Theory and Ideology*, London 1980.

[17] J.H. Dunning, 'Explaining Changing Patterns of International Production: In Defence of Eclectic Theory', *Oxford Bulletin of Economics and Statistics*, No. 41.

[18] Ibid., p.270.

[19] Ibid.

[20] Souza, op. cit.

[21] See J.H. Dunning, K.O. Haberich and J.M. Stopford, *The World Directory of Multinational Enterprises*, London 1981.

[22] Ibid.

[23] Ibid.

[24] See R. Vernon, 'The Product Cycle Hypothesis in a New International Environment', *Oxford Bulletin of Economics and Statistics*, No. 41.

[25] J.H. Dunning and R.D. Pearce, *The World's Largest Industrial Enterprises*, Farnborough 1981.

[26] Ibid.

[27] See United Nations, *Transnational Corporations in World Development: A Re-examination*, New York 1978.

[28] Dunning, op. cit., p.272.

[29] See J.H. Dunning, *International Production and the Multinational Enterprise*, London 1981.

[30] See J.W. Vaupel and J.P. Curhan, *The World's Multinational Enterprises*, Cambridge Mass. 1973.

[31] See van den Bulcke *et al.*, *Investment and Divestment Policies of Multinational Corporations in Europe*, Farnborough 1979.

[32] See Dunning, 'Explaining Changing Patterns of International Production'.

[33] R. Vernon, 'The Product Cycle Hypothesis in a New International Environment', *Oxford Bulletin of Economics and Statistics*, 1979, No. 41, p.265.

[34] Dunning, 'Explaining Changing Patterns of International Production', p.283.

[35] See International Labour Organisation, *Employment Effects of Multinational Enterprises in Industrial Countries*, Geneva 1981.

[36] J.M. Stopford, 'Employment Effects of Multinational Enterprises in the United Kingdom', ILO Working Paper No. 5, Geneva 1979.

[37] *British Business*, 27 February 1981, *Bank of England Bulletin*, 1980, pp.42-55.

[38] M. Panic and P.L. Joyce, 'UK Manufacturing Industry: International Integration and Trade Performance'.

[39] See *British Business*, 3 July 1981.

[40] J.H. Dunning, *US Industry in Britain*, London 1976.

[41] See British Business, 3 July 1981.

[42] J.M. Stopford, 'Changing Perspectives on Investment by British Manufacturing Multinationals', *Journal of International Business Studies*, 1976.

[43] R.B. Hawkins, N. Mintz and M. Provissiero, 'Government Takeovers of US Foreign Affiliates', *Journal of International Business Studies* I, Spring 1976.

[44] P.G. Bradley, 'Managing Against Expropriation', *Harvard Business Review*, July-August 1977.

[45] M.L. Williams, 'The Extent and Significance of the Nationalisation of Foreign-Owned Assets in Developing Countries, 1956-1972', *Oxford Economic Papers*, 1976.

[46] United Nations, *Permanent Sovereignty over National Resources: Report of the Economic and Social Council*, New York 1974, and *Transnational Corporations in World Development: A Re-examination*, New York 1978.

[47] Vaupel and Curhan, op. cit. and J.P. Curhan *et al.*, *Tracing the Multinationals*, Cambridge Mass. 1977.

[48] See United Nations, *Permanent Sovereignty* ...

[49] United Nations, *Transnational Corporations*.

[50] Ibid.

[51] Ibid.

[52] M. Hodges, *Multinational Corporations and National Government: A Case Study of the United Kingdom's Experience 1964-70*, Farnborough 1974, p.285.

[53] Stopford, 'Employment Effects ... ', loc. cit.

Chapter 4

Banks and Industry in the UK: The 'Blocking Thesis'

The particular characteristics of British industry's modern history and present position are bound up with the particular connection, or lack of connection, that it has with finance. It is a commonplace that the special character of the City has weakened British industry in comparison to German, French and Japanese industry where the relations between industry and finance have a structure quite different from the British. Although the argument is, at first sight, intuitively plausible at a general level, the different strands it comprises have to be disentangled and examined in detail if the generalisations are to have any solid foundation. In Chapter 2 we have examined one aspect, the influence of the City on government policies. Here we look at a different element in the argument, the thesis that the financial system has contributed to industrial weakness by failing to provide sufficient finance and by providing it on the wrong terms. Has the City failed industry by diverting to other uses (foreign investment or property being particularly strong candidates) funds that would otherwise have financed real investment in British industry? And has it failed because the money it did provide was on inappropriate terms: was it too much oriented towards the short term, and were the conditions lenders and shareholders imposed upon firms a hindrance to industrial growth?

These questions relate to the whole financial system for the operations of all its main institutions, however different, have a direct or indirect bearing upon the provision of finance for industry. Banks are the most significant source of direct loans to industry: pension funds, insurance companies, investment trusts and unit trusts are the most significant source of share capital and bond finance (that is, the type of finance that is organised with the stock market at its centre); and building societies, the other great financial institutions, control vast sums of personal savings which, by being loaned out as mortgages for house purchase, are prevented from entering directly the pool of funds available for industrial finance. Concern over the responsibility of finance for British industry's straits relates to the operations of all those financial institutions. When the question is, as it has often been, whether the financiers' horizon was too short-term for industry's long-term needs it asks whether banks' loans are too much dominated by short-term overdrafts, whether pension funds and insurance companies too strongly favour shares in those companies that will pay high dividends quickly or yield quick capital gains, *and* whether the growth of building societies is an indication that the financial system has faith only in property rather than industry as a safe repository for long-term funds. Nevertheless, here we shall concentrate on the relations between *banks* and industry, for the relationships between banks and industry are a critical part of the whole. One reason is the size of the banking sector. At the end of 1981 the assets in the hands of banks (including their loans to industry, loans to the state, loans to individuals, and all their other assets) comprised 60 per cent of the total assets of City institutions.[1] Another reason is that banks control, in addition to that treasure, a proportion of the funds of other institutions. In particular, banks have *de facto* control of the investments made by many pension funds. As a result, although banks own a negligible amount of company shares, their control of pension funds' investments has given them control of an estimated 22 per cent of the listed shares in UK companies.[2]

We argue that banks' finance of British industry has contributed to the latter's special weakness although the effect has not arisen in a straightforward way. It is not that the total amount of finance banks have been willing to supply has been inadequate, nor that, favouring the short-term, they have failed to supply the long-term finance industry demanded. Indeed, in a sense, the problem has been the opposite. The banks have met industry's demand for credit all too comfortably and, as a result, have developed a special relationship with industry which has given them a blocking role. They have not used the relationship to stimulate and take a role in industrial development, but at the same time the adequacy of the credit they provided has prevented outside forces, such as the state, which could have combined financial provision with leverage over investment from having an impact on it.

This blocking role of the banks, which has had seriously deleterious effects in the long term, is related to the terms on which banks have provided industrial finance, but its origins are diverse. They stem from the period between 1878 and 1914 when the banking system of Britain's nineteenth century industrialisation was transformed into a twentieth century one that then remained virtually unchanged from 1914 to the 1960s. The system that was constructed then put the banks in a position where they acted as a block against the external forces that were necessary for industry's growth, and it has been the structure of the system rather than the attitudes and choices of bankers that has been at the root of the problem.

The bank amalgamation movement that occurred between 1878 and 1914 produced the type of bank that has dominated the modern system, giant commercial banks with a presence in every high street. Barclays, Lloyds, the Midland, and the predecessors of the National Westminster (the National Provincial and the Westminster) were all formed in that period. The construction of such a highly-centralised system produced two features which marked and affected the banks' relationship with industry for a good half century after 1914 brought the nineteenth century firmly to a close. First, the banks combined their commercial functions with their role as providers of finance in a manner which favoured industrial caution and stagnation. Second, and related to the ways in which commercial and financing functions were combined, the new banks' structure combined local presence and local knowledge of industry with central, head office direction in ways that yielded the worst of both worlds. Not until the late 1970s did these structural weaknesses of the British banks begin to shift, and then it was only under the pressure of competition from American banks lending in Britain and the pressure of the crisis in British manufacturing industry.

In the following pages we shall outline the character of the 1878 to 1914 changes that produced the modern system

(Section 1); examine the mechanisms in banks' industrial lending that have subsequently sustained and characterised banks' blocking role with respect to industry (Section 2); consider the widespread view that the banks' relationship with industry has been marked by a failure to provide sufficient long-term funds (Section 3); and, finally, discuss the changes that have occurred in that relationship as both finance and industry have reacted to the dramatic restructuring of world capitalism since 1970.

The Origins of Twentieth Century Banking: 1878-1918

An influential analysis of the political roots of Britain's modern predicament has emphasised the persistence of the strength of pre-industrial classes in the class alliances that have held state power. Since the eighteenth century the aristocracy has been able to change itself and make alliances to preserve its influence and thereby deny effective political power and cultural domination to the industrial bourgeoisie. It was able to do this because it could ally with other capitalist interests, and particularly finance and the City. In this view, then, the dichotomy between finance and industry has existed for three centuries since the rise of industrial capitalism, and it is often presented as if it were an unchanging division whose character was laid down then. In fact, both industry and finance have subsequently been through major transformations which have affected all aspects of their relationship. The City's orientation to international finance (generally emphasised as a historic contradiction between the City and industry) has been transformed and reconstructed several times, as has the character of the narrower lending and commercial connections between the City and industry. The banks' direct relations with industry were transformed, in particular, between 1878 and 1918; the 'amalgamation movement' is a refutation of any easy assumption that the city-industry distinction has been unchanging and persistent down the centuries.

At the end of the 1870s there was a large number of banks, many of which had been formed in a twenty year upsurge of bank promotions that had started in 1860. In this period, the highly-localised nature of banking began to break down and branch banking became well-established with the average number of branches per bank more or less doubling between 1861 and 1881. Nevertheless, according to one modern authority 'in the late 1870s only the National Provincial had a branch network which extended over most parts of the English economy'.[3] Thus, a concentration on particular regions and particular types of business customer for their deposits and their lending remained a feature of both private and joint-stock banks. Even banks with a relatively strong branch network had definite local roots and their operations did not embrace the whole economy.

By 1918, banking was completely changed. A series of bank amalgamations had created a network of large banks dominated by the 'Big Five'. Whereas the top five banks in England and Wales accounted for only one-quarter (26.4 per cent) of all bank deposits in 1880, a full 80 per cent of deposits were in their hands in 1920. If we include also the next largest banks, the top ten banks were the repositories of almost all bank deposits (96.6 per cent) in England and Wales by 1920.[4] The decline of small banks and the growth of the new giants had been achieved by the disappearance of a large number of banks (323 between 1878 and 1921 according to one estimate) and a series of mergers (225 by the same estimate).[5] The year 1878 was an initial peak; thereafter the most rapid reshaping of the system took place between 1888 and 1902. A final peak of activity came in 1918, when the Big Five were finally created by mergers between banks that were already large.

The amalgamation movement was not a single phenomenon. London banks were not the same as each other; provincial and country banks were even less homogeneous and each merger or disappearance of a bank was unique, reflecting a number of individual and specific factors. Nevertheless, the overall effect was as clear as if a single force had been working relentlessly to produce concentration and centralisation. The outcome was that banking in England and Wales was almost wholly in the hands of a small number of commercial banks, each having headquarters in London and covering the nation with a network of branches. The provinces, towns and suburbs now had branch managers instead of their own local bankers. This change led to banking practices that underpinned the relations between banks and industry in the twentieth century. They were not practices that enabled the banks to act as a dynamic force within industry, but on the other hand they put banks into a comfortable relationship with industry leaving no financial space for the state to step in and push industry toward rationalisation and modernisation. What was the nature of the relationship between industrial firms and their banks after the amalgamation movement? And how had it changed from pre-amalgamation days?

Banks' links with industry comprise two types of activities. First, they lend to industry through overdrafts, through discounting bills and by other means; they also borrow from industry. Second, banks operate the payments system enabling firms to transfer and receive money by clearing their cheques, paying standing orders, and buying and selling foreign exchange for them. The two types of activity are essentially very different: lending and borrowing involves financial capital and its profit comes in the form of interest; clearing cheques, keeping accounts and transferring money is more like the activity of a merchant rather than a financier and its profit comes as the fees (bank charges and commissions) which are the price the bank charges for its services. The daily business of banks is a fusion of both these types of activity, and the way in which they are joined in British banks has affected their ability to play a dynamic role with respect to industry.

Nineteenth-century banks operated the nation's payments system on a local basis and handled the payments of national and international trade through a system of links between correspondent banks. The system was adequate when trade ran smoothly, but prone to crises whenever a panic or an interruption to trade disturbed the flow of cash around the system or, particularly, between London and the rest of the country. Closely related to their provision of these money transfer services was the banks' lending to finance firms' trade; buying and selling commodities and holding stocks of goods for this purpose could easily be financed by bank credit. Because the local banker held the firm's account, the receipt from a sale would pass through his hands and it was a small matter to make a loan and earn interest on it until the money came in. But for longer-term loans to finance capital investment, there were two divergent trends. Some followed the 1850 advice of Thomas Bullion to restrict themselves to the short-term financing of trade and ensure they are always well-covered by holding a readily-encashable collateral.[6] Others, however, did make long-term loans to industry. These were both to finance new investment (such as the Barnsley Bank's financing of new coal-mining in its area) and to support enterprises that were hard hit by depression (such as the Preston Bank's loans to local cotton masters in the 1860s).[7]

To the extent that they provided long-term finance for industrial investment, banks were continuing a practice that was, in fact, significant in the Industrial Revolution before 1830. However, in the nineteenth century there was a fundamental tension between concentrating on short-term credit and offering long-term loans, and the amalgamation movement partially resolved it by shifting the balance toward short-term lending for much of the twentieth century.

Whether making short or long-term loans, the nineteenth century banker based his protection upon the fact that the firm's current account, payments and receipts were in his hands and their fluctuations gave him a direct overview of the firm's position. But that, in itself, could never be enough, for the firm's prospects also depended on what was happening within the firm (labour relations and management efficiency), what was happening to its competitors, and how the industry was changing (the development of new technology and new markets). Bankers needed then, and still need today, a way of obtaining this type of information, or reducing their risks if they don't have it. In the nineteenth century they sought to protect themselves largely by assessing the quality of the industrialists, the owners, to whom they lent. That was very much a local knowledge derived from the links between these essentially local banks and the local businessmen. To take one example:

> The Barnsley Bank, like many of the joint stock banks formed in the 1830s was very much a local concern: its directors and managers knew personally most of their clients and through such knowledge determined their credit-worthiness. The nature of the relationship is illustrated by the case of a possible overdraft to a farmer: the bank's directors mentioned the transaction to the farmer's grandfather, 'who said we should be all right in letting him have it'.[8]

They sometimes sought to protect themselves, too, by taking

a collateral, the right to appropriate and sell some of the firm's assets if the loan failed. But there was disagreement over the type of collateral, for some were more easily encashable than others, and if they were not readily liquid there was always the danger that the banker would be sucked into the firm's affairs to protect himself. The view adopted by some bankers on the need for an arm's length relationship protected by liquid collateral was expressed most strongly by 'Bullion': 'reject ... everything that is not readily convertible into money. In short, turn over a new leaf and mind your own business.'[9]

Thus the banks' loans to industry in the middle and late nineteenth century were protected, or so the banks hoped, by the banker's knowledge of the men he was lending to and the knowledge gained through having the firm's payments and receipts pass through his hands. For some, with or without collateral, this was a basis for long-term lending and the finance of capital investment, but others steered clear. The amalgamation movement decided the issue; it forced a withdrawal from long-term lending. In doing so it took over the system's reliance on the local banker's knowledge and, especially, on its privileged position in control of the payments system, and it made these relationships into a highly conservative force.

The new giant banks created between 1878 and 1918 had the potential to finance a new era of accumulation, a rejuvenation of British industry on a footing to compete with Germany and other countries' new industries. The creation of national branch networks out of individual local banks opened the way for the mobilising of money from any sector or region to finance investment in any part of the country. And this branch network, with its inheritance of local presence, could have provided the basis for a close tie between banker and borrower. With the power of a national bank behind him, the local banker, now personified by the branch manager, could have ensured the profitability and security of the bank's loans by developing an involvement in the borrower's affairs. Making long-term loans or taking an equity stake would involve risks, but they were risks which national banks could take more easily than their local predecessors and they would have been counterbalanced by participation (for example, through non-executive directorships) in the firm's affairs. That participation would have been possible because the national banks' branches gave them as much local presence as their predecessors, and if they had loaned venture capital they would have had to use their involvement to push for modernisation and rationalisation. But, although the creation of national banks opened up that possibility, it also exerted a pressure in the opposite direction, toward a greater distancing from the hard industrial decisions. In the event, the latter was the course taken.

The creation of big banks necessitated the creation of a management structure, for the new local bankers had to be answerable to the centre instead of being their own bosses. The structure which was created regulated their lending by a set of negative rules designed to minimise the damage that could be done if a loan failed, rather than one which gave managers (either at local, regional, or national level) the support of the hierarchy in making informed judgements for a positive programme of financing industrial growth. The conservative system that was adopted hinged on two factors. First, each manager was able to lend only up to a certain limit, the level of which was sometimes very low, and in general precluded any branch from backing a significant industrial investment. Moreover, because these limits were partly designed to ensure a spread of lending across the country instead of a concentration on one sector, they were accompanied by an unwillingness of the head office and regional head office themselves to approve large commitments to major projects. Second, as a general rule, loans had to be covered now by a collateral that would enable the bank to recover its money if the borrower failed. Bankers continued to dispute over the relative merits of different types of collateral but all the national banks adopted the practice that borrowers had to provide sound collateral.

The new national banks lent to industry securely on the basis of these negative management rules. And they believed that additional strength was given by two inherited features: the local banker's ability to assess the quality of the people running the firms and the bank's monitoring of the firms' current accounts, a surveillance strengthened by the amalgamation movement's creation of an integrated national payments system in the hands of the banks. This lending was conservative in nature not because it starved industry of funds (although the reliance on local bank managers' knowledge of the people in charge of the firms made it difficult for new ventures to overcome their lack of a track record), but because its comfortable security prevented banks from having to take an active involvement in stimulating industrial productivity and growth. In fact, as we shall argue below it was the easy availability of bank finance rather than its shortage that contributed to industry's weakness.

The Practice of Banking After 1918

The conservative lending practices laid down by 1918, the negative rules to control the lending of branch managers, persisted throughout the next half century. They greatly weakened the radicalising pressures that could have trans- formed British industry in the periods when it was partially restructured, the slump of the 1930s and the boom of the 1950s and 60s. Through the decades the banks relied predominantly upon a 'liquidation' or 'gone concern' approach which so strongly protected them against loss if the borrower went broke that they had no need to intervene in industry: 'attack is the best form of defence' against industrial frailty was not a relevant concept. The main practices of this approach were: the provisions of finance through overdrafts rather than other types of bank loans; and the securing of these loans by 'charges' on firms' assets (especially floating charges).

Firms' external finance until the 1970s came from three sources, new shares, the sale of new bonds and bills (long and short-term loan instruments respectively) and bank loans. The bank loans consisted almost entirely of overdrafts, and in this respect British banks have been quite different from banks in, say West Germany, France and Japan. The overdraft is a peculiarly British form of bank lending to industry. It involves granting a maximum limit to the loan rather than giving a loan of a single amount; the amount borrowed is determined by the amount the firm (or individual) chooses to draw (up to the maximum limit) and interest is charged only on the amounts drawn rather than on the total permissible under this credit line; the bank has the legal right to demand at any time, immediate repayment of the amount borrowed.

These characteristics of the overdraft conform with and reinforce certain characteristics of both industrial firms and banks in the UK. The flexibility of the overdraft reinforced firms' lack of strategic planning of investment, production and finance. At different times this century various factors (for example, the stop-go demand management policies of the 1950s and 60s) have reinforced firms' reluctance to formulate long-term plans,[10] but if bank finance had been available only to finance forward-looking production and accumulation plans it would have acted as a strong influence in the opposite direction. Overdrafts, however, are at the other extreme, for they enable firms to adjust their borrowing in accordance with immediate rather than planned needs and to do so without cost. As far as the banks were concerned, overdraft financing enabled them to maintain the 'liquidity' and flexibility of assets at the highest level, achieving a form of industrial lending that best satisfies the drive that financial capital everywhere has to free itself from constraints and ties. This liquidity resulted from the fact that overdrafts are repayable to the banks on demand, at least in principle.

The overdraft, therefore, has been an essential element in the 'blocking' role of bank finance. It has meant that firms have been able to meet their financial needs without turning to external sources of funds, such as the state, that would exert a strong interventionist discipline over their operations. And, in principle, it has meant that banks have been able to lend with little apparent risk and so do not have to intervene in order to protect their loans. In reality, overdrafts have been less liquid than in principle, for a high proportion have been 'hard core', credit which is regularly renewed and outstanding for long periods rather than short-term. The effect has been to strengthen the effect of overdraft financing on firms (for it has meant that their long-term financial needs, even for expansion, could be partly financed by this flexible method without rigorous planning) while weakening the overdraft's ability to act as banks' ideal form of flexible capital.

The second element of the banks' approach to industry after the amalgamation movement, however, underpinned their ability to lend to industry without involvement. That is their reliance upon collateral in the form of charges upon the borrowers' assets. United States banks claim to secure their industrial loans generally by agreeing conditions with the borrowers on the firms' operations during the course of the loan, setting out targets (or constraints) on the firm's performance and its financial structure; UK banks' reliance on collateral is at the opposite extreme for it pins the banks' concern on what happens when the firm collapses rather than how it operates when alive. It has enabled banks to obtain priority in confiscating and selling a bankrupt firm's assets. It thereby enabled them to avoid involvement with the firms during the course of the loan, and to avoid acting as an external discipline on them, for, even if their overdrafts became core sources of finance and lose their liquidity, the banks are protected against industry's weakness by their collateral.

Banks' collateral has taken two forms, fixed and floating charges. The first means that the bank can take possession of a specific named asset in case of default (in the same way that a building society can take possession of the borrower's house), and, since 1978, one such asset may be the debts owing to the company. Floating charges give the bank more general powers to secure their loans, for they enable the bank to take possession of any of a bankrupt borrowers' assets, and to place a company in receivership if it appears to have defaulted on a loan. Floating charges were first introduced in England (but not Scotland) in 1870, but their significance stems from the establishment of negative rules as the norm of the giant branch banks established at the start of this century.

The predominance of overdraft financing secured by charges has been significant for banks' 'blocking' role. It has also led to two incorrect interpretations. It has caused some to assume that UK banks have financed industry *only* through overdrafts and other 'short-term' loans without involvement in monitoring borrowers' operations.[11] In reality, however, banks have provided other forms of finance and even held shares in industrial firms, and have monitored and advised on the firms' operations. In most cases the monitoring has been more of a fiction than a reality, relying on the views of bank managers with no understanding of industrial capital, but in the economic crises of the 1930s and early 1980s banks have become actively involved in restructuring a (small) number of the industrial and commercial companies that were in difficulties. It should also be borne in mind that the characteristics outlined here are those of the commercial banks, particularly the Big Four. Merchant banks have a greater involvement with industry advising on financial restructuring, controlling sources of long-term funds, and in some cases (such as the restructuring of the ferrous foundry industry) producing schemes for the rationalisation of production. The second incorrent implication that can be drawn from the banks' reliance on overdrafts is that they have contributed to starving industry of the long-term funds it needs and demands to finance long-term investment plans. We turn now to that question of capital shortage and banks' role in it.

Has There Been a Shortage?

Commentators on the special character of British capital have often identified a shortage of industrial finance (or long-term industrial finance) as one source of industrial weakness. Two phenomena have been noted; industry's high reliance on internal funds (retained profits) to finance accumulation and the City's orientation toward foreign investment. Their coexistence appears to be more than coincidental and is often interpreted as the City starving industry of funds while it invests abroad (and in other 'unproductive' sectors such as landed property). The low level of long-term funds invested in industry is then, on this interpretation, a specific element in this shortage restricting the supply of long term finance. In fact this would be a false interpretation of the role of banks and the City with respect to industry, for the banks' blocking role has arisen for reasons which are the very opposite of a shortage; the banks have supplied industry with the funds it wants thereby precluding the state or other external sources of finance from gaining a financial foothold as a basis for strategic intervention in industrial accumulation.

It is true that banks have had a strong international orientation with overseas lending being a major source of profits, and that industry has relied heavily upon internally generated funds. Regarding the first, the international lending of banks in the UK was 46 per cent of their total lending in 1970, and by 1982 it had risen to 70 per cent.[12] This figure is for the lending of all banks in the UK including foreign-owned banks located in London (which accounted for four-fifths of London's foreign lending in 1982); the Big Four and other commercial banks directed a lower percentage of their lending abroad, but it was still unusually high in comparison to other advanced capitalist countries. For example, in 1981, 39.3 per cent of the profits of Barclays, the largest UK banking group, came from the various types of lending and other business conducted by its international division.

At the same time, the retained profits of industrial and commercial firms have been the main source of finance for fixed investment. Over the 1960s, for example, retained earnings were equivalent, on one estimate, to 99 per cent of the funds industry and commerce invested in new plant and other assets (whereas in France and West Germany comparable approximate proportions were 60 and 80 per cent respectively). The same phenomenon is partly the cause of UK firms' low capital gearing. In 1972, for example, the ratio of external debt to shareholders' own capital was 55 per cent, reflecting low external debt compared with France (a gearing ratio of 126 per cent), West Germany (97 per cent) and Japan (325 per cent).[13]

But these facts do not mean that industrial firms have faced a shortage of bank finance in general or of medium-term bank finance, nor that they have faced a shortage of external finance as a whole, and there is no evidence of such shortages. Evidence of shortage could be of two kinds: either firms systematically finding that the amount of credit they want at the going interest rate is not available, or that, even if the credit they seek is readily available, they cut the amount they want because the going interest rate is too high. It is difficult to get hard evidence of either, but what evidence there is suggests no shortage.

Assessments of the first type of shortage (non-availability) have been made on the basis of surveys. The Wilson Committee is the latest of three major enquiries to have touched this question since the 1930s. Although its theoretical framework is seriously flawed,[14] its surveys and evidence do not indicate that banks or the financial system have been unable to meet firms' demand for finance at the going interest rate.[15] (The only exception the Committee found was that small companies had difficulty obtaining finance, but the subsequent performance of the loan guarantee scheme, a scheme proposed by the Committee, suggests that small companies' credit requirements were not for viable investment in industrial capital.[16]) Surveys of particular industrial sectors, such as the mechanical engineering industry, confirm that firms themselves do not consider that they have been unable to obtain the quantities and types of bank credit they seek.[17]

To assess the second type of shortage, high interest rates, comparisons have to be made. Since we are concerned with the special factors affecting British capital – a particularly British shortage of credit – an important comparison is between British and overseas interest rates. Historically, market interest rates (yields on bonds and bills) in London have moved in line with those in New York, Europe and, in recent decades, the Far East, rather than being systematically higher. In the absence of state controls over the international movement of finance, the tendency for interest rates to be in line with each other in the major capitalist countries (allowing for different rates of inflation and exchange rate depreciation) is an expression of financial capital's main characteristic, its flexibility and its need to free itself from local ties and boundaries. These market interest rates are not the same as the interest charged on the specific part of financial capital we are concerned with here, bank credit to industry, but there is no evidence that those rates have been exceptional. The rate on banks' medium-term loans to companies is often fixed as a margin over the market rate for short term inter-bank loans (LIBOR); the latter keeps in line with international movements while the margin varies from company to company. The little evidence that there is suggests that the margins are not high by international standards; according to Jerry Coakley's 1983 survey of mechanical engineering, the banks' margin was between $\frac{3}{8}$ per cent for the largest companies and $1\frac{3}{4}$ per cent for the smaller. Overdraft facilities carried a standardised rate calculated as 1 per cent over banks' base rate (the latter moving in line with market rates).

Thus there is no evidence either of exceptionally high interest rates or of the non-availability of credit to suggest that banks have starved industry of the funds it has sought and the high proportions of banks' foreign lending and of firms' internal financing are parts of a more complex phenomenon.

This empirical conclusion is consistent with our theoretical conception of the financial system and the emphasis we have placed on the importance for financial capital of independence and flexibility (see Chapter 1). Independence is conceived by some writers as independence from British industry and, hence as the basis of a thesis of inexorable overseas expansion at the expense of British industry's financial needs, but the full independence that financial capital seeks is, in fact, independence from any one sector; a capital flight away from British industry which over the decades locks the City wholly into financing foreign industries and governments (or the British state and property) would have given the banks no more independence that if they were wholly locked into financing Northern mills and Midlands factories. Thus financial capital's flexibility is the essence of its independence and it also ensures that there is unlikely to be a systematic failure to supply the credit which industry demands. Nor is there likely to be a failure to supply the type of credit demanded; if industry demands medium-term loans to finance investment, either banks will supply it or the flexibility of finance will ensure that other finance houses will. It would be easy to imagine that banks' need for independence must make them unwilling to contemplate medium-term financing and concentrate on overdraft lending because only the latter enables them to avoid being locked in to industrial capital, but that would be incorrect. As we have noted, overdrafts have in fact become core, long-term finance for many companies so that they do not enable the lender to avoid becoming locked in despite the formal ability to call the loan in at any time. And medium-term finance need not tie the particular lender to the particular borrower, for arrangements can be made for one bank to sell to others the debt owed to it by a firm.

Recent Changes in Bank Lending to Industry

The banks' blocking role in industrial finance developed on the basis of the amalgamation and centralisation of bank capital which created Britain's banking monopolies, and the relationship between banks and industry was maintained almost unchanged until the late 1970s. Changes did occur but they were either temporary and did not fundamentally affect the position or they were extensions of the same relationships as before (such as the mergers of the 1960s). The most important of the former were the powers the state exercised, through the Bank of England, to regulate bank lending and direct it toward particular sectors of industry and trade during and after the Second World War. These essentially negative controls did not alter the underlying relation between banks and firms and, although some broad directives on the direction of loans were used as late as the 1960s, the banks' comfortable relationship with borrowers blocking the potential for state finance and state rationalisation of industry was unchanged. The long period of continuity determined the character of bank finance in the years that the seeds of Britain's recent industrial weakness were being sown. But the economic crises of the 1970s and early 1980s, and the restructuring of the capitalist world's economy that they have marked, have generated intense changes in the City and transformed the operation of the financial system, while at the same time increasing the probability of a financial crash. Has this broken the old bank-industry relationship and shaken its stultifying blocking role?

The banks have been at the forefront of changes in the financial system and their lending to industry has changed, but the changes do not suggest that the structure of industrial finance in the UK will have any greater ability to act as a rational dynamic force upon industrial capital than it has in the past.

The world economic crisis was associated with a particularly dramatic decline in the rate of profit of firms operating in the UK which forced industry and commerce to rely less on internal financing and more on credit.[18] The sources of new funds for firms can be divided into internal and external sources. In the period 1963-69 the average ratio of new internal funds (such as retained profits) to new external (such as bank credit) was 2.2; but in 1970 to 1982 its average level was only 1.4. And banks were a prime source of these increasingly important external funds for, apart from anything else, firms were unwilling to borrow by issuing bonds on the stock market in the high interest rate years after 1972. Thus, 40 per cent of firms' external funds were borrowed from banks in 1963 to 1969, but a considerably greater proportion, 54 per cent, came from banks in 1970-82.

Firms' increased reliance on bank credit as internal funds and other sources of external funds dried up in the economic crisis is, at one level, a mark of the blocking role banks have continued to have through being the source of easily available funds. However, there have been substantial changes in the form this bank lending has taken which raise the question of whether bank lending now is more oriented toward acting as an external discipline and rationalising force upon industrial capital. Some changes have been in purely technical financial arrangements. For example, in the 1970s (until 1984) the tax system made it advantageous for financial groups (owned by banks) to lease machinery, plant and vehicles to firms instead of lending them the funds to buy the capital equipment themselves (so that financial institutions became the formal owners of large blocks of productive capital as long as the tax system favoured it). Another example of purely technical changes in bank financing was the 'disintermediation' that occurred in the late 1970s when banks (to avoid government regulations on their borrowing) provided facilities for firms to borow directly from lenders instead of receiving deposits and lending them on themselves. Changes which have been more than technical have been the growth of lending to UK firms by American banks and the growth of medium-term loans with less reliance placed on collateral and more on performance conditions as a means of securing them. These do represent significance changes, but they do not fundamentally change the basic position of banks with respect to industry; they remain the principal source of external finance, blocking others, but do not have a role in the rational supervision of and strategic planning of industry.

Since the beginning of the 1960s, and particularly since 1963, the presence of foreign banks in the City has substantially increased, and US banks have led the movement. The main impetus for the establishment of London offices came from the growing internationalisation of capital. The international spread of industrial and commercial capital through foreign investment by US multinationals (MNCs) led US banks to establish branches to service the financial needs in Europe of their customer MNCs. And the internationalisation of financial capital which created the Eurodollar markets led

US banks to set up in London to participate in them. But these banks also actively developed a line in lending to industry and commerce in the UK and increased their role in the 1970s. Whereas in 1970 the proportion of the assets of US banks in London accounted for by loans to the UK private sector was 5.6 per cent, by 1982 it was 11.7 per cent of their assets. The historical development of US banking has given those banks an orientation toward 'wholesale' banking (borrowing and lending in large amounts) rather than the 'retail' operations that have typified British 'high street branch' banking. Consistently with this, the US banks concentrated on lending to the largest corporations within the UK and targeted their loans on a few main sectors (such as commodity traders, North Sea Oil, chemicals and electronics).[19]

The US bank loans to industry and commerce have been the medium-term loans typical of wholesale banking. Unlike overdrafts, the term of the loan is fixed (between 1 and 10 years), the full amount of the credit line is committed (rather than only a maximum limit being set), and, unlike many overdrafts, a written agreement specifies the conditions of the loan. Since the US banks promoted such loans, the British commercial banks have themselves made an increasing number of their industrial loans on this basis, although the switch of emphasis away from overdrafts became substantial only at the end of the 1970s. As a result of such developments, the historic reliance of industry and commerce on overdraft bank finance has been superseded to a large extent. In a survey of mechanical engineering companies it was found that at the end of their 1980 financial year, 46.6 per cent of their bank credit (which, in total, was itself 78 per cent of their external finance) was in the form of medium term loans.[20]

These changes, however, have not led to any shift in the banks' blocking position with respect to industrial finance. On one hand, the availability of bank credit has proved adequate to meet firms' demand for it (even when the latter sharply increased); on the other, the new types of bank lending have not been on terms which increase the banks' strategic, rational organising role. Medium-term loans specify conditions on borrowers quite different from the traditional 'collateral against liquidation' security. The firms have to conduct their business in accordance with the conditions. But this does not involve the banks any more closely in the supervision of industrial capital since the conditions concern only the financial balance sheet aspects of the firm rather than its production and trading. Some financial aspects, such as the level of profits, are the result of the firms' 'real' operations, but the aspects specified in the banks' loan agreements are not tightly linked in that way but can, instead, be varied by purely financial operations. They concern such things as the ratios of different types of finance used by the firm (gearing ratio, current assets/current liabilities ratio etc). When it comes to assessing the production and trading operations of the borrowers, the US banks as much as the traditional UK banks, rely upon 'subjective' assessments of the management team and their past profits rather than informed assessment of the firm's capital equipment or industrial relations system.

Conclusion

Commentators from a wide spectrum have pointed to the 'hardness' of British bankers as a source of industrial weakness. They have argued that bankers have created a shortage of medium-term finance and have been at the forefront of 'disciplining' industry because they have taken the lead in calling in the receiver to companies hit by recession (in the first ten months of 1980 the London Clearing Banks appointed 400 receivers compared with an average of about 150 a year in the preceding decade). We have argued that each aspect of this critique is wrong.[21]

First it is not bankers as such but the structure of the banking *system* that has shaped the relationship between banks and industry. In this the historical roots of the structure are to be found in the amalgamation movement that ended in 1918 and, through intense centralisation, created giant monopolistic banks. The importance of this has not been the degree of monopoly itself; in fact, on several measures of bank concentration, banks in England and Wales were less monopolistic than those in Japan, Italy, West Germany, France, and Switzerland.[22] The characteristics it gave rise to stemmed from the manner in which the monopolies were constructed rather than their size itself.

Second, bank finance has met the demands industry has

placed on it and, third, it has not acted as an external discipline or strategic rational force upon industrial capital. It is for these reasons, rather than their opposite, that banks have contributed to the special weakness of industrial capital in Britain. Because of the adequacy of bank finance there has been no pressure on the state to intervene in financing industry itself and hence nothing to force the state to develop financial strategies as an element in the rational planning of industry itself. It has been a case of a monopolistic banking sector thereby hindering the rise of a rational planned capitalism. Recent changes do not alter that and a programme for industrial development can only be constructed as part of a socialist plan for control of finance.

Notes

[1] J. Coakley and L. Harris, *The City of Capital*, Oxford 1983, p.5.

[2] Ibid., p.111.

[3] P.L. Cottrell, *Industrial Finance, 1830-1914*, London 1980, p.196.

[4] F. Capie and G. Roderick-Bali, 'Concentration in British Banking, 1870-1920', *Business History*, Vol.24, No.3, November 1982, p.287.

[5] Ibid., p.283

[6] 'Thomas Bullion', *The Internal Management of a Country Bank*, 1850, quoted in Cottrell, op. cit., p.2.

[7] Cottrell, op. cit., pp.215-8.

[8] Ibid., pp.213-4.

[9] Quoted in ibid., p.211.

[10] R.E. Caves, *Britain's Economic Prospects*, Washington DC 1968.

[11] Labour Party Financial Institutions Study Group, *The City: A Socialist Approach*, London 1982.

[12] J. Coakley, 'The Internationalisation of Banking Capital', *Capital and Class*, No, 23 Summer 1984.

[13] These figures give only an approximate indication since all data on gearing ratios are weak.

[14] J. Coakley and L. Harris, 'Evaluating the Role of the Financial System' in D. Currie and M. Sawyer (eds), *Socialist Economic Review 1982*, London 1982.

[15] Wilson Report: Committee to Review the Functioning of Financial Institutions, *Report*, London 1980.

[16] See L. Harris, 'British Capital: Manufacturing, Finance and Multinational Corporations' in D. Coates, G. Johnston and R. Bush (eds), *A Socialist Anatomy of Britain*, Oxford 1985.

[17] Surveys conducted by J. Coakley, to be published in J. Coakley, T. Evans and L. Harris (eds), *New Perspectives on the Financial System*, London forthcoming.

[18] W.E. Martin (ed.), *The Economics of the Profits Crisis*, London 1981.

[19] Surveys conducted by J. Coakley, *loc. cit*

[20] J. Coakley, *loc. cit*.

[21] Bank of England, 'Corporate Insolvency', *Bank of England Quarterly Bulletin*, Vol.20, No.4, 1980, pp.430-6.

[22] P. Honohan and R.P. Kinsella, 'Comparing Bank Concentration Across Countries' *Journal of Banking and Finance*, Vol.6, No.2, 1982, pp.255-62.

II State and Industry

Chapter 5

The Nationalised Industries

Since the Second World War, nationalised industries (NIs) have played an important part in the British economy. Currently, they account for about 7 per cent of the country's labour force, 14 per cent of total fixed investment and 10 per cent of net output. Although nationalisation as a form of state economic intervention has not been the exclusive policy instrument of Labour governments in the UK, it has tended to be associated with those professing a socialist ideology and politics. Those to the right tend to view nationalisation as a necessary evil, something which is inevitable rather than desirable. This political compromise has been questioned by Margaret Thatcher's Tory government which, as part of its commitment to the freeing of market forces, has implemented policies of denationalisation as well as the privatisation of welfare services.[1] That it has embarked on this course and achieved some successs requires an explanation that goes beyond the appeal of 'Thatcherism' as an ideology. The development of the NIs must be examined historically to reveal why they have been particularly susceptible to such policies.

Theoretical Considerations

Despite the economic, political and ideological significance of NIs, they have suffered from a lack of both theoretical and empirical analysis. Indeed, the treatment of NIs in orthodox economic theory has always been considered inadequate even by those sympathetic to this approach.[2] It has failed to explain,

---

This chapter was written by Ben Fine and Kathy O'Donnell.

for example, why nationalisations have taken place and why NIs develop in the way that they do. A further peculiarity is that the theory has had very little impact on policy formulation. In this respect there is a contrast with other economic doctrines (for example, Keynesianism), which have provided a theoretical basis for policymakers. It will be instructive to examine why the orthodox theory of NIs has failed to have a similar impact.

The orthodox theory depends upon a rigid separation between economy and society.[3] This permits the economy to be analysed in isolation from society, thus allowing 'economically efficient' outcomes to be identified. The result is to raise two considerations. The first is to enable decisionmakers to satisfy what are termed 'social criteria', for example, the running of unprofitable but socially desirable local transport facilities. Where services are provided under social criteria, it is argued that NIs should be subsidised to compensate for the commercial loss that they bear. The second consideration is to identify what are termed 'economic criteria'. For example, NIs should set their prices equal to long run marginal cost and new investment should be required to obtain a designated rate of return.

These economic criteria are within a perspective which assumes that the market is both desirable and efficient in normal circumstances. Given this starting point, state economic intervention only becomes necessary under certain restrictive conditions. A notable example is the existence of economies of scale which give rise to a natural monopoly; for example, in the case of public utilities like water supply. Since unregulated private ownership would result in allocative and technical inefficiencies, state intervention is required in order to create a benevolent monopoly which exploits economies of scale in production without exercising market power.[4] In such cases of 'market failure', state intervention is supposed to guarantee the smooth and efficient operation of the market economy.[5] However, the analysis fails to explain why such conditions have in practice led to state *ownership* rather than other forms of state *regulation*.

The inability to explain why nationalisation is necessary concedes much to the advocates of the *laissez-faire* economy. The latter have sought to deny the generality and significance of the conditions in which the market is liable to operate inefficiently. Even when this is conceded, forms of state intervention other than nationalisation, such as the issuing of public licences, are considered a sufficient remedy. The advantages of such regulations are set against the various disadvantages of state ownership, associated with which is the erosion of the profit motive, and the loss of intrepreneurial initiative.[6] Finally, nationalisations have been regarded as market imperfections created by ideological and political commitment to socialist principles. As such they are a source of inefficiency and are falsely justified as a means to satisfy social criteria or as a mechanism to control the economy.

These observations concerning the orthodox analysis help to explain why it has failed to act as a practical guide to the running of the NIs. Although it constructs a set of criteria by which the NIs should be operated, it totally neglects the mechanisms by which they are to be implemented. This approach rests upon the absence of conflict in the theory, both within economic and social relations and between them. Once it is recognised that conflicts of interest exist and have to be resolved, then the question of control rather than the question of criteria becomes *central*. Within the *laissez-faire* theory of the capitalist economy, the market harmoniously coordinates different interests and imposes a discipline of profitability upon individual capitalists. These control mechanisms are absent, however, in the orthodox theory of NIs. Instead it implicitly assumes that some other mechanism exists which translates social and economic criteria into the appropriate outcomes. The question of how this process occurs is relegated to the area of practicalities beyond the scope of economic theory. Thus it is not surprising that the theory has been unable to provide a satisfactory account of the NIs' particular histories and development.

The clearest demonstration of these arguments comes from the divergence between economic and financial objectives.[7] Economic objectives correspond to economic criteria. Financial objectives contain within them an economic criterion. For example, over a five year period a NI should break even, or over twelve months not exceed a cash limit. These criteria, and they have been important in the running of the industries, have no obvious and immediate correspondence to economic efficiency and would lead an orthodox economist to despair, particularly as they will in general contradict other economic criteria. Yet, their very importance derives from their role in control, in limiting the operations of the NIs in the same way that profitability ultimately limits the operations of private capital.

The significance of financial control of the NIs can be overemphasised. There are other forms of control, such as pricing, to which we return later. What financial control does is to make clear the significance of state-ownership in distinguishing NIs from private capital. For the latter, whether through low wages, unfair competition, high productivity or even government subsidy, a condition for their reproduction as capital is the generation of profit over time, and this is the mechanism by which private capital is controlled. The same is not true for the reproduction of the NIs, and this explains the need for financial and other objectives, i.e. control. NIs can make losses, irrespective of the validity of the accountancy practices by which they do so, and continue to survive. Profitability is not a mechanism of control, precisely because of state-ownership, even if it is used as a criterion for policy.

Despite our negative conclusions, an assessment of the orthodox theory of NIs is useful because it provides the basis for an alternative approach. An analysis of NIs must recognise that they result from and develop upon a basis of conflict in which economic and political relations have been intimately intertwined. Moreover the structure of control over the NIs is both complex and diverse which means that a general theory of NIs is unhelpful. Consequently, the historical and social conditions within which a particular nationalisation has proceeded should provide a starting point for analysis. Although some of these conditions may be uniform across the NIs as a whole, each industry will exhibit its own peculiarities which will render the significance and effect of these common conditions to be quite diverse. We discuss this later in the context of cash limits. By contrast, orthodox analysis presents a general theory and consequently fails to address the existence and concrete experience of NIs in anything other than name.

Similar conclusions concerning the impossibility of a general theory of NIs can be obtained by a different route. Although NIs need not generate a profit, this does not automatically prevent them from constituting capital. At the most abstract level of theory, capital involves social relations guaranteeing the production of surplus value, for which profit is the usual but not the only nor the necessary form in exchange. NIs could show a deficit but remain a source of surplus value by transferring it, for example, to other capitals in the form of cheap inputs, or to the state of interest payments. This is not so for public corporations such as the British Broadcasting Corporation (BBC) which cannot be considered to employ wage labour to produce commodities embodying surplus value. On the other hand, enterprises like the National Coal Board (NCB) and the British Steel Corporation (BSC) are, in many respects, integrated into the economy like private capital. Finally, there are those NIs like the Post Office and British Rail, which appear to occupy an intermediate position as far as exhibiting the conditions associated with capitalist production is concerned.

The juxtaposition of these empirical examples with the theoretical problem of what constitutes capital reveals the fallacy of approaching the NIs in terms of whether they are capital or not. To do so is to confront concretely organised productive activity with an ideal concept of capital (and hence non-capital) and classifying each industry according to its proximity to this model. Not surprisingly some industries cannot be comfortably fitted into this classification. The theoretical difficulty posed by state-ownership is that the mechanism by which the reproduction of private capital is identified is absent since profitability is not a mechanism of control. The absence of this mechanism can reflect the removal of an NI from organisation as capital, when, for example, its products are no longer (sold as) commodities. The capital/non-capital approach to the classification of state-run enterprises essentially seeks to substitute some criteria other than profitability for it to be theoretically operational. But it is the absence of the profitability criterion and mechanism of control that necessarily leads to economic and *political* conditions of organisation that are diverse.

The presence of the political factor, reflecting the extent of state involvement, suggests that a more satisfying approach is to recognise that increasing state economic intervention and expenditure has exhibited two different tendencies. One has led to the expansion of unproductive, i.e. non-capital expenditure to guarantee economic and social reproduction.

This is usually examined under the rubric of the welfare state. The other tendency has been the state's interventions to facilitate the reorganisation of productive capital. Both tendencies reflect the increasing socialisation of capitalist society and can lead to state ownership in particular circumstances. However, the intervention of the two tendencies yields complex and diverse results which makes a general analysis inapplicable. Categories of expenditure within the welfare state cannot be satisfactorily analysed as a homogeneous mass. At the other extreme, where nationalisation preserves the accumulation of capital, the significance of state ownership is not general but contingent upon the political and economic conditions within which competition mediates the conflicts with labour and with other capitals. As already observed, state-run enterprises scarcely fall within these two ideally conceived extremes so that the fallacy of a general theory of NIs is confirmed.

The significance of these remarks is not confined to orthodox theory, for they apply equally to much analysis within the Marxist tradition. General theories of state expenditure and of the state as capitalist have been advanced. They tend to reproduce the separation between the economic and the political which is characteristic of orthodox analysis. In place of economic efficiency and social criteria, these two levels are then determined by the balance of class conflict with the functional needs of capital to provide general conditions for accumulation, including the moderation of class struggle, to the forefront.[8]

Such an approach to state expenditure, and by corollary to NIs, takes too much for granted. The separation between economic and political is inappropriate, as evidenced, for example, by the role of cash limits which constitute a political control with an essential economic content. Moreover, the relationship between the economic and political is not fixed but open to class conflict, as revealed in the struggle for nationalisation as well as over the established NIs. Struggles over nationalisation and the NIs can reflect within capitalism a challenge to the relations under which production is organised. These struggles may have a formal similarity to those undertaken within private capital, by workers over wages, conditions of work and redundancy, by capitalists for market shares, credit and even government aid. But the content of the struggles can be different. For private capital, the survival of production and capital are synonymous whereas for the NIs the two are quite distinct (although the latter requires the former). In short, whereas the reproduction of private capital involves the struggle to make production profitable, the NIs are first involved in establishing the extent to which production is capitalistic. This process is important to bear in mind in any analysis of nationalisation in practice.

Nationalisation in the UK

In Britain, we can identify three periods when nationalisation has taken place. In the inter-war period, there were a number of politically uncontroversial nationalisations, for example, the electricity grid and coal royalties, whereas the struggle to nationalise the coal mines was fiercely and successfully resisted. The post-war Labour government saw the first major wave of nationalisations and, after 1967 with the renationalisation of BSC, there have been a number of further nationalisations or at least the taking of industries into state-ownership. The first nationalisations of the post-war Labour government were relatively unopposed. By contrast, there was fierce resistance to the later proposals to nationalise steel, road transport, sugar and cement, which were not nationalised or were denationalised by the subsequent Tory government. The lack of substantial conflict over those industries which were permanently nationalised is explained both by long term developments as well as by immediate economic and political circumstances. The inter-war period had witnessed an erosion of capitalist forms of control over the industries and this had been consolidated by war-time regulations. Private capital was unable to reorganise the industries on a profitable basis. The problem was not simply a temporary loss of profitability – something which is quite normal for capital during a recession – but rather it signalled a fundamental decline of capitalist relations of production. The acts of nationalisation represented the culmination of these developments.

The erosion of capitalist relations can be recognised in a number of ways, quite apart from the immediate problems of profitability. The industries were, for example, burdened by worn-out and obsolescent machinery which rendered them uncompetitive. The scale of reorganisation necessary to restore competitiveness would have necessitated massive closures as well as extensive capital expenditure. Moreover, the industries could not have been reorganised by private capital, even with state aid, because of the political and industrial strength of the labour movement in the immediate post-war period which was committed to nationalisation, as is illustrated elsewhere by our analysis of the coal industry. Although the post-war nationalisations were contingent upon a favourable swing in the balance of power towards the labour movement, they were based upon longer term developments which represented the erosion of capitalist relations. The acts of nationalisation could not reverse the effects of those developments at a single blow and make good the elements of capitalist control that had been eroded. Subsequently, the development of the NIs has been a history of the reversal of the processes that created them. Capitalist mechanisms of control have been increasingly restored to the industries. Following nationalisation the industries were subject to a period of reconstruction and planning to reorganise and replace defunct machinery. The elimination of the anarchy between individual producers in competition and the backing of state credit to finance investment was an important factor in making this a success. It was also accomplished without the labour movement challenging the hierarchical forms of control that were being established both within and over the industries. By 1952 parliamentary concern over the running of the industries led to the setting up of a Select Committee which has since reported on them at regular intervals until it was abolished in 1979.[9] In 1956 the Herbert Committee on the Electricity Industry recommended a restoration of certain commercial criteria whether by denying provision of a service to rural areas or by the purchase of capital equipment from abroad if cheaper. In 1958 the National Coal Board and British Rail began their long-term rundown of labour. 1961 saw the first White Paper on the industries' economic and financial obligations which introduced commercial criteria, repeated in the 1967 White Paper and subsequently, with an emphasis on target rates of return for investment projects, pricing policy and financial targets.[10]

These developments largely concern the relationship between government and the NIs; the need for industries to be accountable for performance and to be instructed on objectives. Moreover, concern lay in establishing the mechanisms for the exercise of social criteria and the limitation of social criteria. This has been discussed in terms of the need to allow management the day-to-day discretion to run the enterprises efficiently but for overall policy objectives to be determined by parliament. In practice, rather than a balance between economic and social criteria being established by the so-called arm's length of ministerial control, a dual structure of control has been created whereby the political intervention of the minister tends to consolidate the capitalistic organisation of the industries at the lower level of management of the enterprises. These institutional forms have two further effects. They give the impression that they exist to provide for an appropriate balance between economic and social criteria with the minister and management operating as a counter-balance to each other. The minister imposes social criteria and checks the commercial performance, the manager supposedly advises on the commercial implications of social criteria and imposes commercial criteria. We have emphasised the unity of objectives between the two levels of control. Nevertheless, the 'relative autonomy' from profitability also has the effect of cushioning management from the forces of competition and of permitting the NIs to be used by government for political purposes, a matter we return to later.

The means of re-establishing capitalist production to the nationalised industries has not been confined to the relations between government and enterprise. There has been no discontinuity in the formal relationship between capital and labour since wage labour has been employed to produce goods for sale. Further, competition has been established through market relations. This has been facilitated by the failure to provide an integrated policy for energy and transport services so that the NIs are in competition with each other as well as directly with private capital. Some of the industries have also been subject to competition through their own internal organisation, with one plant, division or region set against another by measures of productivity and with wage settlements linked to productivity deals. Furthermore, the introduction of large scale fixed investment – and significantly each nationalised industry reached an investment peak during the period 1963-70 – is itself often a means of controlling the pace of work by the pace of machinery. This and its associated patterns of work, deskilling and redundancy more than anything demonstrate the affinity of NIs to capital.

Paradoxically, it is in competition for finance that the adoption of commercial criteria has been most limited, at least in so far as the industries are restricted from behaving like private capital, since their source of funds has been essentially restricted to internally generated surpluses and loans or subsidies from central government. Prohibiting borrowing from the private sector is a means of preventing the nationalised industries from extending and expanding operations in competition with private capital. Moreover legal restrictions on the diversification of the NIs into areas of competition with private capital is established by the very Acts which established them, and is a readily forgotten counterpart to their supposed monopolisation of a particular sector. In addition, financial control of the industries has provided a mechanism for triggering political control since corporations are scrutinised when seeking further finance either to cover losses or fund new investment projects. The role of financial control demonstrates very clearly that the process of developing economic control has not been at the expense of, nor moderated by political control.

We have suggested that developed forms of political control are an essential instrument in the regulation of NIs in the absence of the mechanism of profitability. The very existence of these controls, which owe their origin to state-ownership, implies that they can, however, be appropriated for other purposes, to reverse the chain of command and utilise the NIs as an instrument to influence the economy as a whole. As a result, the NIs have been used from time to time to pursue more general policy objectives. For example, in the late 1960s investment projects appeared to be delayed and even sacrificed in the pursuit of deflation; in the late 1960s and early 1970s price rises were held back for the supposed purpose of reducing inflation, whereas now price rises are being accelerated to reduce the budget deficit. The NIs have also played a leading role in the formation and implementation of wages policy.

These examples demonstrate that the NIs have been used as a mechanism for regulating the private economy rather than providing the basis upon which the economy as a whole can be planned. This illustrates not only the divorce between the NIs and the objectives of socialism, but also explains the limited role that the NIs have played in the UK in the formation of capitalist industrial policy. The development of individual NIs, as well as coordinated planning amongst them and the rest of the economy, has been subordinated to macroeconomic objectives such as the reduction of inflation or reducing public expenditure.[11] That NIs have been used in this way by successive UK governments does not mean, however, that this is the only role for NIs under capitalism. A comparison of Western European policies towards public enterprises, as illustrated by the differential subsidies to the coal, steel and railway industries, shows the variance with British policy.

The weakness of government commitment to the NIs in the UK cannot be explained adequately by referring to the hostility towards social ownership, although it may be justified by it under Tory Governments. It is a specific example of the more general weakness rather than extent of state industrial policy. Consequently, policy towards the NIs has reflected financial and international interests rather than the progress of domestic accumulation, through the priority accorded to macro-economic objectives with the NIs as instruments. Equally, the weakness of the labour movement in challenging the political forms of control over the NIs stands in sharp contrast to the role played at the time of the nationalisations.

More recent nationalisations in the UK, starting with the renationalisation of the steel industry in 1967, have been of a different character than those following the war. Profitability of these has often been impaired but not as the culmination of the overall weakening of capitalist relations of production. Accordingly, state ownership has been the instrument of reorganisation rather than restoration of capitalist forms of control. This is particularly illustrated by the brief life of the National Enterprise Board (NEB).

The NEB was set up by the Labour government in 1975. Despite great confidence in its ability to promote industrial policy through state ownership, the effectiveness of the NEB was limited both by its limited access to finance and its obligation to satisfy both commercial criteria and ministerial directions. Leaving aside British Leyland, Rolls Royce and Alfred Herbert which were major government rescues only nominally under the control of the NEB, 67 shareholdings of a total book value of only £155 million had been gathered by November 1979 when the Tory policy of major denationalising from the NEB was imminent. The Tory policy made explicit what had been implicit in the NEB's practice. This is illustrated by reference to the NEB's Report of 1979:

> The Government has accepted the need for a continuing NEB. The broad purposes for which the NEB was set up and which are stated in the Industry Act of 1975 remained unchanged, but its functions are to change. Public ownership for the sake of public ownership is no longer a function and, instead, the NEB is to have the function of disposing of assets in order to increase private sector involvement wherever possible. The notion that the NEB could be a major instrument of industrial reorganisation and rationalisation has also gone.

The supposedly new role for the NEB was described as 'a catalytic investment role, especially in connection with advanced technology and increasingly in partnership with the private sector, as well as its regional and small firms.' The NEB was informally merged with the National Research Development Corporation (NRDC) during 1981 to form the British Technology Group (BTG). The NRDC has existed since 1949 and its expansion to include the NEB provided a convenient resting place for the latter after its short, noisy but ineffectual life.

The major industries nationalised during the 1970s were essentially outside the control of the NEB. This prevented the NEB from coordinating the development of the car and toolmaking industries. The decline of British Leyland proceeded side by side with the decline of Herbert, the major British toolmaker, even though both were formally under the control of the NEB. At its peak in the 1970s, Herbert employed over 8,000. In 1980, whilst wholly owned by the NEB, it went into liquidation and was sold off. By April 1983, at most four or five hundred workers were able to expect continuing employment following a further business collapse.[12]

Current Developments Within the Nationalised Industries

Since the election of the Tory government in 1979, the NIs have suffered a continuing decline in employment and output partly as a result of the depressed state of manufacturing production. This has been felt most severely by British Steel and British Leyland. BSC has halved its employment over the period of depressed demand whilst BL had shed 30,000 jobs by the end of 1980. In the context of the NIs, the Tory government has become known for its free market policies towards the NIs, through the use of stringent cash limits and through proposals for denationalisation.

The use of cash limits for the NIs is only a new form of financial control since limits over borrowing have always existed. Cash limits were first introduced in 1976 and restrict the NIs' external borrowing requirement, the difference between their capital expenditure and their internally generated financial resources. Increases in cash limits can only be made by the Minister responsible for the NI concerned, with an announcement to Parliament. The government Public Expenditure Plans for 1980/81-1983/84 set out to change NIs' external borrowing requirement of £2.3 billion in 1979/80 into a net surplus of £0.4 billion by 1983/84 at the same time as increasing investment by 15 per cent. This implies that within four years the internal finance of the nationalised sector would rise from £1.95 billion, which is less than half of investment, to £5.3 billion, leaving a surplus over investment of £0.4 billion.[13] The overal significance of this change in policy can be seen by comparing the £2.7 billion turnaround in the NIs' finances with other proposed changes in public expenditure which amounted to a net reduction of £2.8 billion. Thus the government's plan to reduce the size of the Public Sector Borrowing Requirement depended to a great extent upon the NIs' ability to stay within their external financing limits. The Chancellor of the Exchequer, in evidence to the Treasury and Civil Service Committee, stated that the nationalised industries would achieve their targets in the following way: 25 per cent of the required £2.7 billion would be funded by increasing the prices of gas and electricity by more than the rate of inflation; 40 per cent by productivity and rationalisation in the loss-making industries of steel, shipbuilding, coal and rail with the remaining one third from cashflow changes and the increased profitability of the British National Oil Corporation.[14] However, the Public Expenditure White Paper did not provide detailed support for these projections and even admitted that 'the figures are ... highly sensitive to assumptions about such factors as pricing, productivity and demand.'[15]

In general the Tory government's financial plans for the NIs were not taken too seriously (indeed, even some Tory members of the Commons Public Expenditure Committee were sceptical).[16] In the event, the plans have already proved hopelessly optimistic. The plans in the following year for 1981/2 recognised a need for external finance of over £2.9 billion and anticipated a reduction to only £1.4 billion for 1982/83. This was, however, revised upwards to £2.7 billion within the year and for 1983/84 the anticipated level of external finance is over £3 billion.[17]

The complete incoherence of the cash limits as a method of planning raises the question of assessing their significance. As a mechanism of financial control cash limits have a dual purpose in the running of the NIs. Since the NIs are not subjected to the discipline of the threat of bankruptcy, cash limits represent a quasi-market force consolidating economic control. At the same time the operation of cash limits exerts political control especially when the limits are violated as each request for an extension is subjected to scrutiny. However, the effect of cash limits on the NIs is not uniform. It depends upon the ability of individual industries to increase their internal finance (though this is usually at the cost of either price increases or redundancies), hence such corporations as British Rail which are largely dependent on revenue subsidies receive closer supervision than the self-financing industries.

The two-fold nature of the cash limits is well illustrated by the steel strike of 1981 over wages. The so-called non-intervention of the government was illusory since it effectively intervened by refusing to ease the cash limit of £450 million thus constraining British Steel Corporation's 'ability to pay'. However, the prolonged strike produced a final settlement of 16 per cent overall. At the end of the financial year 1979/80 the government, in the light of the £545 million loss, was faced with the choice of either allowing BSC to go bankrupt or to relax the cash limit. It chose the latter course. Subsequently, BSC's cash limit for 1980/81 was further extended to £971 million. In contrast, the Electricity Council met little resistance when seeking a further £300 million to finance investment plans which could not be self-financed due to a fall in revenue resulting from the mild winter and the building up of fuel stocks. On the other hand, British Airways' low profitability in 1978/79 was used as the reason for delaying their investment programme. These examples illustrate that cash limits are not rigidly applied and, more importantly, they act as a trigger for government reassessment. The chairmen of the NIs, in criticising cash limits, have argued that they place too much attention on short-term investment plans. The chairmen not only want the removal of cash limits; they are also requesting the freedom to borrow on the open market instead of being solely reliant on the government for funds. The government has agreed to make such limits more flexible in so much as the industries may borrow ahead provided that the following year's cash limit is adjusted. Nevertheless, in revising the cash limits for 1982/3, the Chancellor only allowed approximately half of the NIs' bid for additional finance, suggesting that there will be breaches of the cash limits in the future. These will trigger intervention by the government despite its and the cash limits' supposed association with *laissez-faire*.

The Tory government is strongly committed to denationalisation and this has played an important ideological role in its populist politics. To some extent, this has meant that policies implemented have been symbolic, and even antagonistic to its more general economic objectives. The selling of state-owned shares in British Aerospace, BP and BNOC is not liable to have any great direct impact on the running of these companies since the government retains a substantial degree of control. Selling the shares has yielded a lump sum in place of dividends or their equivalent and has been disadvantageous in that the price obtained has been poor because of the large number sold at one time. Denationalisation has been more significant where the effective transfer of control of production has occurred or is planned.

In general, this has occurred at the boundaries between different industrial sectors. For example, the British Gas

Corporation has been forced to sell off its interests in oilfields and to allow private companies to use gas pipe-lines. British Rail has merged its interests in hotels and Sealink ferries and hovercrafts with Hoverlloyd. The pressures behind these changes can be understood by reference to the changing division of labour within and between capitalist firms. Vertical and other forms of integration result from the accumulation of capital and are intensified by the reorganisation induced by crises. With the critical reorganisation of capitalist production in the 1970s and 1980s, the boundaries between industrial sectors are being redrawn and they cut across the traditional monopolies of the NIs. This has been particularly the case where new technology has been involved. In this light, the government's plans to denationalise British Telecommunications (BT) and to revoke its monopoly of the telephone system can be explained. The accumulation of capital in the information and communications business is contingent upon a reorganised relationship between it and BT. After separating BT from the postal service in 1981, the government is now issuing licences for the provision of network services in competition with BT which use the BT network. It has also helped to promote the Mercury system, a predominantly privately-financed venture, aimed at developing a communications network covering major business centres and utilising the most advanced optical fibres laid alongside BR track.[18]

It is the reorganisation of the division of labour across sectors, and hence across firms and so between the public and the private sector that has been instrumental, as much as the ideology of Thatcherism, in promoting a policy of denationalisation. It is a policy prompted by the crisis of the 1970s and the introduction of new technology that have fuelled the extent of the redivision of labour. The rolling back of the public sector, in this perspective is not so much a radical departure from past policy which has always served to hold back the public sector in industry whilst the redivision of labour remained less drastic. Denationalisation has its counterpart in the past, when NIs have been confined to the broadly defined sectors to which they belong. The NCB, for example, has been instrumental in developing mining machinery but has passed the benefits onto private producers, whilst finished steelmaking has remained primarily a preserve of private capital. These are just two of many such examples. In the case of BT, Tory government or not, sectoral redivisions between information and communication would have to have been accommodated. There is little in the experience of Labour governments in the past to suggest that this would have been met by an aggressive expansion of the public at the expense of the private sector.

The major argument used against the nationalised industries is that they have failed in their performance relative to private industry. To some extent this is an ironic paradox, because it is the very failure of private industry that has resulted in nationalisation. In addition, the argument depends for its verification upon the construction of criteria of success which are common to both private and state-owned industry and it is not clear what these criteria should be as like is not being compared with like. In general, criteria are selected and applied in ways that are more favourable to private capital, although this bears further, more detailed analysis, than is presented here.

One criterion of success is the balance on accounts which are subject to a much closer scrutiny for their final figure of surplus or deficit than for the way in which they are actually made up. This is often a case of heads they win, tails we lose, for a loss is taken to indicate inefficiency and a profit the use of a monopoly power to charge high prices. To assess the NIs, the accounts must be examined closely. To begin with, they often include interest payments for government loan capital which may originate from compensation payments. While it might be argued that original compensation payments from capital expenditures must have become negligible, in proportion to the growth in the NI and relative to inflation, or have been written off by the present time, this is not entirely the case, since the interest payments have a depressing effect on the current account ensuring further borrowing in order to finance investment and current operations. Relative to private industry, the whole process by which the capital stock is valued and revalued is quite different both in terms of the material reorganisation of the industries themselves (bankruptcy, acquisition and merger for the private sector with a Darwinian bias towards the survival of the fittest) and in terms of the associated accountancy practices.[19] Even so, despite popular opinion, the nationalised industries transfer a positive balance to the government exchequer although along with private capital, surpluses have fallen in the current recession. Between 1963 and 1968, seven of the major nationalised industries showed a combined profit of £1,223 million (of interest, tax and dividend payments over revenue subsidies and capital write-offs), with a further £1,821 million between 1969 and 1974. British Rail and the National Coal Board, however, showed a combined deficit of £749 million and £2,683 million over the respective periods, yielding an overall deficit for the nationalised industries as a whole over the second period.

This requires some explanation. First, subsidies as well as capital write-offs are also made available to private industry as investment grants, etc., while the nationalised industries must also be subsidised for social criteria that they fulfil. Second, the accounts are constructed on the basis of bourgeois criteria of profit-making for private companies. Quite apart from the failure to consider social criteria this means that the industries are regarded as if they were private companies in assessing their contribution to the exchequer. In fact, and this holds for private companies as well, the exchequer also receives a surplus in the form of income tax from wages and national insurance contributions. But these are treated as payments from the private individual rather than from the company. These payments are, however, part of the surplus produced and are appropriated and redistributed through the state.[20] A distinguishing characteristic of the National Coal Board and British Rail (and also National Buses, National Freight Corporation and the postal services of the Post Office) is that they have a lower capital intensity than manufacturing industry as a whole. As a result, they pay proportionately more to the Exchequer in the form of 'labour' taxes. On a rough calculation the National Coal Board paid in 1975 £25 million more in income tax than would have been paid by the average manufacturer. It is only the accounting convention of private companies that leads to the exclusion of these payments from the annual accounts of NIs. In fact, of course, even institutionally these payments are indeed made by the employer to the Exchequer rather than by the employee who never sees national insurance or PAYE contributions. Significantly it is considerations of this type that are felt for by the labour movement in making estimates of the costs of closures within the NIs.[21]

It would be over-simplistic to identify the successes of the NIs with the limited planning that they have experienced and to blame their increasingly capitalistic organisation for their deficiencies. Nevertheless, this review of the NIs demonstrates the limited commitment to industrial planning in the UK at the point where it might have been expected to be at its strongest – state ownership of industry. The current Tory government's plans for stringent cash limits and denationalisations have been frequently cited as a radical break with past policy. Whilst true on the face of it in terms of the measures adopted, these developments represent a significant continuity with the past in the critical conditions currently governing the British economy. The use of the NIs is to continue as an instrument to further the development of private capital whilst cuts in their levels of operation, under the ideology of economic discipline and social sacrifice, neatly combines the functions of reorganisation of production and attacks on living standards. It is simultaneously a further withdrawal from coherent industrial planning that can only serve to consolidate the weakness of the British economy.

Notes

[1] For a discussion, with empirical examples, of the policies and effects of privatisation, see S. Hastings and H. Levie *Privatisation?*, Nottingham 1983 and D. Heald and D. Steel, 'The Privatisation of UK Public Enterprises', *Annals of Public and Cooperative Economy*, Vol.52, No.3.

[2] See, for example, M. Peston, 'Aspects of Pricing Policy of the Nationalised Industries' in J. Margolis and H. Guitton (eds.), *Public Economics*, London 1969, and G. Polanyi, *Comparative Returns from Investment in Nationalised Industries*, London 1968. For a more detailed exposition of the orthodox approach, see R. Rees, *Public Enterprise Economics*, London 1976.

[3] For a critique of this separation see J. Holloway and S. Picciotto (eds.), *State and Capital: A Marxist Debate*, London 1978, and for an assessment of the theory of industrial policy from a similar perspective, see M. Williams, 'Industrial Policy and the Neutrality of the State', *Journal of Public Economics*, Vol.19.

[4] See M.A. Crew and P.R. Kleindorfer, *Public Utility Economics*, London 1979.

[5] For a classification of the forms of market failure, see F.M. Bator, 'The Anatomy of Market Failure', *The Quarterly Journal of Economics*, Vol. LXXII, No.1.

[6] See, for example, the debate between Lipton and Redwood in *Lloyds Bank Review*. M. Lipton, 'What is Nationalisation For?', loc. cit., July 1976; J. Redwood, 'Government and the Nationalised Industries' and 'The Future of the Nationalised Industries', loc. cit., April and October 1976.

[7] See D. Heald 'The Economic and Financial Control of the UK Nationalised Industries', *Economic Journal*, June 1980, for an account from an orthodox point of view of the confusions which exist for these over the theory and policy of NIs. The confusions must exist because of the divergence between control and criteria in orthodox theory.

[8] See, for example, I. Gough, *The Political Economy of the Welfare State*, London 1979, and, for a critique, E. Wilson, 'Marxism and the "Welfare State" ', *New Left Review*, No.122.

[9] The committee was replaced by Select Committees attached to Ministries, such as the Select Committee on Energy which has reported on the NCB, for example, together with possible reference to the Monopolies and Mergers Commission, as for the CEGB, for example.

[10] *The Financial and Economic Objectives of the Nationalised Industries*, 1961 Cmnd.1337; *Nationalised Industries: A Review of Economic and Financial Objectives*, 1967 Cmnd.3437; *The Nationalised Industries*, 1978 Cmnd.7131.

[11] See R. Millward 'Price Restraint and Anti-Inflation Policy and Public and Private Industry in the UK 1947-73', *Economic Journal* Vol.86, for the restricting role played by pricing policy.

[12] For an account of the disappointing role of the NEB, written from a labour movement perspective, see Coventry, Liverpool, Newcastle and North Tyneside Trade Councils, *State Intervention in Industry: A Workers' Inquiry*, Nottingham 1982.

[13] *Government Public Expenditure Plans for 1980/81-1983/84*, 1980 Cmnd.7841.

[14] *Treasury and Civil Service Committee 1979-80*, 3 April 1980.

[15] Op. cit., p.55.

[16] See the report of the Treasury and Civil Service Committee.

[17] See Cmnd.8175.

[18] For an analysis if the proposals for BT, see Counter Information Services, *Private Line: The Future of British Telecom*, London 1982, and, for privatisation more generally, see Hastings and Levie, op.cit.

[19] The continuous revision of profitability figures suggests that there is little potential for comparing the NIs and private capital accurately. At a theoretical level, to take account of stock appreciation, etc., equilibrium concepts must be utilised for which rates of profit would in any case be equalised!

[20] This proposition is not uncontroversial. See Gough, op. cit., and B. Fine and L. Harris, 'State Expenditure in Advanced Capitalism: A Critique', *New Left Review*, No.98, who take the positions that taxes on wages form a reduction from wages and a part of surplus value respectively, although each recognises that these taxes may be a mechanism for reducing wages.

[21] See R.A. Bryer, T.J. Brignall and A.R. Maunders, *Accounting for British Steel: A Financial Analysis of the British Steel Corporation 1966-1980, and Who Was to Blame*, Farnborough 1982.

Chapter 6

Coal After Nationalisation

Nationalisation has brought significant changes to the coal industry. To some extent these changes are revealed in aggregate statistics. Between 1947 and 1981-82 output from NCB mines fell from 187.5 million to 108.9 million tonnes.[1] In the same period employment fell from over 700,000 to just under 220,000. Output per manshift rose from 1.09 to 2.40 tonnes yet these figures understate the true extent of the growth of productivity. Coal is now extracted from deeper pits with longer tunnels from the shaft, and the burden of haulage has risen substantially.[2]

These changes have been accompanied by a revolution in the organisation of work. At the time of nationalisation, the predominant method of working coal depended upon a cycle of operations organised around mechanical coal-cutting.[3] Three sequential shifts involved preparatory work, cutting, and loading and conveying of the coal respectively. Smooth operation of the cycle depended upon the satisfactory completion of the work associated with each shift. By contrast, current mining operations have been tending towards continuous mining in which all those operations of the previous cycle are undertaken on each shift. The vast bulk of mining is based upon two or more coal-cutting shifts through the use of power-loading machines which simultaneously cut and load coal.[4] This has been made possible by other technical innovations, the most important of which are self-advancing pit-props, steel roof-supports and more powerful and robust conveyors and cutters, whether the latter be for the coal itself or to drive tunnels.

This chapter was written by Ben Fine, Kathy O'Donnell and Martha Prevezer.

These changes have been accompanied by vast improvements in working conditions. Since 1947 the accident rate per manshift has fallen between four and five times.[5] Facilities at the pit-head, such as canteens and showers, have been improved. A five-day working week with guaranteed pensions, and increased holidays and earlier retirement have been won together with more extensive compensation for industrial diseases.[6] The NCB has been a major provider of housing in order to make up local deficiencies.[7] In addition, the wages system has been radically transformed. The complex system of locally-negotiated allowances has been abolished and replaced by national wage-bargaining.

The concern of this chapter is to examine how these changes have been brought about. Although existing histories of the NCB recognise the developments described here, they tend to place them in a perspective which emphasises the changing conditions of demand.[8] In particular three distinct periods are identified. The first period, between 1947 and 1956, was marked by a shortage of energy so that coal, as the main energy source, was in excess demand. Between 1956 and 1974, output declined as oil and gas displaced coal in energy markets. Since 1974, however, the demand for coal has been maintained by a substantial increase in the relative price of oil, but economic stagnation in the UK has left large excess capacity in energy provision. These fluctuations in demand have to be set against an overall decline in output as coal's share of primary inland energy consumption has fallen from over 90 per cent to 36 per cent between 1947 and 1982. The absolute and relative decline in the use of coal has seen electricity generation become its single most important customer, as is revealed in Table 1. As much as 80 per cent of electricity is now generated by burning coal.

With a focus upon demand, the effect of nationalisation tends to be gauged by the NCB's ability to respond to fluctuations and long term changes in market conditions. Industrial performance is thus assessed in terms of whether closures have proceeded rapidly enough in response to changes in demand. Our analysis, in contrast, suggests that the role of demand in shaping the industry's development is exaggerated. Instead, emphasis is given to the role of changing technology and work organisation, payment systems and

Table 1

Changing Pattern of Coal Consumption

Percentage of total output	1947	1957	1974	1981
Power Stations	14.3	21.0	57.4	70.1
Cokeovens & Gasworks	22.4	25.9	16.0	9.0
Domestic	19.3	16.4	10.4	6.8
Other Inland	41.3	33.2	14.4	10.1
Exports	2.8	3.6	1.7	3.8
TOTAL OUTPUT (million tonnes)	200.0	227.2	108.8	126.6

Source: NCB Accounts.

government policy in influencing the pattern of the industry's growth. Nationalisation is thus viewed as bringing an end to the stalemate in the economic organisation of the industry and opening up a period of substantial reconstruction.

Nationalisation and Reconstruction

In chapter eleven it will be argued that the structure of the inter-war coal industry was highly fragmented, reflecting the low levels of amalgamation, rationalisation and mechanisation. This created divisions both among miners and mineowners. Differing work practices and the uneven spread of mechanisation rendered trade union organisation and unity difficult to accomplish, while mineowners were unable to concede reforms because of their differential effect upon profitability. Rather than introducing measures to increase productivity, they relied upon minimising wage costs, a strategy aided by high levels of unemployment. In the 1930s the industry was supported by a state-organised cartel that maintained prices by allocating output-quotas to individual mines.

The competitiveness of the industry continued to decline during the Second World War.[9] Initially, the government's stance towards the industry was heavily influenced by the attitude of the mineowners who wished to limit the extent of government control. The mineowners feared that greater regulation would either prove irreversible and lead to nationalisation or, as happened after the relaxing of controls in 1921, generate industrial conflict. But, as the war economy went into full swing, coal shortages emerged and the government was forced to reconsider its policy of non-intervention. The situation was exacerbated by the large number of miners who took the opportunity to leave the industry by enrolling in the armed forces.[10] In an attempt to bolster coal output the government imposed an Essential Works Order (EWO) which prevented miners from leaving the industry either for alternative employment or even to join the forces. By guaranteeing work and removing the threat of dismissal, the EWO strengthened the position of the miners. Because of the war effort, however, their improved bargaining power could not be translated into higher wages. Consequently, industrial strife increased and culminated in the illegal strike at the Betteshanger Colliery in Kent in 1941.[11]

Despite the imposition of the EWO, coal output continued to decline. The government, acting on the basis of the Board of Trade's White Paper[12] took immediate steps to increase production and to eliminate unnecessary consumption of coal. This involved the introduction of a dual system of control in which the government determined output, distribution, prices and wages at the national level, while colliery companies organised production within the mines. Although profitability was guaranteed through a subsidy from the Coal Charges Account,[13] the mineowners were opposed to the policy because they disliked government intervention. The miners were also dissatisfied since the policy fell short of immediate nationalisation. Churchill, however, remained firmly opposed to nationalisation, stating 'everything for the war, whether controversial or not, and nothing controversial that is not *bona fide* needed for the war'.[14] Despite this reassurance, the mineowners were fully aware of the Labour Party's commitment to nationalisation and the spectre of public ownership hung over the industry. Consequently, they were reluctant to invest in new machinery or major capital reconstruction, particularly since profitability was already guaranteed. Given the overriding objective of maximising output the existing capital stock of both cutting machines and haulage and transport equipment was used to full capacity. The deterioration in physical assets and the inadequate replacement of capital equipment further weakened the industry.

At the same time, the miners' union reorganised itself in anticipation of nationalisation. In 1944, the National Union of Mineworkers (NUM) was formed and replaced the earlier federation of district unions (MFGB). In name at least, the miners were united on a national basis.[15]

Recognising the decline in the industry, the government set up the Reid Commission to investigate its technical condition.[16] The Report recommended a radical reorganisation of the industry involving the creation of larger mines with better layouts and more effective haulage techniques. Although the Report did not consider the form of ownership under which the reorganisation should be carried out, it did specify that effective powers were a cardinal necessity. This was possibly in recognition of the failure of previous attempts to rationalise the industry under private ownership, such as the Coal Mines Reorganisation Committee.[17] In an attempt to placate the widespread criticisms of the private ownership of the industry Robert Foot, Chairman of the Mineowners' Association, prepared a plan to rationalise the industry.[18] But the Plan, which proposed that the industry should be organised into a single cartel, was universally dismissed. It was described by Harold Wilson as a scheme of Bourbon self-government – government of the coalowners by the coalowners for the coalowners – with no provision for representation of the miners, the consumers or the government.[19]

The election of the Labour government with a large majority in 1945 made nationalisation certain. By creating a single employer, nationalisation permitted a greater degree of coherence in the organisation of the industry, in contrast to the previous experiences of government interventions. The Morrisonian concept of public ownership was adopted and written into the legislation by constraining the National Coal Board (NCB) to break even, taking one year with another.[20] Thus any social obligations, either to workers or consumers, were restricted by the necessity to operate within a commercial framework. Financial constraints have had considerable influence upon the operation of the NCB. In order to maintain total costs below total revenue, there has been pressure to hold down wage-increases. As a commercial discipline, this mechanism of control is supposed to mirror the competitive pressures on a private corporation. In practice it has acted more as a parody than a reflection of the behaviour of private commerce, since the financial constraint has also served to reduce funds for investment. Whereas private companies are free to borrow or to utilise an internally-generated surplus, these sources of funds have not been readily available to the NCB. As a result, the restrictions on investment have reduced the purchase of machinery and restricted mine development. This has intensified the pressure upon wage costs to reduce unit costs of production. Apart from the financial mechanism, the other systematic form of control over the industry has been the plan for the level of output. In the absence of adequate financial provision, demands for increased output have tended to worsen the industry's performance, since production has been forced upon high-cost mines. The latter should not be viewed as an inevitable consequence of geological conditions but rather as a product of low levels of investment.

These remarks are borne out by considering the first decade of nationalisation during which the NCB pursued a two-pronged plan. In the short term, existing collieries were geared up to maximum production. This involved completing the shift to mechanical coal-cutters and also removing other constraints upon output and productivity underground, particularly haulage. Indicative of this was the doubling of the total mileage of conveyors underground to 1,734 miles between 1947 and 1953. Until such improvements had been made there was little point cutting down more coal per shift since it could not be removed from the colliery. Additional output was obtained by extending hours of work: the NCB pressed for 'voluntary' Saturday working and overtime was common. At the same time the bonus system penalised absenteeism.

In the longer term, production was increasingly switched to collieries, new or old, where major investments had been made. This strategy dictated that a number of collieries would, after ten years, be suitable for further development, while others would be abandoned irrespective of the prevailing conditions of demand. According to Schumacher, the Board's economic adviser, the collieries were divided into four groups. By 1955 their respective shares of total output were as follows:[21]

Table 2

Percentage Output 1955

Group A	4.8
Group B	57.4
Group C	23.0
Group D	14.8

Of these, Group A comprised new mines and completed reconstructions, Group B mines which were scheduled for reconstruction, Group C were pits operated without major change and Group D pits that were expected to close. As Table 2 reveals the vast majority of coal was to be produced from collieries for which construction had yet to be completed in 1955. By then 167 schemes had been embarked upon, but only twenty completed.

The Wages System

During the first decade, as well as reorganising production within the industry, the NCB set about revising its complex system of wages. A new structure was developed because the old system was riddled with anomalies. Perhaps more importantly, however, the control of work within coal-mining is highly dependent upon the payment scheme. This is because limitations in working space make it more difficult to supervise production directly. In view of this the NCB attempted to design a wage structure which was compatible with both its short and long-run strategies. In other words an ideal payment system would encourage maximum production initially, while facilitating in the longer run changes in the organisation of work. At the same time, given the operation of financial controls, the NCB had to devise a system which kept wage costs to a minimum.

Upon nationalisation the basic division in the wage system was between piece-rate and day-wage workers which corresponded roughly to the division between faceworkers and other miners (both underground and surface) respectively.[22] In 1947, 40 per cent of the work-force was on piece-rates. Piece-rates were of three separate types: a bonus on top of a basic wage, payment by result according to price lists specifying rates for each task undertaken, and a comprehensive all-in price list for a complete set of tasks.[23] Price lists were supplemented by allowances at the pit, these being regulated by the management in compensation for abnormally difficult or unpleasant working conditions. Piece-rates were primarily negotiated at pit level through revisions in price lists and changes in allowances. However, after 1951, local price list revisions were not allowed, so wage increases were largely dependent upon allowances being raised, and these became an important component of total earnings.

Throughout the period, the NCB faced the task of controlling piece-rates while having to depend upon local negotiations because of lack of uniformity of working and other labour market conditions. Existing anomalies in differentials remained and were compounded by the method of increasing wages. Initially, the Board relied almost exclusively upon the discretion of local managers, and in this period piece-workers gained advantageous wage increases.[24] But the NCB was faced with a conflict between the autonomy and sometimes permissiveness of local management on the one hand and the authority and often inflexibility of central control on the other. In the first decade, a series of centralising and decentralising measures were taken to evolve a system of local and central management. In 1951, local price list revisions were disallowed, while in 1953 a general policy of decentralised decision-making was adopted although the 1951 price list directive was maintained. Following the Fleck Report,[25] recommending centralisation of control, the 1953 directive was cancelled.[26]

The impact on industrial relations was considerable. Conflicts over allowances[27] resulted in numerous stoppages, with an average of 800 strikes per annum between 1945 and 1957, and over 1,400 in 1954 and 2,200 in 1957. After this the number of strikes fell quite sharply as district wage agreements were introduced; Clegg has explained this pattern of strike activity in terms of changes in the structure of collective bargaining and the extent of earnings fluctuations.[28] In the earlier period face-workers' wages were negotiated at pit level and varied significantly as work conditions changed and this encouraged many localised short-term stoppages. According to Clegg these declined in frequency as responsibility for wage negotiations shifted away from the colliery to area management and also as wages became more dependent upon a fixed rate.[29] But, as we shall discuss below, it was not the wages system as such that encouraged conflict: the wages system was an element in and product of the struggle over the level of wages.[30] That is to say, it reflected a conscious choice of management to keep wages down, given the organisation of the industry at that time.

During this period demands for wages were increasingly frustrated at a national level by the claim of inability to pay. This was justified by reference to the need to balance the accounts. But they were more an instrument of control than an indicator of performance, as a few of the more important examples illustrate.[31] Pricing policy was subject to government veto and directly affected revenue in conditions of energy shortage; from 1947 to 1958 the NCB made ten applications for price increases. Of these, one was refused outright, four were decreased below the level deemed necessary and five began later than the dates requested. Prices were below those prevailing on world markets, as the Board learnt at its own expense. It was instructed by the government to import coal and sell it at the lower regulated domestic price until 1956, thus making a cumulative loss of £72 million. This compares with the Board's own definition of a major capital expenditure of £250,000 and a total expenditure on major schemes over this period of £174 million. Inability to pay either for wages or for colliery investment was a product of government policy, as implemented by the Board, and not a result of the industry's performance.

Although face-workers constituted a minority of the work-force, they were the leading section of the miners, particularly because of their control over the pace of work. The coal that they cut determined the intensity of labour, particularly for those paid by the day. The pressure to work off the face was dictated by managerial supervision and even by face-workers who had an incentive under piece-rates to see that operations elsewhere underground encountered no obstacles. The position of those on day-wages meant that the Board could adopt a different strategy towards these workers in the attempt to minimise the wage bill. From the outset, a concerted attempt was made to rationalise the day-wage pay structure by moving towards a greater uniformity of wages. Between 1947 and 1955 wages were increased by a series of seven flat-rate national increases, thereby reducing relative differentials. These increases, however, only fully applied to those on the nationally-agreed minimum; those above the minimum received a proportionally lower increase bounded by an upper limit. By this method, before 1956, the hourly earnings of surface day-wage workers were kept roughly just over 10 per cent below the manufacturing average. Those underground lost over half their 20 per cent earnings advantage over the surface workers.

By the early 1950s, the NCB had begun to investigate the possibilities of a national wage structure for day-wage workers and, with the NUM's co-operation, a grading exercise was embarked upon. Initially 6,000 different jobs were discovered, although this was reduced to 350 after negotiation with the NUM and after taking account of local names for comparable jobs. These jobs were allocated to five underground, four surface and three craftsmen grades.

Whilst this process had been completed by 1952, the day-wage structure to which it was attached was not finally agreed until April 1955. The delay is illustrative of the Board's policy of minimising the wage bill. In implementing the new day-wage structure the NCB was faced with a number of objectives: establishing differentials on new grades, preserving regional differentials and permitting a wage increase to as many workers as possible. As the existing distribution of wages exhibited considerable divergence from the hierarchy explicit in the regrading, it was an extremely complex task to satisfy these objectives at a low cost. Accordingly, the agreement was implemented only after the NCB had evaluated the effects of over a hundred possible schemes.

The award of flat-rate increases bounded by upper limits narrowed differentials and therefore reduced the costs of the scheme. A comparison of the distribution of wages in the various grades before and after the scheme was introduced is most revealing.[32] It shows that the greater proportion of the £14 million cost of the scheme was used to finance a general wage increase with those already earning wages above their grade level being held to a much lower increase. Thus, whilst 93 per cent of day-wage workers received some increase, and this facilitated the introduction of the scheme, the integration of the workers into the new structure was achieved at a remarkably low cost.

The Transition to Full Mechanisation

In the early 1950s, a new power-loader, the Anderton-Shearer Loader, was invented and introduced into the coalfields.[33] It transformed the industry very rapidly. By 1968 over 90 per cent of coal in Britain was extracted by the use of power-loaders. The machine both cuts the coal and loads it onto conveyors mechanically. For longwall mining (subject to roof-support, tunnelling and preparatory operations around the side of the face) the machine can run along the seam cutting and despatching the coal. The pace of work is thus potentially transformed by the pace of the machine along the face and also by the ancillary operations which allow the face to advance. But it is important to stress that the introduction of the power-loader did not by itself radically transform conditions of control over the labour process. It merely joined together what were previously separate tasks, cutting and conveying, while eliminating the intermediate task of hand-filling.

The full benefits of power-loading could only be obtained by maximum operation of the machines. Reconstruction of the mines overcame technical constraints on removal of the coal. The remaining task was to impose new conditions of work upon the miners, particularly at the face, in order to minimise their ability and their incentive to interrupt continuous mining. Because this process accompanied the introduction of the power-loaders, the new machines are sometimes considered to have appropriated work-place control from the hewers.[34] Although new machinery transforms the conditions of work, it also involves changing work-place control which is subject to struggle. The introduction of machinery is of advantage to the employer but does not determine the balance and form of control. As noted above, the problems of direct supervision in coalmining are enormous, with or without machinery, because of the simple limitations in working space which make it difficult to oversee work. Control is therefore much more dependent upon the type of payment scheme than in many other industries.

Initially, the NCB adopted a strategy of introducing power-loaders on a pit-by-pit basis but quickly moved to the negotiation of District Power Loading Agreements (DPLAs). These varied between districts where a choice was given between the systems of piece-rates or day-wages. Only Scotland and Durham opted for the day-wage system, but did so in dissimilar ways. Both schemes allowed for bonuses for task completion, but in Scotland the basic rate formed a higher proportion of pay. The other areas opted for a continuing piece-rate system except for Lancashire and Kent. The former refused to negotiate a DPLA, retaining pit autonomy over the choice of payment system and Kent negotiated a DPLA only in 1965. In terms of work organisation, the major conflict concerned whether method study should be applied to the men or to the machines. The NCB favoured the former which would imply management specification of the tasks to be performed by the men. The miners favoured the latter since the organisation of tasks within the team as well as the size of the team would still be open to negotiation. Consequently, the miners tended to favour machine study with a day-wage and the NCB to favour 'man-study' with piece-rates.

As a result, the process of introducing the machinery yielded a mixture of payment and work-control systems. The primary task for the Board was to ensure that powerloaders were accepted. In addition, it could press through method study for as much control as possible over the work process. The introduction of the power-loaders was facilitated by an unprecedented increase in the wages paid to piece-workers between 1956 and 1959. In that time, their pay, relative to other miners, increased by almost 10 per cent. This stands in contrast to the trend from 1950 to 1976 during which these workers suffered a 60 per cent decline in this relativity. General wage increases were necessary to all piece-workers since the DPLAs had to be acceptable to the unions and not only to those working the new technology. In addition there was, against previous and subsequent trends, a widening of differentials across occupations and regions, with piece-workers in the districts most advanced in power-loading benefiting the most. This was a result of the district and local influence on the implementation of the agreements. It explains why there is no simple cross-section correlation between wage increases and the introduction of powerloaders.[35]

Having paid for the introduction of power-loading the NCB reverted to the principle of minimising wage costs. In the early 1950s the Board was under extreme pressure to hold down the 'wage drift' of piece-workers.[36] It undertook an exercise, comparable to that for the day-wage structure, to investigate the grades remuneration of piece-workers. Not surprisingly, it found an enormous variation of wages with little relationship between task performed and pay. In 1955, however, 89 per cent of piece-workers were concentrated in only twelve jobs and this compares with 83 per cent of day-wage men on 100 jobs. From a purely administrative point of view, the piece-workers could have been placed on a national structure more easily than the day-wage men. Despite the use of £2 million to undertake the piece-worker review, no move was made by the NCB towards a national pay structure for piece-workers.[37] The reasons were firstly, that the cost of regrading would have been enormous, if patterns of regional and occupational differentials were to be maintained without some workers suffering a decrease in pay. Secondly, although the rationale for a national wage structure lay in the removal of anomalies in differentials and the elimination of locally-negotiated allowances, there was little guarantee that this could be achieved given the heterogeneous conditions of work and work organisation. Finally, in the mid-1950s, the drive to introduce power-loading was gathering pace, creating initially greater diversity in work conditions whilst opening the prospect of much greater homogeneity in the future.

Within a decade, the situation had been transformed with the successful negotiation and implementation of DPLAs. This increased dispersion of wage rates and also opened up the potential for wage savings under a national wage agreement. The higher-paid districts could have minimal wage increases whilst the lower paid districts caught up. Equally such an agreement could wipe out locally negotiated allowances. Finally, a national agreement of a day-wage for power-loading teams was attractive, if method study by the men were to be accepted. With management and machine dictating the pace of work, the need for piece-rate incentives was reduced. Piece-rates were also a potential source of localised grievance and wage drift. With power-loading in place the NCB could reverse its stance, adopted for the DPLA, of favouring piece-rates, and favour a day-wage system for face-workers at the national level.

Paradoxically a reversal of policy was also to be exhibited by the miners. At a district level, method study had been generally opposed to allow full scope to negotiate local pay increases, an objective which also made piece-work attractive. At a national level, however, the miners had a long-standing commitment both to national wage determination and the abolition of piece-work.[38] Motivated by the ideology of equal pay for equal work and by concerns for safety, the NUM pressed for a day-wage agreement for face-workers. Day-wages also presented great potential for unity across the coalfields and, as was to be proven in the early 1970s, represented a continuing objective of the left within the union. But day-wages also implied that the miners should be subject to method study so that equal work could be evaluated as the basis for equal pay. With the NCB pursuing wage and work control and the NUM pursuing nationally-negotiated wage agreements, the National Power Loading Agreement (NPLA) was signed in June 1966 placing power-loading teams onto a day-wage system.[39] Nearly all negotiations over allowances were abolished and none remained at the colliery level. Over a five-year period wage rates would be brought into uniformity, with the lowest-paid areas catching up the highest-paid, Kent, which would suffer a wage freeze. The spectrum of tasks covered by power-loading teams was widened and the size of teams was subject to negotiation, but most jobs within the teams were interchangeable. This had the advantage of flexibility in case of changing geological conditions and absenteeism.[40]

Initially, the real wages of face-workers received a temporary boost, possibly as a result of the large increases to craftsmen who became incorporated into the team and as a result of anomalies within the scheme that could be temporarily utilised to the workers' advantage. Subsequently, the face-workers' real wages resumed their stagnant level that had prevailed from the mid-1950s. Their pay relative to non-face-workers resumed its steep fall. The NPLA failed to yield anticipated increases in productivity. Management expected to be able to devote its attention to work supervision, with the end of localised allowance bargaining, but found itself increasingly involved in negotiating manning levels. The NPLA had removed the incentive element in face-work.[41] The intense pressure on wage levels, particularly in those areas with the higher wages and productivity, was conducive to work-place resistance and reduction of effort.

This created two problems for management. Supervision of face-work had to be stepped up, as was to be expected,[42] but also a form of supervision of workers elsewhere underground was lost with the introduction of NPLA. For the first time in the industry, face-workers had no incentive to coerce work from others elsewhere underground in order to sustain their own piece-rate earnings. Failure to remove coal from the face or to bring forward necessary supplies to it were a positive advantage to the face-workers in so far as work was brought to a standstill. Far from reducing management problems, the NPLA intensified them underground and necessitated an increase in officials. This further antagonised the miners who were now suffering the effects of depressed wages and new work methods. Their own control over production was being challenged through the application of method study by an expanding staff of supervisors.

These developments in wages and working conditions in the late 1960s have to be set against the enormous decline in employment in the industry. As argued earlier, the investment funds available to the Board were constrained by the financial mechanisms of control. It is this, rather than reduced demand through cheaper energy substitutes, that determined the level of the NCB's activities. The notion of diminishing returns in mining is unfounded. Sufficient coal reserves existed to replicate the highest levels of productivity, provided adequate investment was made whether in continuing development of existing mines or exploitation of new ones.

Financial constraints also dictated that the Board would exploit declining employment in the industry to hold wages down to the lowest levels. In short, the industry experienced sharp deterioration in employment, wage and working conditions. In the next section we will show that this coincided with developments conducive to the unity and militancy of the union, leading to an eruption of class conflict.

Intensification of Industrial Conflict

After the war, the material basis for trade union strength was weak within the industry owing to its fragmented and heterogeneous organisation. After nationalisation the union faced a single employer, which was able to develop its policies towards labour on an industry-wide basis. Yet the NUM continued to operate on a federal basis: the different areas continued to be registered as independent trade unions with their own finance and spheres of influence. There were few contacts between areas either at the official or the unofficial level. There were often conflicts between the rank and file and the NUM leaders, exacerbated by the complex relation between wage bargaining at local and national levels. Right-wing leaders, wedded to the idea of co-operation with a state-owned industry, dominated the union from national level down through the areas.[43] Only Scotland, South Wales and Kent were led by left-wing executives.

Disputes within the industry were governed by compulsory and lengthy procedures of arbitration prior to the call for a strike. National wage increases were subject to a National Reference Tribunal which consistently took a pessimistic view of the Board's ability to pay. The result was that strikes were localised and unofficial. This is illustrated by the two main strikes during the early period: the Grimethorpe stint strike in 1947 and the Markham Main dispute in 1955. The first resulted from the NCB and NUM's attempt to impose, without local consultation, an increase in the length of the coal-face worked. Even after the strikers had been sacked the union officials attached great weight to the observance of the union negotiating procedure, seeing the choice as lying between industrial democracy and anarchy. The NUM President, Will Lawther, went so far as to advocate that the strikers should be prosecuted. The 1955 strike in Yorkshire was unofficial and primarily over pay. It resulted from the delay in the revision of price lists and the associated resentment over the heavy reliance upon allowances. The conflict was extensive, and remarkable for the use of official 'panels' of trade union officials for unofficial action and organisation.[44]

The conduct of these disputes was indicative both of the right-wing leadership of the union and the union's lack of unity. The position changed following the drive to introduce power-loading. Piece-workers won large wage increases. From the late 1950s, the number of stoppages per annum fell sharply for the next decade, from the peak of 2,228 in 1957 to an average of 221. Three factors operated sequentially to moderate strike activity in the 1960s. Firstly, there was the effect of the wage increases of the late 1950s. Secondly, the decline in employment in the industry weakened the position of those workers who remained within it whilst employment elsewhere in the economy was sufficiently buoyant to provide jobs for those who left.[45] Thirdly, the NPLA of 1966 represented a temporary resolution of wage grievances through the process of implementing it. These factors were temporary and limited in their effect, and by the end of the 1960s forces operating to intensify class conflict gathered pace.

The NPLA was instrumental in creating unity within the union. As has been frequently emphasised, it was a national agreement, thereby creating a common purpose in wage negotiations.[46] Less obviously, the NPLA broke down division of interest between face and other workers.[47] All workers were now on the day-wage system so that those at the face could no longer increase their own earnings through greater effort at the expense of imposing more work on others on a fixed wage. The work-force as a whole had an incentive to reduce effort and increase wages. The NPLA also created a unity between the high-wage (and often high-productivity) areas and the low-wage areas. It did so by freezing the wages of the higher paid, whilst the lower-paid caught up to bring all face-workers into a common pay scale. This reflected the Board's continuing attempt to minimise the wage bill, an objective also pursued by permitting those holding a high wage only to retain it whilst they remained on the same job and face.[48] Consequently, some workers had an incentive to delay completion of extraction from the faces they were working.

The miners' deteriorating economic circumstances stimulated developments within the union.[49] The most significant occurred in Yorkshire. The unofficial action of the panels in the 1950s and early 1960s led to left-wing leadership, especially in the campaigning from Barnsley and Doncaster, spearheaded by Arthur Scargill. Lawrence Daly, a left-winger, was successfully proposed for the post of General Secretary. The national executive moved towards the left and greater emphasis was placed on wages and employment at national level and as separate issues. Previously, the Board had been able to pursue a strategy of trading moderation in wages and closures as alternatives at the local level.

In the late 1960s the number of strikes dropped drastically, to under a fifth of the previous level. They were, however, far more extensive and different in character. The face-workers were prepared to support surface-workers in their struggle for higher wages even though it was their own relativity that had suffered most, their real take-home pay having stagnated since the mid-1950s and having dropped below the manufacturing average. For surface workers, 'their rate of £10 a week was so low that overtime was all but compulsory'.[50]

In 1970 the union prepared a wage demand of £20 a week for surface workers, £22 for underground workers and £30 for face-workers, representing an overall wage increase of 30 per cent. The South Wales union passed a resolution to pledge the union to strike action if the demand was not met. The National Executive rejected an NCB offer which fell within the Tory government's informal pay increase norm of 12 per cent for the public sector. The NUM failed to gain the two-thirds majority for a strike that its constitution at that time required. Nevertheless, unofficial strike action was taken and this led to an increased offer which, after another pithead ballot, was accepted. In 1971, the union changed its constitution to enable strike action to be official with a 55 per cent majority at a pit-head ballot. The change made a national strike more likely, but it also reflected a different assessment of unity within the union. Previously a two-thirds majority had been necessary to ensure sufficient support in each district to make a successful strike possible. By 1971, sufficient support appeared likely with a lower overall majority because of more uniform voting patterns across districts.

Miners' relative pay continued to decline, in 1971 their

index of wage rates was 7 per cent below the manufacturing average. Over the previous eleven years, real earnings had risen by only 10 per cent compared to an average of 26 per cent in manufacturing. The NUM presented the Tory government in 1972 with a pay claim of £26 a week for surface workers, £28 a week for underground workers and £35 a week for face-workers, an increase of 43 per cent. The government's public sector pay target was 7-8 per cent. In anticipation of a strike the CEGB began to stockpile coal and the NCB preserved its stock of ten million tonnes. To reduce these stocks the NUM implemented an overtime ban from November 1971. This action emphasised to the miners the inadequacy of their basic weekly wage and the extent to which they were dependent upon overtime.

On 9 January 1972 a strike was scheduled to begin, supported by a 59 per cent majority in a ballot. The Tories were committed to waging war against the rights as well as the wages of the labour movement. It had done so with some success. In 1971, Robert Carr, Secretary of State for Employment, had proposed the creation of the National Industrial Relations Court (NIRC) with the power given to the Secretary of State to apply a cooling off period of 60 days whilst disputes were referred to the NIRC. Trade unions were required under the Industrial Relations Act of 1971 to register and had almost universally decided not to do so in protest against the conditions of the Act which heavily penalised picketing. The public sector was the government's chosen battlefield for imposing wage restraint. Between 1970 and 1972, there had been strikes of postmen, power-workers, railwaymen, health workers and local government employees. In two cases, the government had taken the step of declaring a State of Emergency.

Although the miners were successful in ensuring that the pits remained closed in order to make their strike effective, they had to picket power stations and prevent movements of coal and other fuels. They organised flying pickets. Gradually the organisation of the strike emerged, allocating areas of picketing of power stations to particular union areas and it gathered momentum despite the lack of strike pay. The major problem was fighting non-union labour, especially lorry drivers. After a month, once voltage reductions had started, belief in the expendability of coal swayed. Moods on the picket lines hardened as a picket was killed at a power station. There followed the battle of Saltley Gate, a fight to keep closed a coke depot in Birmingham containing 100,000 tons of fuel, where picketing had been ineffective.[51] This was the site of the first mass picket as coachloads were rushed in to boost the numbers of pickets; 15,000 people took part. The government declared a State of Emergency on the 9 February and on 11 February a three-day week was imposed on industry and daily power cuts started.

The Wilberforce Enquiry was set up and concluded that the miners were a special case. Nevertheless, it offered slightly less than the miners' claim.[52] The union got extra concessions on top of the Wilberforce recommendations, which doubled the differential between the minimum underground and surface rates and lessened the percentage lead by coal-face workers over the others underground. The net effect was a settlement that benefited the craftsmen.

However, these gains were partially eroded by inflation at 9.1 per cent in 1972-3 and 16 per cent a year later. The 1972 conference proposed a 30 per cent increase contravening the government's Phase II policy of £1 plus 4 per cent. The government freeze on incomes in November 1972 extended the duration of the Wilberforce settlement. Despite this, the miners voted against strike action in 1973. The situation worsened during 1973. The 1973 conference decided on a pay claim to try to catch up embodying £8-£13 increases against the Phase III maximum allowed by the government of 8 per cent. This entailed increases of 22 per cent for face-workers, 40 per cent for underground workers and 38 per cent for surface workers. This time the majority for strike action at a pit-head ballot proved to be 81 per cent.

The conduct of the strike was much lower key, although the stakes involved appeared much higher. A three-day working week was again introduced and picketing was institutionalised so that a token rather than a physical presence of numbers proved adequate to prevent movement of coal. Heath, the Prime Minister, called a general election, asking 'Who Rules Britain?' The miners continued their strike during the course of the election which produced a narrow victory for the Labour Party. The Pay Board had been instructed by the defeated Tory government to assess the case and again the miners were considered to constitute a special case as their earnings in real terms and relative to manufacturing had fallen so much. The 1974 settlement by the Labour government awarded a 32 per cent rise, higher than the Pay Board recommendation, compared with a 15 per cent average in manufacturing,[53] raising the earnings in mining to 22 per cent above manufacturing.

This settlement brought to a close the period of transition to fully mechanised mining. The Labour government paid the miners handsomely to diffuse an extremely unstable situation and it continued to moderate the labour movement with generous reforms for its first six months of office. It then called a general election and, with an increased majority, embarked upon a strategy of seeking collaboration with the unions through the negotiation of the Social Contract. By doing so, it successfully held down real wages and expenditure on social services during its five-year period of office, paving the way for the return of the Tories in 1979.

The miners' victories in the early 1970s were remarkable in a number of respects. Quite apart from the wage increases that had been won, their national strikes, the first for almost half a century, had ultimately brought down a government. Their successful picketing had been based on new forms that were at times both violent and illegal. The contrast with the results and the methods of 1926 are striking. Equally, however, it must be recognised that the victories had little lasting effect. The militancy and unity of the union was largely a result of the pressures experienced during the transition to mechanised mining, particularly after the NPLA was introduced and as a consequence of the NCB's policy of minimising the wage bill. This militancy was dispersed with the 1974 settlement although wages have to some extent been maintained by the moderate increase in commitment to coal following the oil crisis. Nonetheless, the strikes were based upon the emergence of left-wing leadership in the NUM which consolidated its future position.

Following the NPLA, the NCB found that miners' incentive to work had diminished and it also faced continued difficulties in industrial relations with conflict over manning levels.[54] Inevitably, the NCB sought to restore discipline and incentives within the industry and to fracture the unity of the work-force across districts and between face and other workers. The NUM was able to resist this in the period immediately following the national strikes by insisting upon an incentive scheme that would spread bonuses over the whole work-force within an area or even nationally. The NCB resisted such a proposal because of the dilution of incentives involved. Eventually a narrow vote to reject a pit-based scheme in October 1977 revealed a sharp difference of interest and voting behaviour between those districts which would benefit and those which would lose from the scheme. Despite the vote against it, and encouraged by Gormley's right-wing leadership, incentive schemes were negotiated and implemented at a colliery level in those districts in favour. By May 1978 the scheme was operating throughout the industry. Differences of interest across regions and across occupations had been restored within the work-force, destroying the unity and militancy that had characterised the first half of the 1970s.

Yet that period of intense and dramatic conflict had yielded little permanent advantage to the workforce. It had done nothing to transform the mode of control of the industry. The Board continued to be deprived of finance for investment and to press down on wages where possible. Whether directly from the NUM, or through the Labour Party in office, the labour movement had little impact on the development of the industry. Despite the oil crisis, moderated itself by economic stagnation and low demand for energy, the programme of pit closures and limited investment was soon to be resumed.

Future Prospects

Following the introduction of power-loading, technical developments in mining have been dominated by the object of maximising the use of machinery. From the very beginning, it was understood that the full benefits of mechanisation depended upon continuous and rapid operation of machinery at the face.[55] The tendency has been to concentrate production on fewer, larger, thicker and more rapidly moving faces with the use of multiple coal-cutting shifts. To a great extent, given geological and technical conditions, these objectives cannot all be achieved together. For example, thicker seams have always involved shorter working walls in order to maintain roof control. Rapid extraction and movement of the face operates against multiple coal-cutting shifts because of the need to sustain preparatory work on roadways. By the 1960s the average number of shifts per day had increased to just over two from a level of below one-and-a-half at the end of the 1950s. Subsequently, the level has remained above two and stood at 2.16 in 1982. Average seam thickness has increased from 1.30 to 1.58 metres, average face length from 166 to 198 metres.[56] Equally significant has been the concentration of output onto fewer faces which reduces the number of stand-by faces and machine requirements and maintenance. Between 1967 and 1982, the number of mechanised faces decreased from 1,518 to 606. This compares with a fall in the number of collieries from 376 to 198.

Crucial to these changes have been the use of self-advancing steel pit props and rigid steel roof-supports to allow the powerloaders to perform rapidly and continuously. Powered supports have been installed in nearly all mechanised longwalls. Equally, technology in the driving of tunnels along the ends of the faces has been improved by the development of large and more powerful machines. Nevertheless, together these technical advances have brought to maturity the increases in productivity associated with the use of power-loaders.[57] In the immediate future, subsequent increases in productivity are aimed at through increasing machine available time (MAT) within the bounds of existing technology. The two most important mechanisms for bringing this about are through retreat-mining and computerisation.

Longwall retreat-mining derives its name because tunnels are driven out into the coal measures and the face is then worked back towards the shaft. It has certain advantages in that the roof of the mine can be allowed to collapse from behind the continuing work. More important, the immediate geology of the coal seam is proven in advance in that information is gleaned from the forward tunnelling. Faulting can be detected and, with that knowledge, the route of extraction can be planned. As a method of extraction, retreat-mining has long been available, since it is a plan and not a technology of extraction. But it is only recently that it has been greatly used in Britain, and is now the most favoured form for working new faces. This is from an assessment in the NCB's *Production and Productivity Bulletin*:

> Retreat-mining is producing low risk output at a 42 per cent higher rate per face-day and at twice the (shift) productivity of advancing faces. Opportunities exist to extend retreat-working beyond the current level of 25 per cent of major long-wall output, towards a level of 50 per cent.[58]

By 1982, there were 115 retreating as compared to 455 advancing faces with overall output per day of 927 and 697 tonnes respectively and output per man shift of 28.94 as compared to 14.70 tonnes.[59] To some extent these figures overstate the advantage of retreat-mining because this method has been used in better geological conditions and with better machinery.

The reluctance to adopt retreat-mining in the past can be explained by its disadvantages. It involves a heavy capital outlay long before coal can be extracted and sold, while the greater ease and speed of extraction are only of benefit if the face can be supported and serviced at a comparable rate. The full mechanisation of longwall advancing required developments in technology for roof-support, for example. These advances were then adopted for the even faster pace of retreat-mining, in this case, to pre-empt falls with the added advantage of less roof-support per unit of seam extracted.[60]

Retreat-mining allows the machinery to run more rapidly, more continuously and to reduce the need for reserve faces because of advanced knowledge of faulting. The same effect is intended by the increasing computerisation of mining operations. The motive behind the associated automation is to exercise control over both the technical and human sources of lost MAT. It is estimated that potential coal-cutting time is divided into three roughly equal parts, one during which cutting does take place, another when technical reasons prevent it from doing so, and a final portion in which lost MAT is avoidable given computerised control of men and machines. The first experiments with automatic mining took place in the early 1960s but proved unsuccessful because of the deficiency both in mining and computer technology in the context of combining the two.[61] Improvements in mining technology and the microchip revolution have vastly reduced the difficulties, whilst retreat-mining has facilitated control room steering through advance knowledge of faulting.

Control of the work-force in these circumstances rests upon management underground and computer information above ground that can be used for immediate or longer-term assessment of labour.[62] There is a careful allocation of supervisory staff to different operations and this staff is aided and assessed by detailed analyses of the causes of lost MAT, including that which will be construed as worker indiscipline. The increasing role of supervision is indicated by the following account taken from an NCB manual of 1968:

One colliery working an advance/retreat system with three headings on the maingate side and a conventional tailgate with ripping machine, has the following supervisory staff:

1 Undermanager per day	responsible for the co-ordination of work in the district. To ensure that the daily planned output, 1,500 tons per day, is achieved.
1 Overman per shift	responsible for carrying out the instructions of the Undermanager. To co-ordinate the duties and operations of mechanical, electrical and mining functions in the district.
1 Deputy per shift	responsible for face performance only (excludes face ends).
1 Deputy per shift	responsible for the tailgate advance (ripping machines, slusher, etc.).
1 Deputy per shift	responsible for the maingate advance and drawing off behind the face.
1 Deputy per shift	responsible for the heading drivages.

The face is worked two production shifts, the face ends and heading three shifts.

Total officials per day:　　1 Undermanager
　　　　　　　　　　　　　3 Overmen
　　　　　　　　　　　　　11 Deputies

The introduction of retreat-mining to a colliery requires quite significant changes in organisation, both of manpower and planning.

Very much smaller teams are involved in retreat work, therefore, the ratio of facemen to officials is reduced and it is very quickly found that one limiting factor is the number of officials available to take charge of the developments ...

Computerisation and monitoring of face performance has involved a fine division of causes of lost working time for technical and other reasons. This is illustrated by the figures quoted below from the September 1977 *Production and Productivity Bulletin*. In addition, in 1980 the Commission of the European Communities, in which the NCB has been a major participant, details a code of 526 mechanical delay faults. By doing so, it makes possible the identification of non-mechanical delays through worker indiscipline.[63]

Late Start and Early Finish Lost Time Delays

ACTIVITY	MINUTES
Late Start-Winding Relay	.91
Late Start-Manrider Relay	1.05
Late Start-Excess Travel/Prep.	11.30
Late Start-After Snap	.97
Early Finish	3.30
Wait at Shaft Side (Shift End)	.85
Total for Area	18.38

Another method pursued in the attempt to increase MAT has been to reduce travelling time to and from the face by introducing manriding facilities. The *Production and Productivity Bulletin* reports that distance travelled per shift has increased by nearly 2,000 metres to almost 8,000 metres, over the fifteen years to 1981.[64] This represents an increase of eleven minutes to an average of 89 minutes per shift spent travelling, although walking distance has been decreased slightly to just under 3,000 metres.

Illegal riding on conveyors has been common in the industry and has been a means of saving the workers' own time, even if at the expense of safety. Increase in the official provision of riding will tend to transfer the time saved from the miner to the employer given the close computer-based monitoring of time spent underground.

These are the developments in production that are being introduced in the early 1980s. They represent, for the coal industry, the increasing use of machinery to displace labour in the production process. This motive is well illustrated by the NCB's own account of manpower efficiency schemes away from the face.[65]

This analysis contradicts the commonly-held view that the industry suffers under the burden of diminishing productivity as the best reserves are increasingly exhausted. Such a view leads to the conclusion that coal production must be reduced and uneconomic pits closed as a result of competition from cheapening energy substitutes. Although geological conditions are crucial in mining, they do not alone determine the productivity of a colliery or a hierarchy of collieries. Performance of individual collieries is extremely variable from year to year, whatever the level of mechanisation. In addition, the coal reserves available are sufficient to ensure that there need be no declining productivity. While the poor or declining performance of some collieries does reflect the exhaustion of coal measures, in others it represents the failure to make adequate investment. This diagnosis is unconsciously confirmed by the NCB in their examples of the turn around of colliery performance from deficit to surplus once new investments are made.[66]

Recent plans to close 70 pits within ten years must be examined in this context.[67] The NCB is attempting to remain within its financial constraints whilst producing the planned level of output. The latter depends less upon market forces than upon government policy. The Central Electricity Generating Board has become the industry's primary customer, but has increasingly opted for nuclear power despite its higher cost. Paradoxically, inadequate levels of investment tend to lead the NCB to rely upon high-cost pits, to bring downward pressure on wages and to recreate conditions of insufficient internally generated investment funds.

Although closures are negotiated at local level, the decision to invest, which largely determines the rate of closures, is taken at a national level, primarily by the NCB and the government. With the hint of closure, those best able to do so transfer elsewhere, tending to dilute the quality of the work-force and weaken results. By a number of devices, the NCB is able to manipulate accounts and performance to understate results and potential. Even where resistance to closure is successful, it

Summary of manpower efficiency schemes completed in the fiscal year 1976-77

Types of scheme	Location	Number of Schemes completed	Average job saving per scheme	Average cost per scheme (£)	Cost per job saved (£)
Automation, monitoring and remote control	Underground	223	3.1	11,300	3,700
	Surface	27	2.3	17,300	7,500
Other	Underground	180	6.0	13,400	2,300
	Surface	184	2.9	13,800	4,800

merely tends to pass the pressure onto another colliery. Until March 1984 the NUM was unable to make the closure issue a national one. This is partly a result of the NCB's strategy of differentiating between the central coalfields (the Midlands counties and Yorkshire) and the 'peripheral' areas of South Wales, Kent, Scotland and the North-East. Development of new mines and major reconstruction of old ones has primarily taken place in the central bloc. Because employment is relatively more secure and, under the operation of the Area Incentive Scheme, wages are higher in these coalfields, loss of earnings through strike action has inhibited solidarity with the peripheral areas.

Conclusion

Our study of the coal industry has revealed that prior to nationalisation, capitalist relations of production were weakening. To some extent, this is revealed by the state organised cartel in the 1930s and government control during the war. This view is also borne out by the continuing technological backwardness of the industry by comparison with its competitors as well as by reference to increasing mechanisation in other industries. Further, the gathering economic and political conflicts ensured that private reorganisation of the industry for profitability was impossible at the end of the war.

Nationalisation has reversed this erosion of capitalist relations. The period of reconstruction before 1956 reintegrated the work-force into a hierarchy of management control, maintaining long hours of work and pressing down wage-levels. The unification of ownership made possible many reforms that had proved impossible under fragmented private ownership, including those of benefit to the work-force in the sphere of welfare. This provided the basis on which the drive to full mechanisation could be won. Within twenty years of nationalisation the NCB had entered the age of modern industry. It is one of the successes of British industry, both in extracting coal and in developing technology.

But the development of the industry in the post-war period has been punctuated by periods of intense industrial conflict. The critical events which led to the national strikes of 1972 and

1974 were, in our analysis, the change in the payment system associated with the introduction of power-loading, and the rundown in manpower. The restoration of incentives within little more than a decade signified the temporary ebb of the miners' militancy and, by setting region against region, generated disunity when the miners struck in 1984-85. It also revealed that there is no fixed relationship between methods of production and forms of wage payment. The NCB may restore a day-wage as a mechanism of cost control if it is able to coerce a satisfactory pace of work or in an attempt to establish a new average level of wages.

Despite the increasing automation of mining, the industry cannot be seen as an exemplary model of capitalist development. Quite apart from the differing geological conditions which make homogeneous working practices impossible, the NCB has been controlled through particular financial and commercial mechanisms. Investment has been constrained according to the performance on accounts, which have been manipulated by price controls and other mechanisms to ensure that adequate funds are not available. The NCB has not been permitted to borrow freely from the financial system. In addition, production has been constrained by plans for output. These mechanisms of control do not operate with an iron necessity. At times they are reinforced with other mechanisms, such as target rates of return and corporate plans. At other times the constraints are relaxed, by writing off assets on which interest has to be paid or by the provision of additional subsidies for investment or for relief of unemployment.[68]

Our review of the NCB has revealed the problems faced by the NUM, and of the labour movement in general, in determining the conditions in which the coal industry has developed. Despite some success in its struggle over wages, the NUM has generally failed to secure greater investment funds for the industry. Where investment has been applied, it has revealed the fallacious idea of diminishing returns within the industry. This fallacy has served as an ideology to justify low levels of investment and wages. A unified struggle on the part of the miners and the labour movement as a whole will be required to transform the conditions of control imposed upon and implemented by the NCB. In turn, this depends upon an integrated plan for the energy sector and energy consumption, an overall degree of co-ordination that has been totally lacking within the British economy.[69]

Notes

[1] In 1963 the NCB changed its statistics from a calendar to a fiscal year basis.

[2] There has also been some improvement in the quality of coal because of washing, etc. This has, however, to be set against the higher proportion of small coal now extracted. There used to be a premium on large coal but this has been eroded by developments in furnace technology and the decline of the demand for large coal.

[3] As always, it is dangerous to generalise about mining conditions. The following paragraph is merely intended to give a general picture of the changes wrought under nationalisation.

[4] With the introduction of powerloading, mechanisation of coal cutting alone was given the new name of 'partial mechanisation'.

[5] The number of fatal accidents has declined from 432 in 1949 to 33 in 1981.

[6] That compensation is now paid for what is termed pneumonicosis rather than for silicosis reflects the acceptance that it is not only silica that causes lung disease.

[7] In its first ten years the NCB spent £37 million, over 5 per cent of capital expenditure on housing 'in areas where local authorities could not provide sufficient housing, or where none existed at all' *NCB Report and Accounts 1957*, p.26. Significantly, each of the regional surveys of the coal districts following the war had two sections, one on coal reserves and a section on housing, so serious a problem was this considered.

[8] See, for example, I. Berkovitch, *Coal on the Switchback: The Coal Industry since Nationalisation*, London 1977, M.P. Jackson, *The Price of Coal*, London 1974, G. Manners, *Coal in Britain: An Uncertain Future*, London 1981.

[9] For the official history of the industry during the war, see W.H.B. Court, *Coal*, London 1951.

[10] This was a lesson that was not learnt from the first world war. Then a quarter of a million joined the forces in the first year of the war.

[11] The strike concerned allowances. For an account, see B.J. McCormick, *Industrial Relations in the Coal Industry*, London 1979.

[12] See Board of Trade, 1942, *Memorandum on the Production, Distribution and Rationing of Coal*, Cmnd.6364.

[13] By 1945 the Coal Changes Account stood at £27.5 million.

[14] Quoted in M.W. Kirby, *The British Coal Industry 1870-1946: A Political and Economic History*, London 1977, p.188.

[15] For details, see R.P. Arnot, *The Miners in Crisis and War: from 1930 Onwards*, London 1961.

[16] See Reid Report, 1945, *Report of the Technical Advisory Committee on Coal Mining*, Cmnd.6610.

[17] See E. Gowers, *Coal Industry Nationalisation Compensation Tribunal, Evidence*

Submitted, London 1946, for a retrospective assessment by the Chairman of the CMRC who was drawn to the conclusion that nationalisation was the only answer to the mineowners.

[18] See R. Foot, *A Plan for Coal*, London 1945.

[19] See H. Wilson, *New Deal for Coal*, London 1945.

[20] For a discussion of nationalisation in British politics, see E.E. Barry, *Nationalisation in British Politics*, London 1965, and for the nationalisations of the Labour government, see N. Chester, *The Nationalisation of British Industry, 1945-51*, London 1975.

[21] See E. Schumacher, 'Some Aspects of Coal Board Policy 1947-1967', *Economic Studies*, 1969, and also NCB Reports and Accounts.

[22] Our discussion of wages depends heavily upon L.J. Handy, *Wages Policy in the British Coalmining Industry*, Cambridge 1981, to whom explicit acknowledgement will not be repeated. Our interpretation of the statistics that he produces is, however, different.

[23] See P. Kahn, 'Essay in Oral History: An Interview with Frank Watters', *Society for the Study of Labour History Bulletin*, 1981, No.43.

[24] This helped to create an ideology of acceptance of the new form of ownership despite the appointment to management of previous owners and officers returning from the war (C.E. Jenks, *The Impact of Nationalisation on Working Conditions in British Coalmining*, Ph.D. Thesis, Berkeley: University of California, 1964). See also the then confidential NCB *Attitudes to the Nationalisation of Coal*, Study by Mass Observation, 1948, a survey of miners' attitudes for the Board.

[25] See Fleck, *Report of the Advisory Committee on Organisation*, London 1955, and for a discussion of the Fleck Report, see C.A. Roberts, 'The National Coal Board and the Fleck Report', *Public Administration*, 1957, Vol.35 No.1, and A. Thompson, 'Organisation in Two Nationalised Industries: Fleck vs Herbert', *Scottish Journal of Political Economy*, 1957, Vol.4 No.2. Its contrast with the Herbert Report, 1955, *Committee of Inquiry into the Electricity Supply Industry*, Cmnd. 9672, which recommended decentralisation for the electricity industry is less paradoxical, once the administrative problems of the industries are placed in the necessary wider context. Compared to the coal industry, the electricity industry was relatively homogeneous. The discussion of the Fleck Report focuses almost exclusively on the reversal of the 1953 directive, ignoring the preceding central abolition of local autonomy over price lists. For an account of the authoritarianism of the Fleck Report from the perspective of workers, see H.A. Clegg, 'The Fleck Report', *Public Administration*, 1955, Vol.33, pp.274-75.

[26] The subsequent trend was to increasing centralisation, most notably in the major reorganisation of 1965, see J. Nelson, 'The Fleck Report and the Area Organisation of the National Coal Board', *Public Administration*, 1965, Vol.43, No.1.

[27] G.B. Baldwin, *Beyond Nationalisation: The Labour Problems of British Coal*, Cambridge Mass. 1955, for example found that in 1949 over 80 per cent of work stoppages were accounted for by faceworkers. Handy reports that by 1961, 70 per cent of the faceworkers earned 30 per cent or more of their wages from allowances. As many as 16 per cent earned more from allowances than from basic contract.

[28] See H.A. Clegg, *The Changing System of Industrial Relations in Great Britain*, Oxford 1979.

[29] Ibid.

[30] Although the choice of payment system has an influence on wage levels and strike activity it is not the primary determining factor. If it were so, this would suggest the possibility of harmony in industrial relations through the appropriate wage system. For an account and criticism of orthodox treatments of this aspect of industrial relations, see P.K. Edwards, 'The Pattern of Collective Industrial Action' in G.S. Bain (ed.), *Industrial Relations in Britain*, Oxford 1983.

[31] We have given two examples on the revenue account. Similar examples apply to the cost side. These, for instance, were heavily influenced by the vested assets, for whose compensation interest payments were made. Quite apart from the generous compensation paid to the former owners, the NCB was also made liable for the royalty compensation of £66m plus accrued interest. This was the height of historical irony. Nationalisation of the royalties was always seen as a means of relieving the industry of a burden. See B. Fine, 'Land, Capital and the British Coal Industry Prior to World War II' in M. Ball *et al.*, *Land Rent, Housing and Urban Planning: a European Perspective*, London 1985.

[32] See W.H. Sales and J.L. Davies, 'Introducing a New Wage structure into Coal Mining', *Bulletin of the Oxford University Institute of Statistics* 1955, Vol.19, No.3. A new wage structure for the more skilled craftsmen was negotiated in 1949. This was necessary in order to retain these workers in the industry whilst preventing their increases from dragging up the wages of the general miner on daywage.

[33] For an account of the invention of the powerloader, see J.F. Townsend, 'Innovation in Coal Mining Machinery: The Anderton Shearer Loader – The Role of the NCB and the Supply Industry in its Development', *Science Policy Research Unit Occasional Paper Series No.3*, 1976. Its arrival is often seen as fortuitous. We would argue that by the early fifties, the need for and resources devoted to such a technical development reflected an anticipation of a completion of major schemes of reconstruction. Following these, further progress at the face became essential.

[34] For a critique of this view, see I. Rutledge, 'Changes in the Mode of Production and the Growth of 'Mass Militancy' in the British Mining Industry 1954-74'. *Science and Society*, 1977, Vol.41. The notion that the introduction of power-loading, or other machinery, robbed the miners of work-place control romanticises the benefits of independent hand-working. Most miners welcomed machinery for the relief it brought from physical work.

[35] It is considerations such as these that render extremely misleading the testing by cross-section of simple hypotheses relating wage increases to variables like changes in technology, since wage increases may be paid both to those who do and do not work new technology as a condition of its acceptance. Similar remarks apply to the explanation of strike behaviour. Hence J. Winterton's 'The Trend of Strikes in British Coalmining 1949-79', *Industrial Relations Journal* 1981, Vol.12, No.6, need to rely upon multicausal factors underlying the number and type of strikes.

[36] The pressure came from the National Reference Tribunal which was concerned with the drift of locally negotiated piece-rates.

[37] According to Sales and Davies, op.cit., the former NCB Director of Industrial Relations claimed that 'the problems involved in revising the piece-work structure were themselves so different in kind, and so complex, as to make it impracticable to do both (day-wage and piece-work) simultaneously.' But this does not explain why day-wage was done first and why piece-work was delayed until NPLA.

[38] The Miners' Charter of 1946 committed the NUM to abolishing piece-rates and establishing a national day-wage structure throughout the industry. See R.P. Arnot, *The Miners: One Union One Industry, A History of the National Union of Mineworkers 1939-46*, London 1979.

[39] This runs contrary to the common view that the NCB complied with the wishes of the NUM. Its own interests were served by the NPLA. If the NCB had been concerned with a national wage policy for face-workers, it would have introduced one more than ten years before.

[40] This entailed a transformation and not a reduction in the skills of miners unlike the tendency to deskilling associated with technical change.

[41] See D. Gidwell, 'Wage Systems in the British Coal Mining Industry: An Appraisal', *Industrial Relations Journal*, 1977, Vol.8, No.2 and B.J. McCormick, *Industrial Relations in the Coal Industry*, London, 1979.

[42] In 1968, 7,000 face officials were sent on face management courses.

[43] See T. Hall, *King Coal: Miners, Coal and Britain's Industrial Future*, Harmondsworth 1981. Right-wing positions on economic questions were mirrored in the political field, with the adoption of Cold War and anti-Communist ideologies. See A. Moffat, *My Life with the Miners*, London 1959, A. Horner, *Incorrigible Rebel*, London 1960 and W. Paynter, *My Generation*, London 1972.

[44] See L. Slaughter, 'The Strike of Yorkshire Mineworkers in May 1955', *Sociological Review* 1958, Vol.6 No.2. This experience was repeated in the Water Haigh and Bodsworth dispute of 1961, but by then the nature of industrial relations had already substantially changed. See also Kahn, art.cit.

[45] In 1971 only 36 per cent of the workforce was under the age of 40 compared with 50 per cent in 1958.

[46] See Rutledge, art.cit., P.F. Clark, 'Introducing Productivity Incentives in the British Coal Mining Industry', *Industrial Relations Journal*, 1980, Vol.11 No.2, and V.L. Allen, *The Militancy of British Miners*, Ilkley 1981.

[47] All workers came onto the day-wage system by January 1st 1972, the Third Day-wage Agreement came into operation covering non-face piece-workers who had remained on piece-work following the NPLA in 1966.

[48] A similar condition applied to the First Day-wage Agreement of 1956.

[49] See Allen, op.cit.

[50] See Hall, op.cit.

[51] For an account of Saltley Gate and for a wider assessment of the significance of the strikes of the seventies, see A. Scargill, 'The New Unionism', *New Left Review*, No.92.

[52] See Wilberforce Inquiry, 1972, *Report of a Court of Inquiry into a Dispute between the National Coal Board and the National Union of Mineworkers*, Cmnd.4903.

[53] See Pay Board, 1974, *Special Report: Relative Pay of Mineworkers*, Cmnd.5567.
[54] Both Wilberforce and the Pay Board recommended productivity agreements as a means of justifying increased wages.
[55] See NCB (1961) *Transactions of Production Conference* which emphasises 'obtaining more output from less men', 'the elimination of the cyclic face 'bottleneck' and focuses upon the three main factors of seam section, face length and face advance per day. It also suggests concentration on fewer faces and the benefits of multiple shift coalcutting for reducing peak loading winding.
[56] See NCB *Collieries and other NCB Activities*, Statistics Department, 1983. The increases are not continuous over the period 1967 to 1982 because of the strikes in the early seventies quite apart from other factors reflecting geology and the time profile of investment.
[57] See MRDE Report of 1981.
[58] March 1980. The *Production and Productivity Bulletin* (referred to hereafter as *P & P* is a technical journal of the NCB.
[59] See NCB, *Collieries and other NCB Activities*, London 1983, and NCB (1968) *Longwall Retreat Mining*, Sixth Mining Engineers Conference, for a manual on the virtues of retreat mining. One 'of our major aims as mining engineers is to improve the quality of longwall face capacity by increasing the proportion of retreat-working' P & P September 1981, which gives an example of increased productivity at the Haig colliery from between two and three times as a result of switching to retreat mining.
[60] See *P & P* April 1978 for an emphasis on the importance of powered supports in the sixties. See also G.W. Sanders, 'The Changing Technology of Coal Extraction', *Journal of the Royal Society of Arts*, 1971.
[61] The system was known as ROLF, standing for remotely operated longwall face. See J.F. Townsend, 'Innovation in Coal Mining Machinery: The Anderton Shearer Loader – the role of the NCB and the Supply Industry in its Development, *Science Policy Research Unit Occasional Paper Series No.3*, 1976, and *P & P*, April 1978.
[62] The use of computer facilities in the NCB is extremely well developed involving both localised remote control of mining as the most advanced technology and centralised information available by VDU on all personnel as well as on individual face performance week by week. See *P & P*, September 1977.
[63] This report also finds that since 1942, 8.8 billion tons of coal reserves have been written off because of the selectivity of modern mechanised coal winning methods.
[64] See *P & P*, September 1982 and also *P & P*, September 1977.
[65] See *P & P*, September 1977.
[66] See Monopolies and Mergers Commission, 1983 *National Coal Board: A Report on the efficiency and costs in the Development, Production and Supply of Coal by the NCB*, Cmnd. 8920.
[67] The plan was implicit in the confidential, but leaked, submission of the NCB to the Monopolies and Mergers Commission (1983), ibid. It has subsequently been confirmed.
[68] Subsidies per tonne to coal industries in Europe in 1979 were as follows: UK – £2; Belgium – £106; France – £66; Germany – £36.

[69] By the 1980s the NCB was left with ten million tons of excess capacity of coking coal because of the rundown of British Steel. Investment in the previous decade had provided new capacity for twenty million tons.

Chapter 7

Nuclear Power

1 Introduction

The nuclear power industry involves an extensive and complex interaction between economic, political and social forces.[1] At the economic level, multinational corporations are significant producers within the industry. As is the case for other industries, they are heavily influenced by state economic intervention. We consider their mode of operation in the next section. The state is a major customer, inevitably where the manufacture of weapons is concerned. The state also provides subsidies and direction to sustain and reorganise the industry and is a major contributor to research expenditure. State involvement has frequently led to public ownership of production facilities. This is so where military needs are served but it is also usual for electricity generation and supply. The associated utility companies are the customers for nuclear power stations.

The state is concerned in the nuclear sector through industrial, energy and research and development policy and, in Section 6 we examine the role played by two state agencies, the Central Electricity Generating Board (CEGB) and the Atomic Energy Authority (AEA). Elsewhere the interventions of the state are seen to be ever present. This is a result of factors which set the nuclear industry apart from other sectors of the economy. The presence of political influences are strengthened and complicated by the industry's connection with weaponry. Through serving the military, the development of nuclear power is subject to political forces that are elevated to the international arena. This is discussed in Section 5. Further, nuclear power presents the dangers not only of explosive devices but also of extensive pollution through radiation, even if atomic power were and could be confined to peaceful purposes. This has made the technology of nuclear power a significant factor, quite apart from the economics involved, as is illustrated by the close attention to the choice between reactor types, each distinguished from the others by being denominated in its initials: PWR, AGR, etc.

These then are the major factors that constitute the nuclear power industry: the multinationals, the state, the military, research, international politics, safety and technology. It would be attractive to refer to a 'nuclear-industrial complex' by analogy to the 'military-industrial complex', a term which has been used to characterise certain central characteristics of advanced capitalism from a number of different theoretical perspectives.[2] The terminology has the advantage of suggesting a number of agencies, tightly knit together in a complex set of relationships. But the terminology also has drawbacks which lead us to reject its use. It tends to imply an unchanging structure and hierarchy of influence. In the remainder of this section, we shall demonstrate that this is false by examining the relationship between nuclear power and weaponry. Subsequently, the analysis will confirm the changing balance and structure of forces that operate within the industry.

In its infancy, if not at its birth, the connection between nuclear power and weaponry was to dominate all other considerations. America simply set itself the task of building the first atomic bomb as a means to end, or more exactly to win, the Second World War.[3] There is a necessary technical relation between the peaceful and the military use of nuclear power.[4] The chain reaction that splits the uranium atom creates energy and plutonium.[5] In a critical reaction, the energy is released explosively. Otherwise, the plutonium created can be used to make bombs whether the energy is used to generate electricity or not.

Initially, apart from those used for research, reactors were built exclusively for the manufacture of plutonium for bombs. Indeed, the heat given off was viewed as an embarrassment, rather than a bonus, since it presented cooling problems. By 1956, the first reactor was supplying electricity for commercial use, even though Calder Hall in the UK had been designed and built for the primary purpose of plutonium production.[6] Certainly, in the use of nuclear power, military use can be severed from electricity generation, as it was when weapons were first built. Subsequently, the two uses have been and continue to be connected with each other, with electricity generation growing in importance – but not at the expense of the military. It is not necessary for plutonium to be used for bombs, this depends upon political factors. Indeed, plutonium can be used as a reactor fuel to generate electricity. In short, the relationship between military and non-military uses of nuclear energy has to be understood both socially and historically. It does have a technical component, which is itself subject to change,[7] but this does not determine the military connection. To explain the evolution of the nuclear industry, the technical-military connection must be seen as variable and situated within wider economic and political circumstances. Indeed, it can be the proponents of nuclear power who wish to play down the military connection by reducing it to isolated political and technical relations. Marshall, for example, argues that as there are more convenient ways of making bombs than by reprocessing plutonium, its weapon potential should not be over-emphasised in the context of non-proliferation and security should be sought primarily through political negotiation.[8]

What applies to weaponry applies equally to the other agencies and relations constituting the nuclear industry. They have to be understood as a whole, in which the individual agencies are subject to changing relations and circumstances. We begin by considering the multinational corporations (MNCs) involved.

2 The Multinationals

The construction of nuclear power stations in the capitalist world is dominated by a small and diminishing number of multinational corporations.[9] The countries of origin of the firms are France, West Germany, Italy, Switzerland, the UK, the US and Japan with an average of three companies each, although they are not evenly distributed. The firms have a number of characteristics in common and we will illustrate these by reference to the British industry.

First, they are highly concentrated within their own domestic markets. In the UK, there are three key companies: General

Electrical Company (GEC), Northern Engineering Industries (NEI), and Babcock International. Other companies substantially involved include the Howden Group, Stone Platt and Whessoe. The companies have been formed through a history of acquisition and merger. NEI, for example, the smallest of the three companies, owns or has a majority shareholding in 22 UK companies. It was formed in 1977 through merger of Clarke Chapman and Reyrolle Parsons. GEC was ultimately created in 1968 through the Industrial Reorganisation Corporation with General Electric acquiring Associated Electrical Industries and English Electric. Babcock is unique in that it was disposed of by its American parent Babcock and Wilcox in 1975. The companies that it controls, like GEC, are almost too numerous to count.

Second, the companies are highly diversified in a number of related sectors, particularly those involving electricity, engineering and construction. This is particularly true of GEC, one of the largest companies in the world, which covers the whole range of electrical products as well as other industrial equipment. There is diversification and specialisation, however, within the construction of nuclear power stations alone. Such production can be divided into a number of separate tasks. Power plant manufacturers have had very little to do with the preparation of nuclear fuel, nor have they been heavily involved in waste reprocessing and disposal.[10] In the construction of the stations, GEC and NEI have the capacity to produce turbine generators, NEI and Babcock to manufacture boilers, but all three companies are involved in the manufacture of other nuclear components.

Third, the companies are highly internationalised, being heavily dependent on exports and production overseas. NEI controls as many affiliates overseas as it does within the UK. Of Babcock's £955 million turnover in 1982, only a value of £272 million was produced in Britain. In the same year, GEC's output of £5 billion involved overseas production of £1.3 billion.

Fourth, because production is not for the mass market, business is obtained through tendering for contracts. Tenders frequently involve a consortium of the companies in which one manages the project and the others are subcontractors. Also included in the consortia or subcontracting are other producers, often multinationals, to undertake construction such as site preparation. For example, within a month in 1982, the following three contracts were negotiated: NEI to engineer and manage a package of £231.5 billion in the construction of the Yenliao nuclear power station for the Taiwan Power Company, with business of £40 million for GEC and £15 million for Babcock; NEI and Babcock to convert an oil to a coal-fired station in Brazil for a contract of £280 million; all three to build a coal-fired station in India for £380 million.

These characteristics of the MNCs in the industry have important repercussions. Each firm attempts to fill its order book by obtaining the greatest part of as many contracts as possible. Contracts undertaken may bear a more or less realistic relation to productive capacity since the most important consideration is to win the contracts. Having done so, the work can, if necessary, be subcontracted. Alternatively, it can be delayed. This is also an option when there is overcapacity, particularly if costs are guaranteed with a profit mark-up. Then, production is artificially maintained by keeping a plant under construction through delays.

Cost and completion overruns have been a chronic problem in the domestic production of UK power plants with construction time and expenditure running to as much as twice or more the original plans.[11] This is particularly true of the AGR (advanced gas cooled reactor) stations,[12] especially where completion dates are concerned, as the following table drawn from the Monopolies and Mergers Commission illustrates, none of these stations having been completed by March 1983, although Dungeness was experimenting on half-power.

The final increases in costs will prove even greater with the passage of time. As the Select Committee on Energy observed, referring in this instance to an oil-fired station: 'in effect, contractors at the Isle of Grain have enjoyed a blank cheque which the CEGB have been obliged to honour'. This is hardly an auspicious context within which to view current governmental commitment to a further two AGRs (at Torness and Heysham). These stations are intended to keep the industry in work. In other words, this represents a subsidy to keep the MNCs operating as before, with a particular commitment to nuclear power.

Nuclear Power Stations Under Construction

	original completion date	Sanction date	Cost * £million Original	Estimated
Dungeness 'B'	June 1971	Mar 1965	38.5	128.0
Hartlepool	Oct 1974	May 1967	91.8	127.7
Heysham	Sept 1976	Dec 1969	142.3	229.8

* At prices based on date scheme sanctioned and excluding fuel costs which have risen considerably for fabrication (rather than for uranium ore)

Source: Monopolies and Mergers Commission, *CEGB: Report on the Operation by the Board of its System for the Generation and Supply of Electricity in Bulk*, London 1981.

The problems of completing stations at original cost is frequently blamed upon poor industrial relations and changing technical requirements. The latter follows from design changes resulting from operating experience from earlier nuclear power stations. Labour troubles are the result to a great extent of the system of subcontracting upon which the industry depends. In construction, more generally, subcontracting has been a source of industrial conflict, and inefficiencies, as labour is paid low wages for insecure employment. Whatever the causes of industrial conflict and technical respecification, they remain a convenient peg upon which to hang increased charges and completion times.

This brief description of the UK industry demonstrates the conditions in which competition operates. At the level of the market, there is enormous scope for collusion between the firms because of their small number and because of their necessary collaboration to form consortia. In Britain, there has been plenty of scope for such collusion. It gave birth to the expression 'Buggins' turn next' in the contracting for power stations, as companies appeared to take turns for the major role in each new station.

Collusion within the industry is well illustrated by the evolution of the British consortia for nuclear stations. Initially, in 1954, there were as many as four separate consortia and this even increased to five in 1956. Each consortium combined electrical engineering with construction capacity, thereby including companies such as McAlpine. With the reorganisation of the electricity engineering side into fewer larger companies, the numbers of these consortia was inevitably reduced, to three in 1960 and to two in 1968/69. At the latter date, the companies were the Nuclear Power Group (TNPG) and British Nuclear Design and Construction (BNDC). GEC had a substantial shareholding in each of these since they had been formed around AEI and English Electric, respectively, both of which had been acquired by GEC. In 1973, a single consortium was formed, the National Nuclear Corporation (NNC) with a wholly owned operating company, the Nuclear Power Corporation (NPC). Under this umbrella, the electrical engineering and construction companies were all represented. Consequently, prior to the formation of the NNC, the companies involved needed to come to an arrangement over orders on the Buggins-principle through the collusion between consortia. Subsequently, their co-operation (and conflicts) could be handled within the confines of a single organisation, created for that purpose. Such arrangements have not eliminated competition from the industry, since at times there have been conflicts between the firms to obtain the orders, despite more or less formal methods of sustaining profit margins.

Competition has also been engaged through reorganisation of the industry. The ability to tender for contracts is enhanced by the size and diversity of firms, quite apart from any associated economies of scale. On the other hand, contracts can be met by sub-contracting rather than by relying upon own capacity. The result, through time, has been to create a highly diversified, concentrated and internationalised set of MNCs for whom further reorganisation is extremely complex. Acquisition of capacity in one particular branch of the sector alone cannot be easily achieved through taking over another firm. Such a strategy would land an acquiring firm with additional capacity in other branches of the sector which may be unwanted. This explains why the industry is characterised both by diversity and by subcontracting and consortia. One is the result of acquisitions, the other serves to avoid it. Another consequence is that acquisitions lead to excess capacity in particular branches which then suffer closures. GEC, for example, has gained a reputation as an asset stripper, since it had been particularly active in acquiring firms and retaining only those productive assets that are complementary to its continuing needs. Moreover, the economic structure of the industry creates firms which generate an uneven cash flow. Much finance is needed to pay for fixed equipment at intervals, just as revenue accrues periodically upon completion of and payment for major contracts. As a result, companies can face difficulties in gaining sufficient finance to re-equip, whilst others have ready cash available that can be used for acquisition. GEC over the last five years had the following profile of net increases to liquid funds:

GEC: Net addition to Liquid Funds £ million

1978	146.9
1979	112.4
1980	−130.7
1981	61.6
1982	375.0

The low figures in 1980 and 1981 are associated with expenditures of £149.4 million and £83.6 million, respectively, for the purchase of subsidiaries. The process of acquisition and asset stripping goes hand in hand with the holding and use of liquid balances for those purposes.

3 The Crisis of Nuclear Power

The structure of the power industry described in the previous section has been superimposed upon conditions of acute excess capacity since the world economic crisis of 1974. The crisis presented problems for all industries, but they were particularly severe for electricity supply. The oil crisis encouraged measures of conservation in all sources of energy. Low overall growth rates cut demand for electricity. Meanwhile, the boom in electricity-using consumer durables was reaching saturation point in the advanced capitalist world. The turning point of 1974 found the power plant sector caught with expanding capacity even as their orders, yet to be completed, sufficed to satisfy most of the projected demand for electricity. The situation is illustrated by the comparison between orders and capacity projected for the period 1975-87.

Steam Turbine Generators 1975-87
Average Annual Output and Capacity, GW*

	Output	Capacity
United States	22	41
Japan	6	15
West Germany	5	14
France	6	9
United Kingdom	4	8
Switzerland	2	6
TOTAL	45	93

*Gigawatts (1,000 million watts)
Source: Surrey and Walker, *The European Power Plant Industry*, Brighton 1981.

The situation for nuclear power has been even more drastic. Potter reports that total orders per annum within the capitalist world collapsed from 45GW in 1970-74 to 15.1GW in 1975-79.[13] Nuclear power accounted for approximately 12 per cent of electricity by the 1980s, having grown in supply seven times in the 1970s. The growth was primarily between 1974 and 1976, reflecting the effect of orders placed at an earlier time. According to Bupp, between 1975 and 1980, less than half a dozen reactors were newly under construction, the low figure accounted for by fifty cancellations and a hundred deferrals for between five and ten years.[14] A further index of the collapse in the demand for nuclear power is given by movements in the price of uranium. These tend to lag behind power plant orders since the fuel is only required at a later date. In the 1970s, the price rose to a peak of $45 per pound but had fallen to $17 per pound by 1982, with supply capacity estimated to exceed demand twenty times over.

These aggregate figures conceal some important changes that have occurred in the balance of power within the industry. For power plant as a whole, developments have been similar to many other industries, with the exception that domestic markets tend to be preserved for domestic producers where they exist. The UK and US have lost substantial shares of the world market over the post-war period. These have been taken up by Japan and, to a lesser extent, by France and Germany. This process had, however, been essentially completed by the end of the 1960s except that the US domestic market was being penetrated to an increasing extent and Japan's export share continued to grow, albeit unsteadily, at the expense of the United States.

Shares of World Exports of Electric Power Equipment
Percentages

Table 1

Changing Pattern of Coal Consumption

	1955	1969	1978
UK	22.2	9.4	8.7
France	6.0	9.3	10.2
West Germany	18.5	21.6	22.7
US	31.9	20.3	14.1
Japan	1.3	10.2	15.1

Source: Surrey and Walker, op.cit.

Developments in nuclear power have been both later and sharper. Exports only become significant in the mid-1960s with American companies, particularly Westinghouse and General Electric[15] dominating the scene with the light water reactors (LWR).[16] Their competition came primarily from the Canadian heavy water reactor, CANDU.[17] Between 1968 and 1971 the US was responsible for 90 per cent of exports of nuclear reactors. It had licensed reactor technology in Belgium, France, West Germany, Sweden, Switzerland, Spain, Italy and Japan, with joint ventures also undertaken in France, Belgium and Sweden. The decline in demand for nuclear power stations in 1974 coincided with an accelerating loss of American dominance over technology. In particular, French, German, Japanese and Swiss companies, with others on the horizon, were developing independent capability in the manufacture of nuclear power plant by means of licensed technology. They closed their own domestic markets, or what remained of them, to the American MNCs, and competed for exports. The vast majority of these exports had to be found in the third world because of collapsed demand in the advanced capitalist countries coupled with preference for domestic producers where possible. As the 1982 United Nations report reveals, across the whole range of power-equipment exports, developing countries took an increase in share of over 10 per cent in four out of seven subsectors with resulting share close to or exceeding fifty per cent in four subsectors. This explains the sharp fall in American nuclear exports but the slow growth of exports from elsewhere. Just as the Westinghouse PWR (pressurised water reactor) has taken the greater share of the export market, so it has become the preferred technology of adoption. It accounts for 50 per cent of nuclear power generated as compared to 30 per cent for the GE-associated BWR (boiling water reactor).[18]

Nuclear Power Plant Exports

GW p.a.

	1970-74	1975-79
USA	5.7	1.4
Other	1.3	1.6

Source: Surrey and Walker, op.cit.

4 The Origins of Sizewell

Two notable exceptions to these general developments have taken place in Canada and Britain. Canada has continued to rely upon its indigenously developed reactors accounting for 5 per cent of nuclear power generation in the world. It has benefited from large supplies of natural uranium and a stock of heavy water. Its technology originates from the war, when it was chosen as a site for the manufacture of plutonium through the use of a heavy water reactor. Whilst the HWR (heavy water reactor) generates twice as much plutonium as an LWR, it was graphite moderated reactors that were the source of the plutonium first used in bombs. Nuclear energy remains big business in Canada, with a turnover at well over a billion dollars per annum. 19,000 workers are employed in electricity generation, 11,000 in related construction and 5,000 in uranium mining. Only 10 per cent of the uranium extracted is used for domestic purposes.[19]

Like Canada, Britain had not developed an LWR civil reactor programme. Here the similarity ends. In the UK, shortage of heavy water and enriched uranium immediately after the war dictated that graphite moderated reactors were the shortest route to the manufacture of nuclear weapons in the absence of American co-operation.[20] The resulting technology has ultimately led to the British-designed AGR.[21] France followed a similar path but dropped its own programme of graphite reactors at the end of the sixties.[22] Government approval in the UK for PWR stations some ten years later[23] has led to the view that Britain has lost time and money by remaining committed to the AGR.[24] In this light, the Sizewell 'B' Public Inquiry is the first step towards economic rationality in the British nuclear power programme.[25]

Before examining this view, it is necessary to assess how a PWR programme in the UK would affect the MNCs concerned. The vast bulk of the order for the first British PWR would find its way to Westinghouse which would receive £1 billion for hardware and technology. The PWR does not, in the immediate future, provide British MNCs with business to keep them ticking over and maintaining expertise in nuclear technology. This contrasts with the two AGR stations authorised in 1980 to be built at Heysham and Torness. As far as British MNCs are concerned, the first PWR ordered in Britain does not serve their interests through the business that it provides for them directly. Far more important is the opening that it creates for them in PWR technology. The collapsed market for nuclear power stations has left MNCs desperate for orders. They are better able to obtain them, given the consortia system of tendering and subcontracting, the more they are capable in a diverse range of technologies. A PWR order in Britain is most important for the expertise it provides to British MNCs. Ultimately, they may be able to produce PWRs independently of Westinghouse, as have other MNCs, and a continuing programme of orders in Britain would he helpful. But the main benefit would be felt on the world market. As Weinstock, manager of GEC and an enthusiast for the PWR for a number of years remarked 'there is no possibility of selling anything for AGRs ... Nobody will buy AGRs or components'.[26]

The counterpart to the limited potential of the AGR is the export promise of the PWR[27]. As Sedgemore reveals, as early as 1977 Walter Marshall was negotiating with 'the Iranian Foreign Minister about the possible purchase by Iran from Britain of 20 PWRs, a decision which was to be dependent on the UK opting for the development of PWRs for its own use'.[28] At that time, Marshall was Chief Scientific Adviser to the Department of Energy and Deputy-Chairman of the AEA as well as safety adviser to the Iranian nuclear power programme. He subsequently became Chairman of the AEA before transferring to the CEGB.

The potential benefits of the Sizewell 'B' PWR are already being distributed. The £100 million contract for its turbine generators was won in February 1983 by GEC against fierce competition from NEI. Press reports suggest that both companies were asked to retender for the contract in order to allow GEC to undercut its rival. In this instance, the Buggins-principle does not apply. Work obtained on the PWR will enable GEC to steal a lead in obtaining future orders on the world market. It is a lead that will be hard to catch up in conditions of depressed demand.[29] The commitment to the PWR has also represented a setback to NEI which is a strong supporter of and manufacturer for the AGR, although its disappointment is undoubtedly tempered by the continuing orders for the AGR reactor.

It might be thought, with some justification, that the export potential of PWR technology from the UK is extremely limited given the collapsed state of orders and the long lag in expertise compared to competitors. Apart from planning for the distant future, this fails to take account of cartelisation within the power plant industry at a world level. The IEA (International Electrical Association) has a long history going back to before the Second World War. According to the United Nations report the IEA agreement

stipulates the terms and conditions under which the members sell power equipment, the procedures for submitting tenders and price guidelines for tenders. In certain product categories, provisions exist for the market share of the members. Companies which win the tender are expected to give financial compensation to the other companies. In the case of a breach of agreement, penalties are imposed.

The result is to raise contract prices, especially to third world countries, and it is likely that room will be found for the UK MNCs to provide their share of PWRs despite their lack of expertise. A graphic account of this process is to be found in Mirow and Maurer's work.[30]

By this account, the road to Sizewell has witnessed the victory of PWR over AGR technology. Associated with this, the interests of GEC have come to the fore, particularly at the expense of NEI. Whatever the merits of each reactor, the delay in adoption of the PWR is remarkable given the ample opportunity that there has been to develop it in the past. Indeed, PWR technology is not new to Britain, although it is so in the field of *civil* reactors. Under the 1958 Bilateral Agreement between the UK and US governments, Rolls Royce and Associates Ltd (RR&A)[31] contracted PWR technology from Westinghouse for the construction of a nuclear powered submarine.[32] Westinghouse had built the reactor for *Nautilus*, the first nuclear submarine, launched by the US Navy in 1954. Subsequently, the 'US civil PWR is founded on the bedrock of the US Naval Reactor Programme' and this best explains the great success of the Westinghouse PWR reactor. It has been well-served by spin-off from military contracts.

The first British nuclear submarine, the *Dreadnought*, was launched in April 1963. Fifteen are now operating, eight are under construction and two prototypes are under development. As early as 1967, RR&A were interested in constructing the Dungeness 'B' nuclear power station offering a consortium with English Electric under a Westinghouse licence. RR&A have observed that 'there is no difference of kind between the skills of design and manufacturing required for the naval plants and those required for a civil PWR programme, but there are massive differences of scale and significant differences in detailed technology.'[33] Currently they 'believe that it would be both beneficial to RR&A Ltd, in the national interest, if the experience available within the company were to be used to support any UK civil PWR programme'. Unfortunately for RR&A, GEC's interests are no longer served by collaboration with it, since this would involve a potential rival in the long-run and a share of the spoils in the short run. RR&A has been excluded from the National Nuclear Corporation and has not been consulted by the various authorities concerned with civil reactors despite its long experience with PWR technology. It is attempting to form a consortium with Combustion Engineering, an American company with nuclear capacity. With some justification, but undoubtedly motivated by self-interest, RR&A argues that the small British domestic market, with little export prospects given excess capacity abroad, suggests that importing nuclear power plant would be the better alternative than investment in UK manufacturing capability.

The account of the naval reactor programme confirms that the development of nuclear energy in Britain has involved a compromise and conflict of interest amongst the MNCs concerned. Of itself, this does not explain why the interest of one MNC should predominate over another nor the form in which it does so. To address these issues, it is necessary to examine the other agencies involved in the development of nuclear power. We begin by accounting for the role of international politics. We show that it did present a barrier to technology transfer immediately after the Second World War, but that this was no longer a direct influence by the 1960s. It did exert an indirect effect by necessitating the creation of indigenous technology and its associated interest groups in the interim period.

5 *International Politics and the Military*

Both international politics and military considerations have been important in the development of nuclear power, but their direct influence on reactor choice in Britain remains in the distant past. Following the war, the USA was far in advance of other countries in nuclear technology. To build the atomic bombs that were dropped on Japan, it had given absolute priority to the Manhattan Project. Throughout, 600,000 Americans had been directly involved in the Project and expenditure was running at $100 million per month to fund materials and a staffing level of as many as 50,000. During the course of the Project, interchange of information between personnel was kept to a minimum for security reasons. This also served to limit knowledge available to the British, French and other scientists who were employed in the Allies' collaborative effort under American control. The USA was aware of the post-war potential of nuclear power, particularly for military purposes, and sought to guarantee its privileged position both during and after the war in relation both to its western allies as well as to the Soviet Union.[34] Promises of co-operation and hopes for an international agreement to confine atomic power to peaceful purposes came to nothing. By the end of 1946, the Atomic Energy (McMahon) Act had passed through Congress, forbidding the US to reveal its nuclear technology to other countries.

By the end of 1953, the situation had changed drastically. The Soviet Union had exploded an atomic bomb in 1949 and the UK in 1952. This reflected a heavy commitment to nuclear weapons and success despite the denial of direct access to American technology. It weakened the case for continuing American secrecy, especially as the civil potential of nuclear power was being explored by Britain, France and Canada, the latter having no direct interest in weapon capability. In 1954, President Eisenhower launched the 'Atoms for Peace' proposals to the United Nations. Offers of American technology were contingent upon the placing of orders with American firms whose civil reactor programme was emerging from the spin-offs from submarine and weaponry development.

As these events illustrate, the interests of MNCs in non-military use of nuclear power were to be represented at a very early stage, with the US using its technological and political power to further those interests. LWR reactors were developed in the US out of the war effort and because of the availability of uranium enrichment facilities. In the absence of such facilities and heavy water, Britain developed graphite moderated reactors whilst constructing both enrichment and reprocessing facilities. From the mid-1950s onwards it developed its own programme of Magnox reactors which gave way to the AGR programme in 1965. By that time, after an exceptionally slow start, despite subsidies and cut price offers, the American nuclear technology was beginning to grip the world market. As we have seen, Britain had the option to adopt the PWR technology. Neither political nor military considerations prevented it from doing so, since the technology was made available and the AGR is no more productive of plutonium than LWRs. If plutonium were the primary consideration, both the USA and the UK would have adopted an HWR which produces approximately twice the amount of plutonium as compared to an LWR which itself suffices to provide for approximately twenty bombs per reactor per annum.

In 1974, American policy was reversed once more to deny easy access to its technology. The motive given was the fear that civil reactor facilities could be used for manufacturing nuclear weapons. This fear was well-grounded and has given rise to much discussion on the subject of 'Nuclear Power and non-Proliferation'.[35] But it has been expressed much too late. It is estimated that at least thirty countries could manufacture nuclear weapons relatively quickly from their existing research and civil reactors.[36] The ease of this was demonstrated by India's explosion of a nuclear device in 1974, having relied upon Canadian technology.

Much of the literature is informed by the naïve presumption that the US had unwittingly made a mistake which it should correct by withholding technology and facilities unless it could guarantee against military spin-off. It was a case of closing the stable door after a large number of horses had bolted and trying to hold onto the few still left inside. Such a perspective ignores the economic interests involved, quite apart from the extensive spy network of US intelligence. By 1974, US dominance in nuclear power was already being challenged. It deliberately set about accruing the maximum advantage of its lead in the short time remaining whilst impeding the developments of its rivals. For example, in the case of enrichment facilities the USA had a virtual monopoly, which was known to be short-lived, because two separate Consortia of European States had set up Companies to provide enrichment facilies. These were Eurodif and Urenco and were about to enter production whilst the Soviet Union was also beginning to offer exports.[37] America's policy that emerged in the early 1970s was to refuse to take any further orders for enriched uranium after June 1974 until at least 1982. Customers were forced to place orders with America or face the risk of being caught short of enriched uranium,[38] depending upon the success and policy of Urenco and Eurodif.

The collapse of the nuclear power industry after 1974 brought America into sharp conflict with its competitors. West Germany, in particular, was faced with the request from the USA not to export power stations to Brazil, but honoured its commitment.[39] Paradoxically, France, which had always resisted the hegemony of the United States in foreign policy, conformed more easily in this instance, but was less dependent upon export markets because of its heavy commitment to a domestic programme of nuclear power.[40] By 1980, West Germany had been without a domestic order for a nuclear power station for five years. The conflict between the USA and West Germany signalled the impossibility of the USA determining policy alone because of the breach in its overwhelming technical supremacy. It proved necessary for the USA to share power in the formation of a cartel of the major producers. This materialised in the informal institution of the London Suppliers Group in 1975 which arranged for its members to limit to themselves facilities for enrichment and reprocessing. It promised that customers were to suffer no commercial disadvantage. Significantly, West Germany withdrew its offer of building enrichment and reprocessing plants in Brazil, in line with the policy of the Suppliers Group.[41]

This account of international politics explains how Britain became committed to independent development of nuclear weapons through graphite-moderated reactors that were eventually adapted for electricity generation. France experienced a similar history although it lagged behind the UK, exploding its first bomb in 1960. The historical factors creating the need for independent technology did not last long, as far as the development of civil reactors was concerned, because of the lifting of the US embargo on technology transfer after 1954. The renewal of restrictions in 1974 had little effect on Britain in this respect and did, if anything, bring the USA and UK closer together.[42] The transfer of naval reactor technology in 1958 demonstrated the possibilities that existed for commercial reactors. That this option was not taken up in the form of

British adoption of the PWR technology depended upon internal factors to which we now turn with respect to state agencies.

6 The AEA and the CEGB

The Atomic Energy Authority was the eventual form of the organisation set up after the war to develop British nuclear weapons. It was guaranteed priority in funds, materials and personnel and a virtual monopoly in research. Its activities were certain to place it in a crucial role in the development of nuclear power stations. Inevitably the AEA's commanding position in relation to nuclear weapons was carried over into nuclear power more generally. It has been a continuing major influence on the industry. The power that it exerts derives from its importance to the military, but its motives tend to be more research-orientated. The AEA seeks funding for its continuing scientific work. Initially, this was guaranteed by the need to develop British reactor technology to manufacture plutonium. With American technology coming available, AEA research would have been considerably curtailed, if it had been unable to press successfully for its reactors to be adopted for a power station programme.

Although it was historically inevitable that the AEA should dominate the nuclear power programme, it is not necessary for it to continue to do so. The connections between research and military and civil uses of nuclear power endure but this does not entail policy-making residing with the AEA. For it to lose that role, it would either have to be defeated politically, since its research interests are served by its command over policy, or its own interests would have to be served more or less independently of the immediate needs of energy policy. In France, for example, the equivalent organisation to AEA, the CEA, suffered a substantial defeat in 1969. At the same time that the graphite reactor was dropped and American technology licensed, primary responsibility for nuclear power was handed over to the EDF, the equivalent of the CEGB. In America, MNCs were early introduced into the military programme and were encouraged to develop their own research and technology for nuclear power.

In Britain, the history of the twenty years from 1956 is one of the AEA dominating the nuclear power programme against the wishes of the CEGB.[43] The Magnox programme beginning in 1957 left the CEGB determined not to be burdened with its high costs and in 1960 it pressed for a cut-back in the programme. Lord Hinton, who had been at the AEA before becoming Chairman of the CEGB, recognised the extra cost of nuclear power and considered that it was accepted because of the scare over oil supplies following Suez. The ending of the Magnox programme in 1963 saw the CEGB and AEA in conflict again, with the CEGB favouring foreign nuclear technology against the AGR. When the issue was renewed in 1974, the AEA won a remarkable victory through commitment to the steam generating heavy water reactor (SGHWR) when agreement could not be won for either the AGR or for an LWR. The SGHWR was totally undeveloped, had little connection with existing British technology, and it promised years of funded research. Within two years, the SGHWR was abandoned but the AEA has been amply funded for fast breeder reactor (FBR) research. This is not expected to produce electricity commercially until the next century, so direct AEA influence over nuclear power has been thwarted without substantially damaging its interests, as long as the FBR programme is funded.

Meanwhile, the CEGB had become increasingly committed to nuclear power from a stance of strong opposition. There has been a persistent stream of personnel from the AEA to the CEGB, particularly at the top. Initially, some such as Hinton were sceptical about the costs that would have to be met. The CEGB found, however, that its costs could be met out of revenue or government loans or subsidies such was the commitment to nuclear power. The nuclear industry within the CEGB began to grow and its preferred technology became the PWR. With this technology, it could develop a unique expertise in the country and hope to satisfy its suppliers of power stations given their international interests. Consequently, the CEGB set about pressing the case for nuclear power with the PWR as the preferred technology and the AGR as a second best choice. Its argument rested upon the supposedly cheap electricity that would result.

7 The So-Called Economics of Nuclear Power

Until recently, assessments of the costs of nuclear power have been practically non-existent in the UK. It was more or less presumed that what had been little more than back-of-the-envelope calculations justified enormous expenditure for the firm promise of future, cheaper electricity. From the time of the decision in favour of AGR over LWR technology in the mid-1960s, increasing attention has been paid to costing. Initially, it was devoted to proving that the AGR was disastrously expensive with the possible presumption that the PWR would deliver what the AGR had failed to do.[44] This was quite acceptable to the CEGB, which favoured the PWR, although it preferred to argue that AGRs would also be cheaper than conventional stations in the future on the basis of past experience. Costing has subsequently been taken up by opponents of any type of nuclear power.[45] Doubt has been cast on whether nuclear power of any sort could be justified on grounds of cheaper cost.

The arguments over costing are extremely complex since they depend upon predicting the future demand for electricity, the price of alternative fuels etc. It is debate over these issues which constitutes the economics of nuclear power. It is an extremely narrow analysis.[46] It requires first and foremost that what is to be counted as economic be rigidly separated from everything else which is then put aside. Where that dividing line is drawn can be subject to dispute but drawn it must be. However, the issue of nuclear power combines a multitude of factors many of which are not directly economic and cannot be costed. These are certain to be excluded from consideration. They are factors such as the effect on proliferation and the need for more extensive security and secrecy to pre-empt difficulties from opposition groups or sabotage. Opponents of nuclear power have been relatively generous in drawing the line on what should be costed even where factors are involved which could be partially assessed. These include consideration of the cost of research for safety and waste disposal as well as for design. In contrast to the NCB, the vast majority of such expenditure does not fall upon the CEGB, but upon 'outside' institutions such as the Nuclear Industry Inspectorate and the AEA. Although these are often called upon to make independent nuclear judgements, they have close links – including financial support – from the CEGB. Accordingly, the dispute over the economics of nuclear power has been confined to very narrow ground. Like much cost-benefit analysis, it is better seen as the reasons given to justify a decision already made rather than the method of reaching that decision. Opponents of nuclear power would have broadened their calculus of costs to present their economic case if this had proved necessary. Fortunately for them, the case for nuclear power, as presented by the CEGB, has been so poor that it is their motivation rather than their reason that has been exposed.

This has emerged from the recent reports, one on the CEGB by the Monopolies and Mergers Commission, and the other by the Select Committee on Energy examining the government's proposals for nuclear power. They reveal an appalling lack of sophistication and rigour on the part of the CEGB in its costings. To some extent, this may reflect the lack of any necessity to have been otherwise in the past. A more sinister interpretation is that the CEGB has deliberately presented misleading calculations in order to support its favoured policy.[47] We gather together some of the criticisms made of the CEGB in these reports.

Nuclear power stations command a high initial cost of construction but subsequently run on lower fuel costs as compared to conventional power stations. At its simplest, the economies of nuclear power is reduced to a choice between the various time-profiles of costs from construction and fuel as compared to the benefits from electricity generated. This choice is easily made by use of a discount rate to calculate and compare the present values of two projected power stations. This is the basic method of comparison and, as argued earlier, it depends upon a reduction of social decision to a single dimension of (discounted) monetary value.[48]

Within this calculus of costs and benefits, the CEGB's estimates have exhibited a systematic bias in favour of nuclear power. One example is the estimate of construction costs and time. The CEGB admits to having based its calculations on the minimum technically feasible values even though these have never been achieved in practice and it is recognised that they will not be achieved in the future. Its reason for having done so is the wish to press contractors to produce at agreed cost and time. Whether it could possibly hope to do so by such methods is beside the point. Its estimates for contracting purposes are irrelevant for decision-making purposes.

When nuclear power stations are in place, they are liable to be used on the maximum possible load because of their cheaper running costs. Electricity demand in the UK has both seasonal, weekly and daily variations. As a result, many stations are not run at full capacity all the time. The CEGB has compared *actual* operating costs of nuclear stations against coal stations. Since the former are on full load as compared to the latter, they will appear cheaper. The correct procedure, however, for future stations is to compare the two with each on full load. If the nuclear option were rejected, this is the basis on which conventional stations would be used.

The CEGB has consistently overestimated the future demand for electricity as observed by the Reports and Papadopoulos,[49] and this adds to their case for nuclear power. Their liberal estimate of extra capacity over and above expected peak demand (at 28 per cent) to assure secure supply has the same effect. Once excess capacity is installed then nuclear power will be run on full load and other stations will either be scrapped prematurely or run at low capacity. This creates the impression that they are inefficient as compared to nuclear for the reasons mentioned earlier.

These criticisms, and there are many others, of the CEGB's economics have been accepted in the presentation of its case for Sizewell 'B'. They have served to improve the presentation of its case whilst having no effect on its decision-making. No reason is given to explain how it could have made such flawed calculations in the past. The lack of skill in its reasoning contrasts strongly, for example, with the techniques needed to operate the allocation of load between various power stations. Nevertheless, despite the expenditure of £5 million to state its case for Sizewell, the CEGB's calculations remain seriously deficient.[50] We give some examples.

Construction cost and delay time have been estimated for Sizewell by the CEGB on the basis of average experience for the PWR in the past with a fairly generous allowance on top. This is justified by the treatment of the PWR as a proven technology for which there will be minimal design change during construction. This is questionable quite apart from the economic pressures that might arise to delay construction and increase costs. First of all, nuclear power stations are extremely complex and not subject to straightforward assembly, particularly as the products of different manufactures will need to be co-ordinated. The real cost of construction has been rising rapidly in the 1970s as compared to coal-fired stations. Komanoff presents estimates of capital construction costs.[51]

Construction Costs for Power Stations $/Kilowatt

	1971	1978	1988
Coal	346	583	794
Nuclear	366	887	1374

Second, although it is too early historically to confirm, nuclear power construction tends to move in cycles. On the basis of a given technology, a number of orders are rushed through. This occurred for the PWR ten years ago. These stations then yield a period of operating experience which gives rise to design change both for safety and for improved loading. Power stations at the moment are liable to be subject to these design changes during construction especially as there is no sign of a renewed rush of construction on which a fixed design could be based.

The CEGB recognises that it does not need to start any new construction for a number of years in order to satisfy demand. Its case for a nuclear power station at Sizewell rests on the argument that it will generate electricity so cheaply that it will be worthwhile closing down existing capacity to make way for it. Sizewell 'B' will save the cost of highly expensive coal to such an extent that its capital cost will be justified. This view depends crucially upon assumptions about the price of coal. The CEGB reckons that it will rise in *real terms* by at least 1 per cent per annum. This is far from necessary, since coal can be mined by highly capital-intensive methods, so there is no reason for the real price of coal to rise. Significantly, the CEGB treats the price of coal as exogenous, whereas its own commitment to nuclear power and influence over energy policy affects the investment funds that are made available to the NCB.[52] It should also be observed that high estimates of electricity demand aid the case for nuclear power since more of the expensive existing capacity could be displaced by supposedly cheaper nuclear power.

The above account gives a sample of the problems with CEGB arguments. It suffices to show the arguments are constructed to justify decisions rather than to make them. It is in this respect that the arguments are improved, as in the statement of the case for Sizewell, in answer to criticisms which it is felt must be met. Given the method of assessment, it is also possible to argue the merits of nuclear power on what become non-economic grounds because they have been excluded from cost considerations. One such factor is safety, which is considered to count against nuclear power. Here, we do not wish to assess the technical conditions concerning safety but to emphasise its economic significance.[53] One consideration is the disposal of radio-active waste. At the moment, there is no known and agreed long-term method. Because the problem arises at the end of a station's life, the present discounted value of the costs of disposal are small since they lie thirty or more years into the future. But the research expenditure into waste disposal must be incurred in advance, although it does not count as a cost since it is not undertaken by the CEGB.

Although the CEGB bases its case mainly on economic grounds, it has other non-economic arguments of which the most important concerns diversity to ensure security of electricity supply. This is presented as a search for less risk by using a number of fuel options, but more ominously it has figured as a means of weakening the industrial strength of the miners since coal currently accounts for eight per cent of electricity generation. As Sedgemore reveals, a Tory Cabinet paper of 25 october 1979 argued:

> But a nuclear programme would have the advantage of removing a substantial portion of electricity production from the dangers of disruption by industrial action by coal miners or transport workers.[54]

By this means, the CEGB may gain support for its case, but the substance of the argument is extremely weak. As Sweet has emphasised,[55] even under the most optimistic outcome, nuclear power will continue to provide only a minority share of electricity generation into the next century. Consequently, it can do little to guarantee security of supply and, from an economic point of view, it has extremely risky prospects as compared to other fuels. Indeed, the pursuit of nuclear power appears to go hand in hand with deprivation of finance for investment to the coal industry. This is probably a greater potential source of industrial action than a programme of expansion for coal!

8 Conclusion

Many commentators on the issue of nuclear power have recognised the burden that its development has placed upon the British economy through pre-empting resources for investment and creating high energy costs. This conclusion is practically unavoidable, because of the high generating costs of nuclear power in the past, despite efforts by the CEGB to conceal this and to promise even lower costs in the future. A remedy to what are perceived as mistaken policies is sought. Sometimes this is seen in narrow technical terms, a problem of making correct choices; between PWR and AGR, nuclear and coal, or coal and alternative renewable sources. Others see the problem institutionally. Burn, for example, wishes to see less government interference in decision-making with the CEGB and private companies carrying the authority and bearing the responsibility for reactor choice.[56] Here, he wishes to follow the American and West German models in which research institutions such as the UK AEA play a minimal role and electricity supply is governed by a utility/manufacturer axis. He, together with Henderson emphasises the incompetence of government control in the UK.

None of these approaches gets to the root of the problem. They tend, whilst revealing significant criticisms of the existing system, to ignore the complexity of the industry. In addition, they neglect the simple reality of substantial conflict of interest, which must be accommodated *and* reproduced. It cannot be resolved by appropriate decision-making since contradictory economic and political pressures are certain to operate.

There is, for example, nothing ideal about the American system. Placing economic pressures upon the utility/-manufacturer axis may lead to one or the other being forced into bankruptcy, to higher fuel costs, to neglect of safety, and, almost inevitably, to a return to some form of more extensive state intervention. Such realities have been apparent from the crisis in the industry following the collapse of orders from the mid-1970s. Nor is the West German industry in any better shape with a complete collapse of domestic orders since 1975 making government intervention essential.[57] The role of the state would appear to be unavoidable. Translated to British conditions, a greater degree of autonomy in decision-making, by the CEGB and MNCs may do little that is positive in dealing with problems of construction cost and time overrun. Nor can it be presumed, given the desirability of nuclear power, that such an axis would have been correct in choosing the PWR over the AGR at an earlier date. No doubt, such a choice would have been made, but the AGR was developed and failed in the most disadvantageous circumstances. The PWR may develop equally poorly whatever its record elsewhere. It is, moreover, a reactor chosen to further the interests of British MNCs overseas. As such, it may or may not be advantageous or certain that the reactor perform well here.

In France, in contrast to the rest of the western world, nuclear power has continued to thrive.[58] In the late 1960s, the power of the CEA (the equivalent of the AEA) was defeated. Following de Gaulle's death, France rejected its own technology and adopted American LWR technology. Authority for nuclear power was essentially vested in the EDF (the equivalent of the CEGB) with production facilities concentrated in the state-controlled firm Framatome. A policy was pursued of rapid growth of nuclear power with its proportion of electricity to grow to a half by 1985, having been as little as 7 per cent in 1973. Significantly, the plan was wedded to an energy policy in which electricity was to play a crucial role in the French economy, summarised in the slogan 'tout électrique, tout nucléaire' and leading to electricity use at twice UK levels. The result has been a success in the sense of achieving a major part of these aims, but the economic cost may prove enormous. The political cost has been to create an empire around the EDF which has been dubbed 'a state within a state'. Consequently, the momentum of the nuclear programme will prove difficult to halt whatever its continuing performance.

The coherent direction given to French policy since 1970 stands in sharp contrast to the British experience. From its

origins, responsibility for the programme has shifted from
Ministry to Ministry at a bewildering pace,[59] making room for
the various interest groups to press more readily for their
long-term goals. Opposing these interests even at an
immediate level is difficult and does not yield an alternative
policy, let alone the means by which to implement it. Tony
Benn, whilst Secretary of State for Energy, recognised the
powerful lobby for the PWR in 1978 and was determined to
oppose it.[60] He did so through a compromise that recognised
the merits of both AGR and PWR technology. Ironically, his
stand was soon to become the basis on which to order two
AGR reactors and to condone the CEGB case for a PWR at
Sizewell.

These incidents demonstrate the total exclusion of labour
movement participation in the nuclear decision apart from the
occasional and self-admittedly ineffective intervention by
individuals such as Benn. The parallel with the military is
striking, but even there the labour movement has representation in so far as it can influence foreign policy. Where and
how can the labour movement make its presence felt?
Anti-nuclear protest in the non-military context has been
extremely weak in Britain. It is heavily circumscribed by the
forms that it can take. Sizewell, for example, is a local inquiry
over site use with nothing but the appearance of nuclear power
on trial. As at Windscale/Sellafield, it will be possible for the
decision to favour nuclear power more or less because that is
what the government wants.[61] Even in France and West
Germany, where the anti-nuclear movement is far stronger
and more militant than in the UK, the extent of its effectiveness
must be questioned.[62] Nuclear power proceeds apace in
France. In West Germany, as in the USA, the halts in the
development of nuclear power must be set against the pressure
of economic forces operating in the same direction as protest.
Site approval, which is the main object of conflict, would be
pursued on many fronts simultaneously if there were scope for
rapid growth in nuclear power. In this way, the physical and
financial resources of the protest movement would be severely
stretched. Whilst the anti-nuclear movement has been crucial
in exposing the weakness of the case for nuclear power, it has
thereby demonstrated that its case cannot be won primarily in
the realm of ideas. Nor are workers within the industry a likely

organising force. Whilst they have been involved in conflicts, over both wages and working conditions, these issues have been confined to their own narrow economic interests. In defence of jobs, it has led to support for nuclear power.

To conclude, labour movement participation in decisions over nuclear power will have to come from those who are currently indirectly involved and through policy that is indirectly related. Most obviously, the issue of nuclear power bears fundamentally upon both industrial and energy policy. These areas, in which long-term and coherent planning by the British state has been so weak, must be engaged through strengthening the economic demands of those involved and carrying them through to the political arena. Such abstract formulations do have implications for immediate policy in the UK. There is no immediate need for new nuclear or other power stations. Resources should be devoted to investment in coal, alternative energy sources and conservation. The influence of the MNCs and the structure of supply of power plant necessitates that the facilities in the UK be nationalised together with the construction industry. The role of the AEA and its influence must be diminished and the research effort openly and independently examined. Finally, the operation of the CEGB must be coordinated with other sectors through a plan for energy and industry.

Notes

[1] The term nuclear (or atomic) power has experienced an interesting history. Originally it described the energy released through radiation. With the development of bombs in the Second World War, it became identified with weaponry. Subsequently, with the growing role of nuclear power stations, it is increasingly associated with electricity generation, so that nuclear power refers less to bombs except in the context of the military capacity of a nation, i.e. a political rather than a technical property. The changing meaning is an ideological support for nuclear electricity generation by disconnecting it linguistically from weaponry. Throughout we use nuclear power in its widest sense and the context should make its narrower meaning clear.

[2] The term is particularly associated with J.K. Galbraith. For an account of the elements of the nuclear-industrial complex under the terminology 'nuclear capital' see M. Spence, 'Nuclear Capital', *Capital and Class*, No.16.

[3] For a firsthand account of the Manhattan Project, see L.R. Groves, *Now It Can Be Told: The Story of the Manhattan Project*, London 1963.

[4] For analyses with an emphasis on this, see S. Durie and R. Edwards, *Fuelling the Nuclear Arms Race: The Links Between Nuclear Power and Nuclear Weapons*, London 1982 and R. Papadopoulos, 'Nuclear Power: The Enduring Connection', *Energy Policy*, December 1981.

[5] For a simple account of the nuclear physics involved, see W.C. Paterson, *Nuclear Power*, Harmondsworth 1980.

[6] See M. Gowing, *Independence and Deferrence: Britain and Atomic Energy 1945-1952*, London 1974, who reveals that, until at least 1951, the commercial potential of nuclear power was obstructed if it hindered the maximum and most rapid extraction of plutonium.

[7] For example, it was incorrectly believed that bombs could only be manufactured from plutonium that had been reprocessed after being removed from a reactor, so that the reprocessing facility was a prerequisite of weaponry. Reprocessing involves high technology available only to a few countries.

[8] This is an argument that seeks by analogy to reduce violent crime by preventing the sale only of the most effective personal weapons. Unwittingly, it is a replica of the rationale for the arms trade: Sell all but the most dangerous (atomic) weapons with the justification of otherwise alternative sources of supply. See W. Marshall 'Proliferation and the Recycling of Plutonium' *Atom*, September 1978.

[9] See J. Surrey and W. Walker *The European Power Plant Industry: Structural Responses to International Market Pressures*, Brighton 1981, and United Nations Commission on Transnational Corporations, *Transnational Corporations in the Power Equipment Industry*, New York 1982.

[10] MNCs such as Rio Tinto Zinc are, however, significant in uranium mining.

[11] For an official account of the problems with large site construction, see, for example, the extracts from and references to reports on the question in the Select Committee on Energy, *The Government's Statement on the New Nuclear Power Programme*, London 1981, Vol IV Appendix 73.

[12] Advanced Gas-cooled Reactors are the British designed nuclear power technology.

[13] W.C. Potter, *Nuclear Power and Non-Proliferation*, Cambridge Mass. 1982.

[14] I.C. Bupp, 'The Actual Growth and Probable Future of the Worldwide Nuclear Industry', *International Organisation*, Winter 1981.

[15] The American General Electric is not to be confused with the British GEC.

[16] See Bupp, op. cit. LWRs use ordinary water as a catalyst (known as a moderator) for the nuclear chain reaction. There are two different types, the pressurised water reactor (PWR) originally marketed by Westinghouse, and the boiling water reactor (BWR) associated with General Electric. LWRs use enriched uranium which is produced from natural uranium, itself a product from purification of uranium ore.

[17] Canada uses heavy water as a moderator which is more efficient than ordinary water in sustaining a chain reaction and ultimately converts more uranium into energy (and plutonium). Heavy water is expensive to manufacture but, with it, enriched uranium is not necessary for the reactor.

[18] See CEGB, *Sizewell 'B' Power Station Public Inquiry: CEGB Statement of Case*, Vols. 1 & 2 and Appendices, London 1982.

[19] See R.W. Morrison, *Canada's Nuclear Export Policy*, Ottawa 1978, for an

account of the Canadian industry.

[20] See Gowing op. cit.

[21] For a history of UK nuclear power developments, see R. Williams, *The Nuclear Power Decisions*, London 1980, D. Burn, *The Political Economy of Nuclear Energy*, London 1978, and *Nuclear Power and the Energy Crisis*, London 1980.

[22] For an account of the French industry, see S.R. Weart, *Scientists in Power*, Cambridge, Mass. 1979, N.J.O. Lucas, *Energy in France*, London 1979 and C. Sweet, 'A Study of Nuclear Power in France', *Energy Paper No.2*, 1981.

[23] Reluctant approval for a PWR was given by Tony Benn as Secretary of State for Energy in 1978, in the form of an intention if not a definite order. The commitment to the AGR remained.

[24] See in particular Burn's work for an expression of this view.

[25] The Inquiry is to ascertain whether local planning permission should be granted to build the station.

[26] Select Committee on Energy, op. cit., p.45.

[27] See also Volume IV, p.1075 of the Select Committee Report. In the early 1970s, GEC was in collaboration with Framatome, the French nuclear power company. This avenue was closed off when the UK failed to adopt the PWR, see Volume II, p.464.

[28] B. Sedgemore, *The Secret Constitution*, London 1980, p.107.

[29] The *Financial Times* commented that it was to the disadvantage of NEI in domestic *and* overseas contracts.

[30] K. Mirow and H. Maurer, *Webs of Power: International Cartels and the World Economy*, Boston 1982.

[31] RR&A currently has an equity shared between Rolls Royce (43 per cent), Babcock (19 per cent), Foster Wheeler (19 per cent) and Vickers (19 per cent). It depends heavily upon subcontracting with over one hundred firms benefiting from its orders for parts.

[32] For the account that follows, see Select Committee on Energy, op. cit., Vol. II pp.223-77.

[33] Submarine reactors are approximately one-fortieth of the size of civil reactors.

[34] See this from the British and French perspectives in M. Gowing, *Britain and Atomic Energy, 1939-1945*, London 1964 and Weart, op. cit.

[35] Books by both Brenner and Potter both have this title; see M.J. Brenner, *Nuclear Power and Non Proliferation: The Remaking of US Policy*, Cambridge 1981, and Potter, op. cit.

[36] See A Wohlsetter et al, *Swords From Ploughshares*, Chicago 1979.

[37] See P.L. Joskow, 'The International Nuclear Industry Today', *Foreign Affairs*, Vol. 54, 1976.

[38] Brenner, op. cit., describes these events in great detail but explains them in terms of *internal* domestic conflicts over the degree of state involvement in the control of the nuclear industry.

[39] See E. Häckel, 'The Domestic and International Context of West Germany's 'Nuclear Energy Policy' in E. Häckel et al, op. cit.

[40] See P.P. Lellouche, 'French Nuclear Policy' in E. Häckel et al, op.cit.

[41] For international political reaction to these events, see C.K. Ebinger, *The International Politics of Nuclear Power*, London 1978. Those without nuclear technology saw the nuclear powers extending their monopoly in the sphere

of weapons to the sphere of civil reactors. For the latter it is unclear what is the origin from which 'commercial advantage' or 'disadvantage' could be measured.

[42] The collaboration between the US and UK has been particularly close over weaponry. See Durie and Edwards, op. cit., and for the most recent statement of policy see the Written Answer of the Secretary of State for Energy on 9 March 1983.

[43] This account relies heavily upon Williams, op. cit.

[44] See Burn, op. cit., who prides himself on having anticipated the failure of the AGR and deplores the decision to adopt it. See also P.D. Henderson 'Two British Errors: Their Probable Size and Some Possible Lessons', *Oxford Economics Papers*, July 1977, which compares the AGR programme to the Concorde fiasco.

[45] See in particular J.W. Jeffery's articles 'The Real Costs of Nuclear Power in the UK' and 'The Real Costs of Nuclear Electricity in the UK', *Energy Policy*, December 1980 and June 1982.

[46] For a criticism of cost-benefit analysis, see M. Ball, 'Cost Benefit Analysis: A Critique', F. Green and P. Nore (eds.), *Issues in Political Economy: A Critical Approach*, London 1979.

[47] The Select Committee complains of lack of cooperation from the CEGB in examining its case. A crucial downward revision of electricity demand was not communicated to it. The Select Committee was also denied access to the Central Policy Review Staff Report which recommended the order of two further AGRs. See also Monopolies and Mergers Commission, *CEGB: Report on the Operation by the Board of its System for the Generation and Supply of Electricity in Bulk*, London 1981.

[48] For this reason, there could only be limited application of such methods in socialist planning where a multitude of economic and other criteria enter decision-making. For a discussion of this, see B. Fine, 'Marx on Economic Relations Under Socialism' in B. Matthews (ed.), *Marx: A Hundred Years On*, London 1983.

[49] R. Papadopoulos, 'Growth and Overcapacity in the UK Electricity Industry', *Energy Policy*, June 1981.

[50] See Electricity Consumers' Council Statement of Case to the Sizewell 'B' Public Inquiry' for an assessment and G. MacKerron 'Nuclear Power and the Interests of Consumers', *Electricity Consumers' Council Research Report No. 6*, June 1982 for a summary.

[51] C. Komanoff, *Power Plant Escalation*, New York 1981.

[52] Similar considerations apply to alternative sources of energy. As the Select Committee observed 'We were dismayed to find that, seven years after the first major oil price increases, the Department of Energy has no clear idea of whether investing around £1300 million in a single nuclear plant is as cost-effective as spending a similar sum to promote energy conservation'. The same comment appears to apply to the CEGB.

[53] We have already considered how safety is a factor tending to increase cost and time of construction. During operation, the wish for maximum loading of a station has safety implications. One can be pursued only at the expense of the other.

[54] Sedgemore op. cit., p. 135.

[55] C. Sweet, *The Price of Nuclear Power*, London 1983.

[56] Burn 1978, op. cit.

[57] For a report on recent development in the West German industry, see J. Conrad, 'Future Nuclear Energy Policy – the West German *Enquete* Commission', *Energy Policy*, September 1982.

[58] For developments in France, see Sweet, op. cit., and G. de Carmoy, 'The New French Energy Policy', *Energy Policy*, September 1982.

[59] See Williams, op. cit.

[60] See Sedgemore, op. cit.

[61] For the limitations of the Windscale Inquiry, see D. Pearce et al, *Decision making for Energy Futures*, London 1979. Windscale has obtained such a bad public image, that it has been felt necessary to change its name to Sellafield.

[62] For an account of these anti-nuclear movements, see D. Elkin and M. Pollak, *The Atom Besieged*, Cambridge Mass., 1981.

Chapter 8

Arms, the State and the Economy

The weight of military spending in the British economy is exceptional by the standards of other capitalist economies. During the 1960s and 70s the British state's spending on the military accounted for a greater proportion of the country's output (GDP) than any other NATO state apart from the United States. This phenomenon provides a clear example of the peculiar relation between the state and industry in Britain in the years since the Second World War; although political ambitions rather than economic management account for the high level of state spending on arms this spending illuminates the weakness of post-war Keynesianism and the failure of the British state with regard to industry as a whole. It has had effects on the economy's productive capacity which have hindered the development of industry while simultaneously enabling a small number of multinational corporations to profit fully from close relations with the state apparatuses.

Although the UK's military spending has been nearly the highest in NATO throughout the post war period it has itself fluctuated over these years. The military budget absorbed a declining proportion of national output from the early 1950s to 1979. As imperialist pressures changed their character the military's responsibility for the colonial empire declined, conscription was replaced with smaller professional forces, and, as the economy expanded, the economic burden of military spending fell. However, after 1979 the Conservative governments have systematically increased its size and significance.

Between 1979 and 1983, the British state's spending on the military has climbed. Although the country's total output has fallen because of the international crisis of the capitalist economies (between 1979 and 1981), military spending had, by

1983, risen to absorb 5.3 per cent of the GDP (as compared with 4.4 per cent in 1979).[1] While the government's monetarism has involved severe cuts in housing, education and social budgets, and while the government has planned to hold down its deficit and total spending it has stuck fast to (and even exceeded) a supposed NATO commitment to increase military spending by 3 per cent per year in real terms.

Between fiscal year 1978/79 and 1983/84, the state's military spending rose by 23.3 per cent in real terms, while its expenditure on housing fell by 54.8 per cent and its expenditure on education by 6.4 per cent.[2]

To assess the economic impact of the (over) arming of the British state it is important to be clear what we are talking about. The high level of political activity over nuclear arms makes it easy to imagine that the economics of the military turn only on the cost of the nuclear arms race; for example, such questions as whether 'the country can afford' to spend £10 billion on buying Trident. State spending on nuclear weapons is, indeed an important economic element of the rise of the military, but its role has to be distinguished from that of spending on non-nuclear arms and personnel. And the economic impact of both types of *spending* has to be distinguished from the role of the arms firms' *production*. In this chapter we are concerned with the economic role and significance of all these aspects of armaments spending and production. We focus attention, first, on one activity that relates to all of them, military research and development (R and D).

Impact of State and Military on R and D

Throughout the post-war decades, industry within Britain has used technology which consistently lags behind that of the USA, Japan, West Germany and other advanced capitalist countries. This in turn relates to the particularly distorted character of R and D in Britain which results from the state's policy toward the role of science and technology in the arms industry.

The scientists, engineers and equipment which capitalism requires to develop the productive forces have in Britain been engaged disproportionately on military work. Half a decade after the British rearmament for the Korean war, 40 per cent of all British scientists and engineers engaged on R and D were working on military projects, and that preponderance has remained the pattern since then. In 1978, the Ministry of Defence itself accounted for one-quarter of all the R and D in Britain, and since the corporations selling military equipment have their own R and D programmes, the proportion of the economy's total research absorbed by the military is much higher. By contrast, two of the strongest capitalist economies, West Germany and Japan, devote a much smaller percentage of their total R and D to military purposes.

The post-war history of R and D in Britain has differed from that of most other advanced capitalist countries. In the 1950s and early 1960s Britain appeared to devote much greater resources to Research and Development in total than either West Germany or Japan, but by the 1970s its expenditure on R and D was considerably lower than those countries and (in relative terms) than Sweden, Switzerland and others. Thus, in terms of the *level* of R and D resourcing, Britain's early lead was overtaken as other countries expanded theirs.[3] But the greatest difference between British R and D and other countries' lies in its character.

Firstly, the funding of R and D has been provided by the state to an unusual extent. At the beginning of the 1960s the Japanese state's spending on R and D was one fifth of Britain's, in West Germany it was two fifths and in France three fifths. Over the subsequent decades the amount of state funding in those countries rose to close the gap, but since firms' own funding also expanded faster than in the UK, the high proportion of R and D financed by the state remained exceptional.

Secondly, the distribution of R and D expenditure has been exceptional in Britain; a high proportion, unparalleled in any OECD country apart from the USA, is devoted to military expenditure and, of the rest, most is concentrated on large projects in industries with strong military links such as aircraft and electronics.

Chris Freeman of the Sussex University Science Policy Research Unit summarised both these characteristics as follows:

In examining the pattern of British R and D expenditure and comparing them with other industrial countries, two peculiarities stand out: first the extraordinarily high concentration of British effort in the aircraft industry in comparison with Germany and Japan; second, the very high proportion of total British R and D which is government financed and directed to a few areas of high technology – especially military electronics. The counterpart of these peculiarities is the relatively low (and declining) proportion of British expenditure directed to R and D in machinery.[4]

Freeman demonstrates that these peculiarities were evident as early as the 1950s; in his 1975 Royal Society lecture, Sir Ieuen Maddock pointed to the continuing existence of those peculiarities at the beginning of the 1970s.[5] A comparison between the UK and Japan is well illuminated by two of his diagrams below; the first for the UK and the second for Japan. Each consists of a 'pie chart' showing the importance of each industrial sector's net output in the national total; the antennae attached to each slice show the total amount of R and D in that sector and the proportion financed by the state (the shaded part). The diagrams show at a glance that in the UK a disproportionate amount of R and D has been devoted to two sectors which make a small contribution to national output, electronics and aircraft, and this was heavily financed by the state, whereas in Japan the (largely privately-funded) R and D effort has given much more weight to 'other manufacturing', – motor vehicles, chemicals and other sectors without military orientation. Even the high Japanese spending on electronics R and D is principally privately-funded reflecting its orientation toward 'civil' rather than 'military' products.

One particularly illuminating example of the mismatch Maddock identified between state spending on a sector's R and D and that sector's importance in national output was nuclear energy. In general:

a very large proportion of the total government R and D expenditure is *not* aimed at industrial improvement in any specific way. Where the objective has clearly been an industrial one a significant portion has been aimed at a very small part of the total industrial pattern of the UK and an even smaller part of the total economic pattern. For example … nuclear power was responsible for under 3 per cent of total energy consumption[6]

while almost all the Department of Trade and Industry's

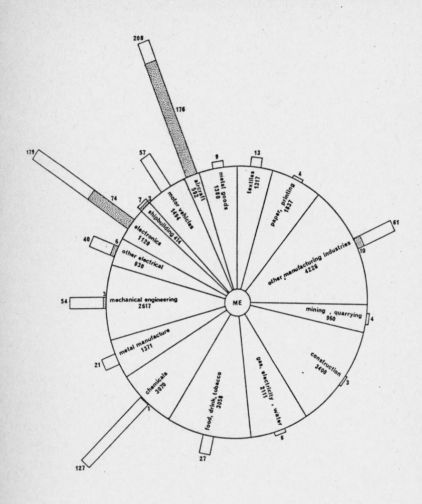

UK: net output and R and D (1972, provisional.) Net output total £28 897 million; R and D total of £820 million (shaded areas indicate government contribution; nuclear £50 million. Sources: net output-business monitoring 1000 census of production provisional results 1972; R and D – Trade and Industry, 5 September 1974; nuclear C.S.O R and D expenditure.

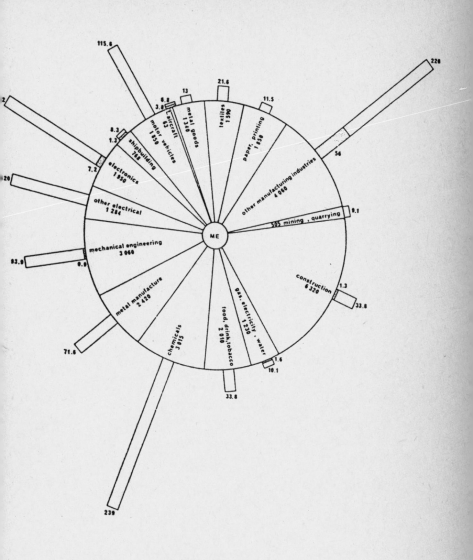

Japan: net output (total £33 315 million) and R and D 1971 (total £1178.3 million (shaded areas indicate government contribution), £1 = 810 yen).

spending on energy R and D in 1973-74 was devoted to nuclear energy. This allocation of R and D appears to be irrational (as Maddock notes, 'In terms of net effect to the economy a comparable benefit could have been obtained by a 3 per cent reduction on energy utilisation by greater efficiency') but our explanation of its logic is twofold; first the development of nuclear power was an essential base for Britain's nuclear military strategy and, second, it was a rational allocation from the point of view of the British multinational corporations involved in nuclear and electrical engineering. We shall argue, below, that the links between the military and multinational corporations in a wider context go a long way toward explaining the economic role of military spending.

Effect of R and D Militarisation

The dominance of R and D by state funded activities (including those carried out in government establishments themselves) has led to its concentration in military and military-related fields and in large high-technology projects at the expense of a wide range of technological development applicable to other industries. That, in itself, does not immediately imply that non-military industries have suffered from technological backwardness, for they may use innovations based on new technologies developed abroad (transfer of technology) and they may benefit from a spin-off from military research to civil industry. In fact, however, industry in Britain has not overcome the effect of the distortions in R and D by either of these routes to technological advance.

A major indication of the technological backwardness of industrial production in Britain is the degree to which industrial exports are based upon high technology, and the extent to which high exports depend on a country's own R and D.

Indications that British manufacturing exports have been marked by products which incorporate relatively low levels of technology have come from sectoral case studies by Pavitt, and by case studies of engineering exports by Saunders and NEDO.[7] The latter showed that German machinery exports had a price/weight ratio twice as high as Britain's in almost every product group indicating that the products themselves were technologically sophisticated. A failure of British exporting industries in general to achieve technical advance by circumventing the weakness in its own R and D conforms with the general pattern. A statistical study of 22 OECD countries by Soete indicates that for most capital goods and chemicals the extent of a country's R and D (measured by the US patents its firms take out) is correlated with its export strength.[8] In Britain, the relationship between R and D (and other measures of technological advance) and trade performance has been examined by Katrak.[9] That study shows that there has been a significant relationship between Britain's foreign trade and its technology inputs. Interestingly, it emphasises that the technology content of Britain's exports became particularly inferior compared with other countries during the 1970s. We conclude that this reflects the skewed pattern of R and D that existed in the 1950s and 60s; the concentration on military and related R and D in that period while countries such as Japan were investing in the long-term technological development of motor vehicles and other manufacturing industries bore fruit in the 1970s with phenomena such as the expansion of Japanese motor car and motor cycle exports.

These indications of a low level of technological development in industry in Britain could not have been a foregone conclusion. Apart from the possibilities for an international transfer of technology, military R and D itself could have had spin-off effects. Indeed, the military interests themselves claim that the funding of their R and D is in the 'national interest' because of those effects. In fact, though, an investigation for NEDO by Sir Ieuen Maddock (formerly Chief Scientist at the Department of Industry) found that non-military production and products in the electronics industries have not gained from that sector's large military research and development.[10] Surveying four types of electronics companies he found that in each, for different reasons, there was little transfer of technology from military-oriented research to civil applications. One aspect of this, either symptom or cause, was the difference in approach of the personnel involved in each type of field:

There can be little doubt that mobility of personnel is one of the most powerful methods of achieving technology transfer but there was very little evidence in the large companies that there was a *deliberate* policy of moving people between the defence and civil fields. Indeed, in most cases there was hostility to the idea because the people in the two fields were regarded as being 'so different', even to the extent of one individual stating emphatically that he would never use an engineer from the civil field on his defence work.

What was striking was the distance between the attitudes of the civil and defence-oriented companies even when they existed within the same large group. There already exists a large culture gap and it is getting even wider.[11]

At a more general level the technological backwardness of British 'civil' industry is unlikely to benefit directly from military technology even if those barriers were to disappear. For the weakness of British industry, its peculiarity of combining both low profits and low wages, relates to its inability to modernise and innovate in the methods of production, but the R and D devoted to military products absorbs scientists and engineers in developing new high technology products rather than production processes (machines, production control instruments etc.).

Economic Significance of Arms

The high degree of state funding of military R and D relates to both the main aspects of the role of arms in the economy, military *spending* and arms *production*. Spending on the military and on arms refers to the state's purchases whether the money is spent on personnel, the output of British arms factories (such as Chieftain tanks) or the output of other countries (such as Trident and Cruise); arms production, by contrast, relates to the output of the large arms industry in Britain irrespective of whether its products are sold to the British state or contribute to the large and growing export trade in arms (the British industry is the world's fourth largest arms exporter). The state's funding of military R and D relates to both aspects, for it is intended to ensure the development and production of the types of arms Britain's armed forces wish to buy while at the same time stimulating technological advances that will attract wider business for the arms firms and support the expansion and profitability of production in those industries. (In fact, however, these two aspects have partially conflicted, as military leaders within the British state have imposed specific and expensive requirements on arms which discourage the development of production for a wider market).

To assess the significance arms have played for British industry we have to take account of both military *spending* and arms *production*. However, several Marxist studies have reached false conclusions by studying one element alone.

The most prominent Marxist approach argues that the state's military spending acts as a stimulus to the economy and to profits because, being a large and crucial contribution to total aggregate demand, it helps capital avoid a crisis produced by an underlying realisation problem.[12] There is, however, no basis to the assumption that economies such as Britain's would suffer from a chronic shortfall of demand in the absence of state spending and, even if there were, there is no reason to think that military spending rather than other types is the most functional remedy. A different approach to the role of military spending sees it, by contrast as irrational for capitalism. The econometric results obtained for 14 OECD countries led to the conclusion that high military spending is correlated with a low level of productive investment in the economy as a whole.[13] Both these approaches suffer from the fact that they are concerned with the effect of state spending alone rather than it together with the effect of arms production.

Another type of analysis is directly concerned only with arms production. It argues that since arms are neither consumption goods for workers nor inputs into other industries (as machines would be) they are 'luxuries' and therefore their production does not contribute to capitalism's inherent tendency for the rate of profit to fall.[14] Therefore, it is argued, arms production benefits Britain's capitalists by absorbing resources which would otherwise speed the decline in industrial profits throughout the economy. These purely theoretical propositions are claimed to derive from Marx's theorems, but that claim is mistaken and in fact there is no basis for the argument.

We consider that none of these approaches is satisfactory for understanding the significance arms have had for Britain's modern economic development. Apart from the fact that they do not comprehend both spending and production, they implicitly or explicitly pose too simple a question: have arms acted as an accelerator or brake for industry in Britain?[15] This question is part of a tradition which attempts to explain Britain's economic position by isolating one or another 'crucial element' to which growth or decline can be directly attributed. By contrast in this book we attempt to account for Britain's peculiarities by identifying and examining the relations between different classes, sections and the state rather than finding a 'crucial element'; and, unlike existing writings on arms and the economy, our approach involves considering the historical turning points and changes. Military spending and arms production are highly significant in this approach, for, since they are an area where the state has had the greatest potential for leading industry along a path of planned and rational production and accumulation, they illuminate most sharply its failure to carry out this role. The character of arms spending and manufacture, and the state's promulgation of R and D in relation to them, illustrate the problematic nature of the state's relation to industrial development in general and, more than being an illustration alone, they are intimately bound up with those problems.

The state's military spending within the UK is enormous. In 1982-83 the Ministry of Defence paid out £6.8 billion on its contracts with the arms industry, it benefited some 10,000 firms (although these were dominated by a few giants) and (in 1980-81) its purchases represented 29 per cent of the output of the electronics industry, 30 per cent of shipbuilding's output, and 39 per cent of the aerospace industry.[16] A proportion of the output of the arms industry is from state-owned establishments such as the Royal Ordnance Factories and Royal Dockyards (now candidates for privatisation). In addition to the 600,000 civil and military personnel employed by the Ministry of Defence itself, the government estimates that another 400,000 jobs in industry depend on its military spending,[17] so that in total some 5 per cent of the UK labour force is related to this expenditure. And, as we have seen, state-funded military and military-related R and D accounts for a high proportion of total industrial R and D. The state could have used this great weight of its military spending as a leading element in long-term strategic planning for industry as a whole. But it has not done so. Military spending and arms production exemplify the peculiarity of the British state's economic role; it has been interventionist but its interventions have been one-sided and unable to provide a rational, planned lead for industrial production and accumulation. This peculiarly ineffective role of the state conforms with two particular forces that have characterised the modern economy: the strength of multinational corporations and the weakness of the labour movement.

Arms and Multinationals

Although military spending benefits some 10,000 companies, it is heavily concentrated on a few giant suppliers of equipment and research. Some twenty two large enterprises (including some state-owned) each received payments from £25 million to more than £100 million for equipment in 1981-82. The list, which follows, is dominated by UK based multinational corporations:

These multinational corporations have had a direct and close relationship with the state itself which is well illustrated by British Aerospace, GEC and Racal.

The largest supplier of aerospace equipment is British Aerospace, a company formed in 1977 by the state taking over, merging and rationalising several private corporations. Under state ownership, British Aerospace was made efficient and profitable enough to be sold back to private capital. The Thatcher government announced its return to private ownership (with minority state share-holding) in 1981. Its profits on sales of aircraft and, to an even greater extent, missiles and space equipment, depend almost entirely on the Ministry of Defence. It receives bigger orders than any other supplier to the Ministry and accounts directly for about one-eighth of all state spending on arms.[18]

The largest supplier of electronic equipment is the GEC, which, too, is a multinational corporation formed by the state in 1968 by encouraging the merger and rationalisation of smaller companies. It has always been privately-owned rather than state-owned. Its main armaments division (GEC-Marconi) monopolises the UK supply of torpedoes and, under state contracts and with state funding, develops and

UK-based Ministry of Defence contractors paid over £25 million for equipment, 1981-82

	Turnover £ million	Defence %	Pre-tax profits £ million
Over £100 million			
British Aerospace (Aircraft)	1,310	66	−9.8
British Aerospace (Dynamics)	743	72	−5.6
British Shipbuilders	1,093	39	−110.4
Ferranti	372	60	30.9
GEC	4,626	17*	670.4
Rolls Royce	1,493	52	−90.9
Royal Ordnance Factories	284	99	68.8
Westland	284	60*	24.6
£50-100 million			
Hunting Associated Industries	169	45	4.1
Philips Electronics	850	7	118.4
Racal Electronics	762	30	114.3
Sperry	215	30	0.3
Thorn EMI	2,716	8	122.0
Vauxhall Motors	1,060	8*	29.5
£25-50 million			
BL	3,072	3*	−223.0
Cable and Wireless	403	15*	146.2
Dowty Group	420	40	40.2
Lucas Industries	1,220	10	35.3
Marshall of Cambridge	95	60*	10.1
Short Brothers	111	39	12.9
Smiths Industries	386	20	26.5
United Scientific Holdings	70*	107	12.5

*estimates

Source: Technology, 7 November 1983, p.14.

supplies radar, radio and electronic systems. GEC is a force throughout the electrical and electronics industries, producing everything from household equipment to microprocessors, but its arms sales are estimated to be one-fifth of its total sales.[19] The second largest manufacturer of electronics, Racal, illustrates the close links between these multinationals and the state – its founder joined the Ministry of Defence as head of Defence Sales.

The close links between the state and the corporations are illustrated even more strongly by interchanges of personnel other than that from Racal. In 1983 Michael Heseltine, as Defence Secretary, announced a review of the methods by which the Ministry of Defence's Procurement Executive (employing 43,000 people) carried out its purchasing policy. The review was to be carried out by a group chaired by the head of one of the leading beneficiaries of military spending, Mr. Peter Levene who was Chairman of United Scientific Holdings, a company where, according to estimates, 70 per cent of its sales were to the Ministry. Subsequently, Mr Levene became an employee of the Ministry of Defence with responsibility for procurement; his salary, at around £100,000, was extraordinary and the Civil Service Commissioner, criticised the remarkable circumstances applying to his appointment. But in fact the close ties between the Ministry and the arms manufacturers are common. The procurement review group was also to include four high level members from the Defence Industries Council, an association of arms-producing firms.[20]

Despite, or perhaps because of this close relationship between the state and the arms industry multinationals, the state has not generally taken any direct role in modernising the firms' production methods. Its concern, instead, has been to specify the product (the ships, tanks, etc.) to meet the particular needs of Britain's military forces, to finance R and D to that end, and to price contracts in such a way as to guarantee the firms' profits as far as possible. In the arms industry, a sector with the closest links to the state, it has had a policy of leaving production and productivity alone and accepting whatever result management produces, virtually guaranteeing profits however inefficient the firms. In the 1970s and early 1980s a high proportion (three quarters in 1980-81) of Ministry of Defence contracts for military equipment or private research, designated 'non-competitive' contracts, are priced on the basis of actual or estimated future costs plus a margin which guarantees the firm a certain rate of profit whatever its efficiency. The formula is intended to ensure that such firms obtain a profit rate equal to the 'normal recent' average for private industry as a whole. This reduces firms' incentive to improve production methods for their rate of profit is guaranteed, but it has proved to be a pricing system that is so loose that it easily generates profits even higher than the industrial average. Intended to produce a real rate of profit of 3.7 per cent in 1980 contractors are estimated to have actually obtained up to 13 per cent in real terms in that year; and in 1982 the Ministry of Defence stated that on £250 million worth of contracts five major firms had obtained profits above the target rate in 75 per cent of their contracts.[21]

Nevertheless, the pricing system for contracts has not been able to guarantee high profitability at all times. It has, on the other hand, relieved managements from competitive pressures to modernise production methods and, when this underlying weakness has led to losses despite the pricing system, the state has had to step in, nationalise and rationalise (as with British Aerospace which was subsequently privatised).

This pattern reflects the role of the state with regard to industry as a whole. Its interventions, under the rules of post-war Keynesianism, were conceived as aiding industry by maintaining demand and improving profits through policies on prices and distribution (in industry as a whole these hinged on incomes policies and on reductions in profits taxes to offset falls in pre-tax profits). It was against the interests of the multinationals (and the City) for the state to intervene directly in production and such interventions were restricted to cases where private capital had to be rescued.

The form taken by state intervention after the war, and the restrictions placed on it in the interests of large private corporations, has been a continuation of the framework established during the late 1930s and in the Second World War itself. The rise of the military aircraft industry in the 1930s typified this. It was dominated by a few giant firms (such as Hawkers and A.V. Roe) organised in a powerful cartel, the Society of British Aircraft Constructors. The increasing orders for the RAF were channelled through this cartel and the terms of the state's purchases conformed to the aims of these large firms. The cost-plus method of contract pricing guaranteed high profits for the members of the cartel while the smaller firms outside it made consistent losses for many years. But the state did not actively intervene in modernising and rationalising production methods themselves; it did not interfere with the prerogatives of private enterprise's own management.[22] Thus, according to one historian of the engineering industry, 'It was not until the second half of the war that anything approaching mass production was applied to aero-engine production'.[23] Even during the period of rearmament and war itself when, under the 'shadow factory' scheme, the state built and equipped factories for private aircraft firms, it took no part in supervising and directing production methods themselves, although it did install Resident Technical Officers with responsibility for the application of R and D to products rather than production methods. The official historian of war production wrote that the Air Ministry

> In general … did little to supervise or to direct the methods of production in the factories of its contractors. Had it tried to do so it would probably have been rebuffed by its contractors.[24]

Arms and the Labour Movement

The most prominent political issue for the labour movement on the question of arms production and military spending is its attitude toward their reduction and 'conversion' of jobs toward other lines of production.[25] But another, related, problem is especially pertinent to understanding the state's role; is its perculiarity due to the labour movement's historical weakness? The immediate post-war years were critical for the construction of the state's role in the modern British economy and the labour movement's weakness in those years (despite or because of its electoral strength and the domination of political debate by socialist ideas) was critical in determining the future limits to the state's interventionism. We have seen those limits in the modern arms sector and the weakness of the labour movement in those years too relates to the state's military spending and arms production. The question for then as for the subsequent years was whether the state could apply to industry more generally the R and D stimulus that it applied in the arms sector.

In the 1930s a strong body of socialist scientists around Bernal, Blackett, Levy, Haldane, Needham and Hogben organised to argue for the rational state planning of science and its application. They were responding to a situation which Bernal described as follows:

> There is a tradition in British industry which is definitely inimical to science ... the Government, despite its zeal for the protection of the products and profits of British industry, would seem to have given no consideration to the safeguarding of its scientific initiative ...[26]

During the war itself the members of this 'visible college' became scientific leaders within the ministries themselves and had their ideas strengthened by the successful experience of planning in the application of science to individual military research projects.

This group held almost a hegemonic position in military science during the war, but in the face of political obstacles it could not achieve its aim of a centralised state plan for science. Nevertheless, the Labour victory of 1945 appeared to offer greater possibilities for the development of a state plan and organisation to stimulate R and D in industry and build outward from the wartime role that state sponsorship of science had played in the arms industries. Their book, *Science and the Nation*,[27] was a major political intervention along these lines, and they actively sought trade union support. The 1945 TUC Annual Congress strongly endorsed these ideas, but the trade union movement never delivered the effective support to back that endorsement. Even formal Congress support was not maintained. The scientists' resolution at the 1947 Congress was referred back and then rejected and so was its 1948 resolution on changing the balance between military and civil research.

The failure of the labour movement to support the scientific planners' proposals in the 1940s was instrumental in ensuring that the post-war role of the state in industry as a whole, being constructed then, would be restricted and confined principally to distributional and demand management policies. In that context it hinged particularly on the role of the state regarding military and civil R and D, but that is an example which illustrates well the general weakness the labour movement showed in the post-war years and its general failure to shape the state in the direction of planning industrial development.[28]

Conclusion

The high military expenditure of the state and the relatively high significance of arms production have been outstanding features of both the British economy and the state's role in it since the Second World War. Its impact is highlighted by its dominance of R and D while civil industry is relatively backward technologically. The special character of the state's role in regard to this parallels the peculiarities of its general position in the economy, and it has to be seen in the context of both the power of large multinational corporations and the particular weaknesses of the labour movement.

Notes

[1] M. Chalmers, *The Cost of Britain's Defence, Peace Studies Papers*, No. 10 School of Peace Studies, Bradford University. (When GDP is calculated at factor cost, the percentage of military spending is even higher.)

[2] The Government's Expenditure Plans 1983/4 to 1985/6, London 1983, Cmnd. 8789-1, Table 1-14.

[3] C. Freeman, 'Technical Innovation and British Trade Performance' in F. Blackaby (ed.), *De-industrialisation*, London 1978.

[4] Freeman, op.cit., p.66.

[5] I. Maddock, 'Science, Technology and Industry' Proceedings of the Royal Society, London, Vol. 345, A pp.295-326 (30 September 1975).

[6] Ibid., p.321.

[7] Quoted in Freeman, op.cit., p.70.

[8] Quoted in ibid., pp.63-5.

[9] H. Katrak, *Labour skills, R and D and capital requirements in the international trade and investment of the United Kingdom 1968-78, National Institute of Economic and Social Research Review*, No.101, August 1982, pp.38-47.

[10] Maddock, *Civil Exploitation of Defence Technology*, London 1983.

[11] Ibid., p.8.

[12] M. Kidron, *Western Capitalism Since the War*, Harmondsworth 1970; P. Baran and P. Sweezy, *Monopoly Capital*, Harmondsworth 1968.

[13] R.P. Smith, 'Military Expenditure and Capitalism', *Cambridge Journal of Economics*, March 1977; R.P. Smith, 'Military Expenditure and Investment in OECD Countries', *Journal of Comparative Economics*, March 1980.

[14] Kidron, op.cit.

[15] This simple question is reviewed in L. Harris. 'The Arms Race: A Burden on the Economy', *World Marxist Review*, Vol. 27, No. 9, September 1984, pp.89-95.

[16] Chalmers, op.cit., p.30.

[17] *Statement on the Defence Estimates 1982*, London Cmnd. 8529-1.

[18] The UK Arms Industry, Anti-Report No. 31, Counter Information Services, London 1982, p.18.

[19] Ibid., p.9.

[20] Financial Times, 21 March 1984, p.1.

[21] *Financial Times*, 24 October 1983, p.5.

[22] R. Croucher, *Engineers at War 1939-45*, London 1982.

[23] Ibid., p.8.

[24] M.M. Postan, *British War Production*, London 1952, p.438 quoted in F. Steward and D. Wield, *Science Planning and the State*, Unit 16, D209, Open University Press, p.31.

[25] See Transport and General Workers' Union, *A Better Future*, London 1983, and Harris, op.cit.

[26] J.D. Bernal, *The Social Function of Science*, London 1939, pp.56-7 quoted in Steward and Wield, op.cit., p.16.

[27] Association of Scientific Workers, *Science and the Nation*, Harmondsworth 1947.

[28] This section's discussion of the history of the scientists' pressure for state leadership in the industrial application of science owes much to Steward and Wield, op.cit., for factual material.

III Specific Sectors

Chapter 9

The Car Industry

The car industry in Britain has been *the* barometer of the manufacturing sector's health. The great expansion in the output of its factories in the West and South Midlands, Dagenham and elsewhere during the 1950s and 1960s were seen as the visible proof of the long post-war boom; those factories' shrinking output and employment in the early 1980s was the mark of the economic crisis. Unemployment and distress made the West Midlands the surprising 1980s equivalent of Jarrow.

The key position of the car industry is not only as a symbol, for the industry has been both a major employer and a major consumer of other industries' products, so that a boom or crisis in cars is not only a product or example of fluctuations in the economy as a whole but also a force in generating them. The linkages which have given the motor industry this central importance arise from the purchase of many components, raw materials and semi-finished parts; a major supplier is the steel industry and an estimated 17 per cent of the British Steel Corporation's output is directed to the motor industry.[1] Although the motor industry's labour force almost halved between 1970 and 1983, it was still 289,000 in 1983 and it is estimated that over one million jobs are directly or indirectly dependent on vehicle manufacture.[2]

The car industry's significance, therefore, makes it in some ways a focus of many of the characteristics of British manufacturing industry; its peculiarities are in microcosm the peculiarities that have marked the British economy. While the recent crisis in British capitalism is special, particularly intractable and not simply a reflection of the international capitalist crisis, so the crisis of the British car industry is the product of the special forces at work in Britain and the way they interact with the changes and difficulties of the world car industry. In this chapter we begin by examining the international changes under way in the capitalist world's car industry. We then discuss the special forces acting on the British industry and generating a crisis as it adjusts in conformity with these international changes. Because of the links between the industry and others, we consider both the car industry itself and its most direct suppliers, the components industry.

The World Context: International Structure

The near halving of jobs in the UK motor industry between 1979 and 1983 was matched by a sharp decline in output. In the late 1960s and early 1970s between 1.5 million and 2 million cars a year were produced in the UK with a peak of 1,921,000 being produced in 1972. In 1982 considerably less than half this number were produced; the output of cars was 872,000 (with some recovery to 1,006,000 in 1983). A similar, but less significant, decline also occurred in commercial vehicle production. It is widely recognised that these changes are only comprehensible in terms of the British industry's international position; car exports shrank by two-thirds (from 723,000 to 237,000) from 1970 to 1983, as did exports of commercial vehicles,while the percentage of the British car market supplied by imports doubled (from 27.4 to 57.1 per cent) between 1973 and 1983.[3] The changing international position was reflected in the fact that in 1977 the UK became a net importer of cars for the first time since the Second World War. These phenomena have a highly visible presence in unemployment and factory closures in the West Midlands coexisting with the motorway traffic jams dominated by Toyotas, Datsuns, BMWs, Renaults and, most significantly, 'British' cars manufactured abroad. Their causes, which are less visible, are both international and domestic. One approach analyses them wholly in terms of world-wide changes so that the position of the industry in one country is simply a product of 'international industrial restructuring' or the new international division of labour; another concentrates almost wholly upon the domestic industry examining the problem in terms of the strategies, choices and constraints of its firms.[4] We are concerned with the interaction between the specifically British aspects of the industry and the powerful world-wide forces within which it is located. We begin with the latter.

As an international system, the car industry is organised under the direction of a few multinational corporations. The eight largest car producers account for some 70 per cent of world output and a high proportion of their output is in countries outside of their 'home' base. The most international firm is Ford with almost 58 per cent of its production outside the USA (in 1980) with Volkswagen having 34 per cent, General Motors 29 per cent and Renault 28 per cent of their output abroad.[5] Although the Japanese companies have accounted for a high proportion of car output without having production facilities abroad, they are increasing the latter and the internationalisation of their operations has taken other forms. Apart from ownership of foreign production facilities, multinational corporations have entered into joint agreements for producing cars (such as the collaboration between Honda and British Leyland for production of the Acclaim) for producing components (such as those developed extensively by Renault, Volkswagen and others) or for marketing. In several cases these joint ventures involve one partner owning part of the other's equity; Renault, for example, owns 46.4 of American Motors and 20 per cent of Volvo's shares.[6]

Not all major corporations in the car industry have substantial ownership of overseas plants or significant collaboration agreements. The two largest Japanese companies, in particular, have not developed significantly in either of these directions while the US firms, Ford and General Motors, have not developed significant collaborations. But overseas operations by multinationals and collaborative agreements have between them been increasingly significant in the recent economic crisis. Collaboration has been especially important for the firms whose size places them in the second rank of world producers. But, looking at the industry as a world system, the significant changes lie in the transnational, cross-border character of its *operations*. Firms' production and marketing are internationalised partly under transnational legal links (ownership of overseas firms or collaborative agreements) partly independent of them and through market relations such as the leading Japanese firms' international expansion through exports. Some of the leading corporations have responded to the collapse of the post-war boom by a fundamental restructuring of their operations towards different and greater forms of international integration in making their products. In doing this, of course, the redivision of production processes and their relocation itself contributes to the redundancies and the fracturing of national economies that mark the crisis in each national economy such as Britain. The restructuring has involved a major switch toward foreign purchases of components for car production plants in any one country ('off-shore sourcing') and toward globally integrated production (production of a 'world car'). Whereas off-shore sourcing aims 'to find the profitable locations to produce particular parts of a vehicle', the world car global integration strategy goes further and aims 'to unify design and engineering of vehicles, to centralize corporate planning, to try and homogenise consumption styles in different countries, and finally to concentrate production of each component in one or two key locations but to have multiple assembly points'.[7] There have been considerable moves in both these directions in recent years, but there have also been limits and difficulties to both methods of internationalising operations.

The lead in off-shore sourcing has been taken particularly by companies producing cars in the USA moving toward importing engines and transmissions from Brazil, Mexico and Japan. American companies' foreign sourcing began with the import of parts from Canada; in 1971, following a bilateral agreement in 1965, US firms controlled 80 per cent of Canada's production of car parts. But European car producers have also developed a major trade in parts and components, either within a single corporation or between firms, so that a high proportion of the content of cars made in Britain, Sweden or other European countries often originates elsewhere in Europe or the world.

Off-shore sourcing is motivated by companies' search for cost-minimising sources and is highly influenced by labour costs per unit, transport costs and government subsidies. The structure of these costs in 1984 permits calculation of both the advantages some countries have and the present limits to the growth of this trend. The relative labour costs of the West German industry in 1982 were 61 per cent of those in the USA;

while Japan's were 27 per cent, Mexico 22 per cent, Brazil's 24 per cent and S. Korea 11 per cent, the advantage US car firms could gain by importing components and parts from such countries varied according to the specific case. Radiators would be more expensive than those produced in the US; the only profitable location for engine wiring harnesses would be Mexico and while that country's low transport costs to the US give it an advantage in many products, Brazil's advantage as a supplier appeared to US firms to be not greater than Japan's.[8]

In the 1980s the two leading US multinational car producers made strides toward producing a world car; General Motors with its J and S cars and Ford with its Erika. But it is recognised that there are immediate limits to parts of the strategy. In particular, differences between national markets in such things as tastes, legal requirements (on pollution control, for example) and replacement cycles limit the extent to which an essentially identical car can be produced for world-wide sales. Ford claim that the economies of scale from producing standardised components for a world car assembled in different countries cannot yet be realised.[9]

Nevertheless, the moves toward off-shore sourcing and a world car have strong implications for both assembly and the components and parts industries. Both are based on the assumption that specialisation in the production of components can generate considerable cost advantages. Apart from the labour cost advantages of some locations (such as Mexico for US off-shore sourcing) these can stem from economies of scale in their production. The implications for the car producers themselves and the components industry relate to the radical changes in technology and the labour process that are accompanying these changes in international structure.

The World Context: New Technology and Methods

From the late 1970s, car producers in Europe and the US, led by competition from Japan, have been radically restructuring their production technology and with it, their labour practices. Seen by some to be as radical as Henry Ford's early adoption of the assembly line, the new methods are widely described as 'neo-Fordism' The technologies underlying them are robot technology and computer aided design and manufacturing systems (CAD/CAM) and they have two distinct implications for production. First their use yields great potential increases in labour productivity or, in other words, great reductions in the direct labour costs of the product. The use of robots has been greatest in spot welding where, at the beginning of the 1980s, one robot could replace three or four workers at a cost saving of more than 80 per cent, and the use of robots elsewhere in assembly and production has the potential to be similarly labour saving. Computer aided design has increased the productivity of design teams; at General Motors, for example, labour productivity is reported to have tripled. Computer aided manufacturing systems, controlling and linking the production processes have generated reductions in labour input and increases in productivity illustrated by the system installed in Fiat's Mirafiori engine plant in 1980 achieving a 33 per cent increase in labour productivity. Secondly, these technologies introduce great flexibility into production, for whereas the technology of car production from Henry Ford to the end of the 1970s gave great advantages to those who could produce long runs because the production and assembly plants were expensive to retool for new lines, the new technology, robots, and computer aided design and manufacturing systems are easily reprogrammed for cars with different specifications. Thus, plants using new technology reach break-even point on a particular car at considerably lower levels of output than under the old technologies.

Technological innovation is more or less continuous in all capitalist industry but some innovations are radical or basic, altering production methods to a degree quite different from others.[10] The car industry's radical new technologies have been adopted, unevenly, incrementally and spasmodically but nevertheless increasingly since the late 1970s. The effects on the labour force have been both an absolute reduction in the numbers employed as corporations have attempted to raise productivity in the midst of an economic crisis which restricts their ability to raise production, and a change in the character (the skill composition, organisation and practices) of the labour force. The latter has occasioned redundancies as much as the former for companies attempting to change the character of the labour force have done so by key dismissals from the old workforce. The overall changes in world-wide employment for eight leading multinational corporations in the industry between 1978 and 1982 are shown in the following table:

Table I

World-wide Employment changes in Leading automotive TNCs, 1978-82[2]

Corporation	1978	1982	% Change
General Motors	839[1]	657	−21.7
Ford	506	404[3]	−20.2
Volkswagen	207	239	15.5
Renault	143[4]	132[4]	6.7
Peugeot (PSA)	265[5]	208	−21.5
Fiat	134	124[3]	−7.5
Toyota	45[6]	56[6]	24.4
Nissan	56[7]	59[7]	5.4

Notes
1 Figures in units of thousands.
2 Data for year end except where otherwise specified.
3 1981.
4 Data for vehicle production and not the whole Renault group (end 1982 employment for the total group approximately 217,000).
5 1979 figure, to include Citröen and Talbot.
6 Figures for June 1978 to June 1982.
7 Figures for March 1979 to March 1983.
Due to substantial differences in company structures and definitions, no comparisons among companies should be made.

Sources: United Nations Industrial Development Organisation, *International Industrial Restructuring and the International Division of Labour in the Automobile Industry*, New York 1984.

To a large extent these labour force changes are being achieved through closure of old plants. This disinvestment has occurred at the same time as the leading corporations have been implementing programmes for investing in new plant and machinery on a very large scale. For example, while General Motors reduced its labour force by more than 20 per cent between 1978 and 1982 and closed plants, it engaged in a five year investment programme of approximately $40 billion up to 1985, more than the total spent on capital projects in the fifteen years prior to 1980.

The technological innovations and the changing internationalisation of the car industry combine to produce highly complex changes which the simple conceptions, widespread in both left and right wing polemics, fail to capture. For example, the view that multinationals are cutting jobs in the old industrial countries in order to employ cheap labour in the Third World is too simple. Apart from the limits to off-shore sourcing we have outlined, the case of Mexico is instructive. It has been estimated that about 30 per cent of that country's automobile jobs were lost in the last eight months of 1982 while at the same time one-fifth of General Motors' large five year capital spending budget was allocated toward Mexico.[11] Similarly, views regarding the run-down, concentration or re-location of car production as such fail to take account of the quite distinct but interrelated changes that are taking place in the different stages of car production. While technological change makes feasible smaller batch production of cars and the 'world car' strategy has not produced a standard car, there are strong drives for economies of scale in production of components and parts, for standardisation, and for concentration in the components industry. Thus, for components such as gear boxes production runs of a million or more are planned, whereas in the 1960s and early 1970s runs of 100,000 were the limit.

These changes at the global level have had different impacts on different countries. Car and components production in Britain have been unable to respond in ways which strengthen their position; on the contrary, the restructuring of the world industry, while precarious for several leading corporations and several economies, has had an exceptional effect in Britain, completely undermining production in this country.

The UK Industry's Special Features

A 1984 TUC study described the contemporary weakness of the UK motor industry as a whole:

the UK, European and world motor industries have been living through a period of intense restructuring. In the UK this restructuring of production has been particularly savage. But it has not left the UK industry in a stronger position. The irony of the last five years of restructuring is that the underlying structural imperfections in the industry remain untouched.' [12]

Within capitalism the restructuring of industries, other productive enterprises and the whole gamut of social and political structures that are linked to them is a powerful regenerative force released and accelerated by economic crises, but its success is never guaranteed for it can fail to lay the foundation for a renewed boom. [13] Its outcome is especially precarious for particular sections of capital. In the present context motor industry production located in Britain has not benefited from the industry's global restructuring. What special characteristics underlay its problems (the existing 'structural imperfections' as the TUC study describes them) and how have they affected the outcome of the recent re-structuring? The fact that the UK industry has ceased to be a major car producer and only faces a prospect of further marginalisation both with regard to other sectors of the British economy and to the world car industry relates to the large role foreign multinational corporations play in it and the failure of the state to formulate and implement a long term strategy for the industry during the years of post-war expansion.

Britain's motor industry is highly concentrated; the four largest firms produced 99.5 per cent of passenger car output in 1980. Only one of these four, BL, is British owned. Two, Ford and Vauxhall (General Motors) are subsidiaries of US multinationals and have been since before the Second World War. The last, Talbot, is a subsidiary of the French multinational PSA (Peugeot, Citröen) after having been part of the US corporation, Chrysler. While the high degree of concentration in the British industry is a common feature of most countries, the industry's domination by the subsidiaries of foreign multinationals distinguishes Britain sharply from other advanced capitalist countries. Whereas car production in Japan, the USA, France and Italy is almost entirely largely controlled by corporations based there, Britain's position has more in common with Spain and some Third World countries. Approximately 60 per cent of UK car output comes from the British subsidiaries of foreign multinationals compared with

31 per cent for West Germany, 3 per cent for the USA, 1 per cent for France and none in Japan, Italy and Sweden.

The fact of foreign ownership itself is not a source of weakness for the industry, but the position of their British plants as subordinate parts of those corporations' world-wide operations is. In particular, it has meant that when faced with the economic crisis and the need to adjust as part of the restructuring of the international industry, the easiest path for British based plants has been to increase their marginal character while the British based components industries have lost their British markets without capturing an equivalent foreign market.

One mark of the industry's greater marginalisation is its weak position in supplying the British market itself. As we noted earlier, the proportion of UK car sales accounted for by imports rose to 57 per cent in 1983 (from 27 per cent in 1973). This compares with import penetration of less than 40 per cent in West Germany, France and Italy (and much less in the US and Japan). The declining level of exports indicates that these imports are not simply the counterpart of an increased orientation toward the world market as the industry internationalises. The principal channels for these imports are the multinational corporations operating in the UK; in particular, Ford and Vauxhall import cars from their plants in Spain, Germany and Belgium to sell under British model names. That the multinationals' imports from their own plants have been central to the British industry's response to the economic crisis is shown by the fact that whereas multinationals' imports of their own cars ('tied imports' or 'intra-firm' imports) accounted for only 6 per cent of car sales in the UK in 1976, they reached 21 per cent in 1982.[14]

Another sign of the multinationals' role in making the UK industry increasingly marginal is their transformation of their production facilities from relatively integrated to relatively fragmented operations. Talbot in particular and, to a considerable extent, Vauxhall, have been largely transformed into assembly plants for imported parts and sub-assemblies which, in the case of Talbot, contrasts sharply with the 1950s structure of the Rootes empire on which it was based. Fragmentation in any one country's industry is in one sense the counterpart to the integration of the car industry at a global level, for independence means greater specialisation of each country's industry. Therefore, the increased specialisation in assembly of the multinationals' British plants could be seen, in principle, as a sign of a stronger role for them in the new international division of labour; moreover, it can be seen as something that would have occurred whether the plants were owned by multinationals or independent. But such interpretations would be wrong, as can be seen by considering the character of the international division of labour and off-shore sourcing which is the particular form it takes within motor industry multinationals.

A highly developed international system with a high degree of specialisation between countries does not imply that each specialised process has equal status. If a US multinational producing cars in Detroit relies on Mexico for engines, Brazil for transmissions and other countries for electrical components, neither the engine factory in Mexico nor the assembly line in Detroit is automatically and *a priori* the most significant part of the firm with a determining influence over the whole. It depends on where the key management decisions are located and aimed at, where the key labour skills are located and the control of technology lies, and on where the financial markets evaluate the corporation as a whole. In the example given there is no doubt that the US multinational's American operations, even if they were primarily the assembly of vehicles, would dominate the whole. The case of foreign multinationals in the UK is different. Their key management decisions have never been located in Britain, and the company's British operations are evaluated by US financial markets as parts of the whole. If they become increasingly oriented to assembling parts made in other countries, as they have done in the recent economic crisis, they have done so to concentrate relatively low-skilled processes in the UK with the key technological advances being located within the firm's plants and suppliers elsewhere. One observation that bears this out is the transfer of key skilled personnel, design teams, to non-UK centres:

In the late 1970s, GM decided to locate its main European car design activities in Germany ... As a result, Vauxhall's design capability has been virtually destroyed ... Similarly, a decision was taken at Talbot UK in 1983 to move its UK design team to Paris.[15]

Regarding technology the lead in installing robots in Britain was taken by BL rather than any of the foreign multinationals operating in the country.

The domination of the UK car industry by foreign multinationals has meant that their head offices have been the source of many of the major decisions determining the character of the UK car industry. The British state itself has implemented policies toward the industry at particular stages, but its influence has been partial, ill-timed and lacking any strategic conception of the industry's role and needs that was required. In this it contrasts strongly with Japan where, the state has regulated the industry's foreign trade and competition from overseas and its finance, and has supported its long term product and process development. It also contrasts with France where the dominant firm, Renault, is state-owned and with West Germany, where Volkswagen was established and built up under state control.

The four main forms of state intervention have been to influence the industry's market conditions; tax and subsidy policies (especially regarding regional locations); the encouragement of mergers; and, finally, nationalisation. These policies have been piecemeal and, having been produced as responses to particular crises in the industry, have invariably been 'too late' in a sense. The absence of a coherent state strategy for the industry and the essentially negative 'crisis-response' character of the policies are well illustrated by developments in the components industry and in BL, the only major British owned producer.

State Intervention: The Case of BL

BL, whose frequent changes of name (BMC, British Motor Holdings, Leyland, BLMC, British Leyland, BL) symbolises its vicissitudes and lack of long-term security or strategy, exemplifies the most developed relation between the state and the motor industry. It therefore exhibits all the weaknesses, distortions and impoverishment of the type of involvement the British state has pursued.

Through the boom years of the 1950s and early 1960s the factor that seemed to dominate the car firms that eventually linked (with commercial vehicles) to form BL was the market.

And the level of demand appeared to be the only consideration affecting the state's policies; while other states were associated with the plant and product development of their main national producers, the British state took positions almost solely on matters affecting the level of demand. In the short-term, these were far from being wholly to the car industry's benefit, for 'credit squeezes' imposed in response to City policies and actions regarding the exchange rate at times restricted the finance for domestic car purchases in an unpredictable way. Nevertheless, the contest over such policies indicated that the aspect of the car industry that was a matter for policy action was only the level of demand and its financing. In the long-run the state gave strong support to the development of that market by providing the stable but liberal conditions in financial markets that permitted the development of consumer credit through new financial intermediaries. But when production conditions failed to match the developing mass consumer market, sustaining demand could not guarantee the firm's future.

The greatest move the state made, before the 1970s, toward encouraging the modernisation and strengthening of production was the arrangement of a merger between the disparate car companies of British Motor Holdings (including the main British volume manufacturers, Austin and Morris) and the profitable but small commercial vehicle manufacturer, Leyland. The creation of BLMC in this way was in accordance with the logic of the Industrial Reorganisation Corporation that promulgated it, for the IRC was established as a state body to promote mergers on the assumption that the creation of large organisations under one ownership would of itself stimulate reorganisation of plant, methods of working and the whole production (and selling) process itself. It was assumed that the creation of giant corporations from smaller ones would lead to innovation, rationalisation and a stronger base without greater state intervention.

In the case of BLMC no such reorganisation of the productive base did result. A new management team was recruited largely from Ford but could not apply that company's strategies in a company with a wide variety of models produced in diverse, non-integrated plants. Although new models were developed and launched in the early 1970s in an attempt to increase the new company's market share, they did not represent any significant product innovation or development. By 1975 this strategy or, from the point of view of state leadership, non-strategy had led to an acute profits crisis or, in fact, a pre-tax loss of £76 million in that year and a rapid increase in short-term borrowing (net short-term debt increasing from £35 million in 1974 to nearly £250 million in 1975) in order to finance operations and investment. At the end of 1974 the state guaranteed a bank loan of £50 million and in 1975 nationalised the assets under a new company BL.

In its nationalised form BL received state support and intervention of a kind that other advanced countries' car industries had received two or three decades earlier, and newly industrialising countries had begun to implement ten years previously. Following the plan put forward by Ryder the state committed itself to a large expansion of investment in new plant and machinery.[15] In the light of Ryder's finding that BL employed fewer fixed assets per worker and older machinery than its competitors, the Labour government committed large sums of money to a £2 billion eight-year development programme. By 1979 the pursuit of this strategy had led to another profits crisis which was a symptom of the problems emanating from the weak and distorted character of the state's intervention, even when that policy had begun to engage with the need to develop and modernise production methods.

One fault with the state's (Ryder) strategy was its over-optimistic assessment of the size of BL's markets; its projections foresaw no difficulties in selling the firm's increased output whereas in fact BL's market shrank. Some writers falsely identify almost the whole history of BL's problems with demand failures and faulty marketing and product strategies.[16] As a result, they see the key problem of the Ryder strategy as a failure to estimate demand accurately, or concentrating on production, to give marketing due consideration. By contrast, we see the false forecasts as an aspect of a more general weakness, the absence of an industrial strategy. Ryder's failure to forecast accurately was shared by all car manufacturers in the unstable markets of the 1970s and early 1980s rather than being due to a 'productionist bias'. The orientation toward the productive base was precisely what had been neglected in the past, and the failure to forecast sales accurately was simply a mark of the state's inability or unwillingness to intervene to secure BL's market. The state's policy toward BL, in other words, was a response to the crisis in a particular company; it did not form part of an industry-wide strategy. If such a strategy had existed it would have included trade and fiscal policies to support a market share for BL which matched the growth of its productive potential.

A second fault evident in the state involvement following Ryder was that it was too late. By 1975 BL's production methods, the quantity and technical age of its machinery and its organisation of the work-force were extremely backward in relation to its overseas competitors. This was reflected in low productivity and high losses, low market share and poor product quality. The strategic medium-term policy adopted on the basis of the Ryder Report involved a rationalisation and strengthening of the productive base that needed to be undertaken during the boom years of the 1950s and early 1960s when market conditions would have supported the increased output that accompanied increased productivity. Instead, Ryder's plan was essentially a strategic policy introduced in response to an immediate crisis; in that sense it ran into difficulties that neither a strategic policy in the context of stable market developments, nor a crash policy in the context of a crisis would have done. In the end, the new management under Michael Edwardes who was installed in 1977, had to institute a crisis-response policy in 1979. In response to a further deterioration of profits, they implemented sharp cut-backs and redundancies and an attack upon existing trade union organisation in the company.

The problem of the Ryder-based state policy was not so much why it failed to restore profitability, but why there had been no such strategic plan in the earlier decades. One factor that bore upon the car firms that made up BL as much as upon the rest of British industry was its reliance on internal funds to finance its investment and on bank credit for residual external funds. At crucial periods internal funds were inadequate to finance a major investment strategy,[17] but the state, capital markets and company all operated in ways which did not disturb these methods of financing, or intrude any of the external discipline that the state could provide through financing strategic investment. And, as we outlined in Chapter 4, bank finance has been based on a principle of non-intervention.

The third weakness of the Ryder plan was that, although it appeared to be a major state intervention in pursuit of a medium-term strategy and one of the first to emulate the policies that more *dirigiste* states have followed with regard to their motor firms, it was in fact too small to warrant such a conception. The Ryder plan claimed to promote a 'massive strategy to modernise plant and equipment at BL' by investing some £2,000 million over eight years. However, that sum was not large compared to the investments in new equipment being made by the leading multi-nationals abroad. And, since Ryder argued for £1,150 million to be allocated to product development and an increase in working capital, the amounts available for building new production facilities were to be very modest.

Thus, BL has been the subject of a considerable degree of state intervention and exemplifies the peculiarities of state industrial policy in Britain. Instead of adopting a strategic responsibility for developing the motor industry, the state has taken partial and crisis-response actions with regard to the individual firm. In the case of other motor firms, the British subsidiaries of foreign multinationals, the state has similarly taken a piecemeal approach, principally a policy of tax relief and subsidies oriented toward regional interests or a straightforward 'rescue package' which as in the case of Chrysler (now Talbot) was on the terms set by the companies. Indeed, the dominance of the UK industry by foreign multinationals has been a major obstacle to the development of a strategic state policy. These multinationals have proved to be a powerful opponent to a state-led strategy for, in order to be effective, it would necessarily imply limits to their freedom of manoeuvre.

The piecemeal character of the state's policies in this industry (even more than in others) is symbolised by the fact that alone among major industries, the car industry or wider motor industry has no Economic Development Committee under the National Economic Development Council to take a strategic overview. The absence of such a strategy is exemplified by the fact that, whatever the policies followed for

BL or other car producers, no complementary policy for adjustment in the components industry was ever developed with them. The changes the UK motor industry has been undergoing in the recent economic crisis have caused the closure of large sections of the components industry and the job losses that accompany closures. These are consistent with the international changes in the car industry. At the world level, the industry has moved toward off-shore sourcing of standardised components produced in large volume. The British components industry had been based on relatively small scale production and model variety so that in the face of international competition a large number of its firms were forced to close. These shifts were precipitated by the sharp falls in output by the firms' traditional customers, the UK motor industry and by that industry's sudden switch toward buying from one supplier instead of from several sources. Only the largest, such as Lucas, were able to switch their role and direct their production toward large volumes and the supply of international markets. But even there the state's lack of an industrial strategy has had an impact, for as we have outlined in Chapter 8, the state's sponsoring of research and development has weakened the R and D effort directed toward lines such as car components. In the case of electronic components produced by firms such as Lucas or Smiths where both military products and car components are produced, this has generated especially severe long term bias.

Notes

[1] See Trades Union Congress, *TUC Motor Industry Study*, London, 1984, p.2. Similar figures apply to the US and EEC motor industries, see United Nations Industrial Development Organisation, (UNIDO) *International Industrial Restructuring and the International Division of Labour in the Automotive Industry*, New York 1984, p.3.

[2] TUC, op.cit., pp.2 and 6

[3] Ibid., pp.4-6

[4] The first approach is exemplified by UNIDO, op.cit. The second by K. Williams, J. Williams and D. Thomas, *Why are the British Bad at Manufacturing?*, London 1983.

[5] UNIDO, op.cit., pp.22-3

[6] Ibid., pp.74-87.

[7] Ibid., pp.87-100.

[8] Ibid.

[9] Ibid., pp.100-101.

[10] See G. Mensch, *Stalemate in Technology: Innovations Overcome the Depression*, New York 1979 and C. Freeman, J. Clark, L. Soete, *Unemployment and Technical Innovation*, London 1982.

[11] UNIDO, op.cit., pp.37-41.

[12] TUC, op.cit., p.37.

[13] See B. Fine and L. Harris, *Rereading 'Capital'*, London 1979.

[14] TUC, op.cit., pp.17-8.

[15] Ibid., p.18.

[16] D. Ryder, *British Leyland: The Next Decade London*, London 1975.

[17] For example, Williams, Williams and Thomas, op.cit.

[18] Ibid., p.227.

Chapter 10
Electronics

There is an industry in Britain whose output has grown at 12 per cent per annum during the 1970s and has even accelerated to 20 per cent in the 1980s. Exports have been growing almost as fast. The industry is Information Technology (IT) and as such includes telecommunications, computing and office equipment. Yet despite these indices of success, NEDO has considered IT to be in a crisis, as is indicated by the title of its 1984 report *Crisis Facing UK Information Technology*.[1]

It sees the very survival of a significant IT sector in the UK at stake:

> the UK IT industry now has such a small share of world markets that it can no longer continue to invest adequately in product development, in marketing or in production facilities.[2]

Although this is the sharpest statement from NEDO of its diagnosis, it is by no means the first. A series of reports have pointed to the deficiencies of the UK IT industry and have posed remedies in terms of coherent and extensive state intervention and support. There has been some response from government but it has remained sorely inadequate.[3]

As a result, whilst employment in the UK remained fairly constant at 150,000 in the 1970s, it began to drop rapidly at the end of that decade and now stands at 120,000. Similarly, there was almost balance of trade in the sector until the late 1970s but now a deficit of £800 million has opened up in a market of almost £5 billion in size.

Whilst exports may account for 44 per cent of UK output, imports take up 54 per cent of the domestic market. The UK growth rate of 12 per cent over the 1970s has to be set against France (19 per cent), West Germany (15 per cent), Japan (23 per cent) and USA (18 per cent). The relatively poor performance of the UK has meant that its share of world markets over the same period has dropped from 9 per cent to a meagre 5 per cent, the major shares being taken by the US (47 per cent) and Japan (19 per cent).

The explosive growth of IT in recent years has depended upon 'new technology'. In the transmission of information, there has been the introduction of satellites, fibre optics and increasingly powerful co-axial cable. The processing of (the transmitted) data has been enhanced thousands of times over by the progress in 'chip' technology. Where, a generation ago, the first electronic chip could hold one piece of information, today a chip of one-fiftieth the thickness of a human hair is expected to hold 256,000 pieces of information. Such chips cost more to produce but it is reckoned that information processing costs of machinery have decreased 1,000 times in the last 25 years.

These two developments in technology, transmission and processing, are independent in principle but they have an intimate practical connection for the mass of data transmitted by electronic, optical or other means could not be decoded or unscrambled without the use of computers. There have been other technical developments also – most familiar to us is the use of liquid crystals in our pocket games and watches. Taken together these products constitute what is termed the 'hardware' of the industry. But to make the hardware do what is wanted, it has to be instructed, a programme has to be written; this is 'software'.

Sometimes, software is incorporated into hardware at the stage of manufacture – as in an electronically controlled cooker, for example, or the standard functions of a personal computer. At other times, software is created for specific applications of the hardware. Such software may be sold as a standardised package which can be used with little amendment – in company payrolls for example.

The character of IT has led to the development of a particular industrial structure. First, it is dominated by multinational corporations. This is inevitable given the enormous research and development costs that have to be laid out prior to manufacture and the often equally large fixed capital costs that are necessary to guarantee economies of scale in hardware production.

Second, the industry is subject to rapid technological change and this tends to influence the industry at all levels. For example, the increasing capacity of the electronic chip has given rise to a whole new generation of microcomputers which are on a par with the mainframe computers of the past. The Fairchild F-8 Microcomputer (1970) can be compared to the leading IBM machine of 1955 (IBM 650). It is 30,000 times smaller, weighs one pound as opposed to 5,650 lbs, consumes 7,000 times less power, employs 20,000 transmitters rather than 2,000 vaccum tubes, calculates five times faster and is 10,000 times more reliable. Not surprisingly, the microcomputer market is blossoming with a growth rate of 50 per cent per annum.[4]

But apart from transforming the quality of computers, the increasing capacity of chips has drastically altered the cost balance between hardware and software. Chip technology has been costly both in terms of research and development (R and D) and fixed capital costs, and its viability depends upon the mass production of standardised components. These are cheap, but to make them work when assembled into hardware increasing reliance has been placed upon the use of software which is skilled-labour-intensive and not subject to mass production. The result has been that, over the past twenty years, software costs of computing have risen from 20 per cent to 60 per cent of total costs and are predicted to rise to over 80 per cent in the next twenty years.

The volatility of the sector following on from its rapid technical change tends to reinforce the role of large multinational corporations. Learning through innovation encourages firms to market at below cost in early years of product development. If this leads to the acceptance of a product as standard, it carries further advantages in the assurance of market share and the knock-on effect of demand for compatible equipment. This has been one of the factors behind IBM's rapid rise to and stability at the top of the computer manufacturing – it produces twice as much as any non-US company. Britain's only remaining computer manufacturer, ICL, has products valued at $1.5 billion compared to IBM's computer products of $26 billion.

The third crucial feature of the IT industry is that, dramatically over more recent years, it is rupturing the traditional divisions across sectors of the economy. Telecommunications, computing and office equipment are becoming a single industry. Again this reinforces the role of large multinationals which have the resources to buy and diversify into the related sectors in which they feel themselves to be weak but able to exploit new opportunities.

The recent takeover of ICL by STC illustrates this point, as does the attempt by IBM and BT to collaborate in the production of telephone (and computer) networks. But these are typical moves in the industry, with Ferranti collaborating with GTE, ICL with Fujitron and Plessey with Stromberg-Carlson being other examples. In short, even multinational corporations are troubled by the need to locate their operations relative to the shifting sands of rapid technical change and the breakdown of traditional sectoral divisions.

This is well illustrated by the production of semi-conductors which are the raw materials of hardware and include chips alone as well as their assembly into units with other components such as transistors. Producers fall into two sorts – those such as IBM and Western Electric, who only produce for their own internal consumption or captive markets, and those such as Texas Instruments and Motorola who sell most of their production on the open market. Altogether for the US producers, the US captive market in 1982 accounted for a 33.5 per cent share (up from 29.3 per cent in 1978) reflecting the extent to which electronic goods manufacturers guarantee security of component supply and of sale in their own final products.

70 per cent of the world's semi-conductors are produced by US firms around the world and 60 per cent of output in the US is accounted for by the four multinationals previously mentioned. The only other major producer is Japan which accounts for almost a quarter of world output. Western Europe accounted for a mere 4.4 per cent of world output.

This relatively poor performance of Western Europe is reflected throughout the whole spectrum of electronic products; over the period from 1978 to 1983, its consumption has been growing at 4 per cent a year, twice the rate of production, its trade balance has worsened from a deficit of £0.7 billion to a deficit of $8.1 billion in a total consumption of $109.4 billion (all at 1982 prices), so that Western Europe now accounts for a third of all consumption of electronic products but only a quarter of production.

This discussion illustrates a fourth fundamental aspect of the electronics sector: whilst it is dominated by a few large multinationals, it also provides a place for specialised producers who are often dependent for component supplies on other companies who may well prove to be their competitors. These dependent companies are often multinationals themselves, for example, both specialising in particular semi-conductors for captive and merchant purposes as well as diversifying across a range of electrical and electronic goods. Currently, fifty billion semi-conductors are produced each year of at least a hundred thousand different types with several hundred thousand different customers. Typically, West European semi-conductor manufacturers have less than 10 per cent of their revenue accounted for by this product. Consequently, a niche is created for them to specialise in particular semi-conductors, but equally this is essential for their own survival in electronic goods more generally lest they become dependent upon their competitive rivals. Significantly, whilst plants sited in Europe account for about a quarter of semi-conductor production, well over half of this output flows from American subsidiaries. In addition, Japanese producers have increasingly threatened Western European producers in recent years.

Not surprisingly, in the face of such competition Western European governments have adopted a variety of industrial policies to support their electronic industries. In the UK, for example, the semi-conductor manufacturer INMOS has been consistently supported. But UK policy stands out as being inadequate in its extent, its direction and its coherence. This has particularly troubled NEDO and has led it to campaign with limited success for greater and more consistent intervention. Even the United States, in response to the Japanese challenge, has responded to the need for industrial policy in response, in particular, to the challenge of the Japanese which has seen the capture of much of the US consumer electronics goods market.

The USA views industrial policy of other countries with a mixture of envy and denunciation as unfair. It is no longer able to claim that an industrial policy is unnecessary by posing the rhetorical question 'Who needs to create world leaders when you have IBM?' Indeed, it is more likely to be confronted with the question 'How can you have an industrial policy when you have IBM?' So great is the influence of this company over the electronics sector, particularly for computers, that the corporate policy of all others is heavily influenced by it. This has been recognised by the anti-trust suit brought against IBM in 1969; the trial, however, only began in 1975, and was dropped in 1982.

Whatever the envy, admiration and hostility with which the USA views the industrial policies of other nations, it holds British policy in an ill-concealed contempt. This emerges from the most comprehensive report on the sector for the United States Congress by the office of Technical Assessment, *International Competitiveness in Electronics*. The USA is looking, against its own (partially false) ideology of non-intervention by the state in business, for models for industrial policy in order to ensure its competitiveness in electronics. It finds that 'since the beginning of the 1970s UK industrial policy has been a hodge-podge'.[5] It puts this down to the large number of unco-ordinated bodies responsible for policy that have come and gone – such as the IRC, NEB, Ministry of Technology etc. 'The number of government bodies involved in industrial policy provides one explanation for the random approach to programs in electronics,'[6] creating a 'grab-bag character of UK policies toward electronics,'[7] (for which, as we shall see, US companies are partly responsible).

This has harmed UK policy through lack of coherence. This is illustrated in the case of INMOS, the government-created chip manufacturer started up in 1978 by the NEB. Whenever requiring further investment funds, it has met a stormy passage sometimes complicated by the dictates (rightly or wrongly) of regional policy in determining plant location. The height of irony was reached in 1980 when there was a seven-month delay in approving an investment tranche to INMOS, at a cost to the company calculated at £300,000 per day. At the same time, with no attendant conflict, the government distributed £14 million to multinationals establishing chip production in the UK. ITT semiconductor, National Semiconductor, Motorola and General Instruments all received over £2 million each for expansion.[8]

This episode is related to a further weakness in the formation of policy which depends upon and supports the proliferation of unco-ordinated decision making institutions. The current government, in pursuing policies of allowing the market to decide, has incorporated the competitive multi-nationals onto committees designed to determine industrial policy. Such positions can be used as a base from which to oppose government policy with which they disagree and to press for policy in their own interests. As if this were not enough, there is always room for dirtier tactics. IBM, for example, is known to have employed a 'Project Knock-Off' team in the UK to publicise and spread criticisms of the British computer company ICL.[9]

A further weakness of the British effort in electronics has been in its R and D policy. This has been insufficient and since R and D expenditure has been dominated by military needs, misdirected. Although defence R & D may have been the origin of much innovation in 'new technology', this has long since been surpassed as a source of commercial gain through spin-off. As the US Report observes, 'Today, military electronic systems are seldom as advanced as civilian; it has been years since Federal spending has had much influence over electronics technology or competitiveness,'[10] This is reflected in the changing balance of electronic sales in the USA where, from 50 per cent of output in 1960, the military share had by 1980 fallen to under 10 per cent. Computer and industrial sales increased their share from 40 per cent to 60 per cent with the balance of 10 and 30 per cent being taken up by consumer goods.

Yet, in the UK, in 1982 arms were responsible for 30 per cent of electronic goods (and 40 per cent of ships and 50 per cent of aerospace) revealing the burden that such expenditure places on the ability to pursue competitive commercial applications. This is reinforced by R & D policy for which in 1978, for example, £312 million was spent on electronics – all but £20 million on defence! Nor do private firms make up the difference; in 1975, for example, public corporations spent £36 million on electronics, the government £130 million and the private sector a mere £113 million. As the Report drily summarises: 'in the United States, the impact of military spending on electronics have been far overshadowed by the vigour of the commercial industry; the British case has been vastly different.'[11] And, we may note, vastly inferior and unsuccessful.

To sum up, electronics has been dominated by multi-nationals, particularly from the US and increasingly from Japan, so that European producers, including multinationals themselves, have been placed in an exposed and subordinate position. In the case of the UK, this has been compounded by chaotic industrial policy and over-commitment to military products. Multinationals locating production facilities in the UK have focused on the less skill and capital intensive products in organising their operations on a global basis. They have plundered rather than contributed to the UK research potential and effort. UK producers are confined to a precarious existence amongst the interstices of electronic manufacturers depending upon specialised products and component supplies from their potential competitors.

As argued in the opening chapter, different options depend upon a system of industrial planning that includes but goes far beyond the electronics sector. For electronics is not simply a sector with products but has applications in, and must be integrated with, other sectors, quite apart from training needs.

That a co-ordinated strategy for the adoption of new technology can be successful is illustrated by the development of new technology in coal-mining, where the physical conditions of work make its application most difficult. By analysing the success of British industry in this field we are able to throw into relief the weaknesses of industrial policy more generally. Throughout, the National Coal Board (NCB) has been prominent in developing new technology and a programme for its implementation through its research organisation, the Mining Research and Development Establishment. Initially, computerised mining was limited by the inadequacy both of heavy machinery and the monitoring capacity of electronic technology. Both have been improved, the latter dramatically, since the relatively unsuccessful experiments with ROLF (Remotely Operated Coupwall Face) in 1963. A 1983 report indicates that ROLF was a prestige project ahead of its time, reflecting Chairman Robens' ego, so that coal was placed by hand prior to a demonstration of the new technology.[12]

Subsequently, the NCB has developed and is implementing a programme for the new technology, MINOS (Mine Operating System). Broadly, it covers five areas of operation, each of which can be subdivided into a number of processes. The plan has involved covering more and more of these processes and creating a management system to co-ordinate them. Distinct stages of progress are designated by 'V', so that V3 signifies the third stage. By the beginning of 1984, V4 was in operation. The following table demonstrates the progress made –

	Number of Processes Computerised				Schemes Currently Operational/ Commissioned	Delivered/ Ordered
	V1	V2	V3	V4		
Coal Clearance	3	7	9	10	31	11
Production Monitoring (FIDO)	0	0	4	5	28	1
Environmental	3	6	7	8	10	8
Fixed Plant	0	0	2	5	2	1
Management Information	2	3	5	7	17	7
Total	11	16	27	35	78	32

Whilst MRDE has been heavily involved in research, manufacture of equipment has been privately undertaken. In 1976, for standardisation and cost effectiveness, the NCB reduced its suppliers of electronic components to four – Huwood, Hawker–Siddeley Dynamics Engineering, Transmitton Ltd. and Westinghouse Brake and Signal Co. Babcock International had acquired Huwood in February 1974, but Transmitton was acquired by BICC (cable, construction and electrical engineering) in November 1976. Hawker-Siddeley acquired Westinghouse (no relation to the US electrical company) in December 1978 'out of the blue' with its largest ever take-over bid of £40.5 million, making use of the £120 million compensation that it had received for the 1977 state take-over of its aerospace interests. One of the motives for the acquisition of these companies by large MNCs is for the latter to obtain experience and production in electronics the better to be able to diversify from its other products into new technology. BICC, for example, anticipates its share of electronics turnover to increase between 1981 and 1990 from 4 to 25 per cent and acquired the US company Sealectro for £38.5 million to support the effort. Apart from the contribution to be made from the companies acquired there is the indirect contribution from the research of the NCB's MRDE.

In short, under the co-ordination of the MRDE, the introduction of new technology into mining has achieved considerable success both for mining itself and also for the companies manufacturing machinery. To give another example, MRDE developed a sensor to guide coal-cutting automatically (the AM500); it has been manufactured by Anderson Strathclyde, creating a world record for cutting in South Africa and national records elsewhere, as well as a £13.4 million export contract with China. Yet it is precisely this co-ordination that is absent from the development of new technology more generally. As we have seen, potential in the area is appropriated through acquisitions according to the particular diversifying interests of different MNCs and the availability of finance at the right time.

Notes

[1] NEDO, *Crisis Facing UK Information Technology*, London 1984.
[2] Ibid., p.2.
[3] See Chapter 1 for details of other NEDO reports.
[4] For much of the information here, apart from NEDO reports, see Congress of the United States, Office of Technical Assessment, *International Competitiveness in Electronics*, Washington DC 1983.
[5] Ibid., p.401.
[6] Ibid.
[7] Ibid., p.404.
[8] See J. Hills, *Information Technology and Industrial Policy*, London 1984.
[9] Ibid., p.21 and p.162.
[10] Congress of the United States ... , op. cit., p.46.
[11] Ibid., p.403. See also Chapter 8 on the arms industry and on military expenditure.
[12] *Colliery Guardian*, January 1983.

Chapter 11
Coal Before Nationalisation

The development of the British coal industry in the years leading up to 1947 was marked by periods of contrasting fortunes. Before the First World War the industry expanded rapidly with output increasing from 60 million to 300 million tons between 1850 and 1913; in the same period employment in the industry rose from 250,000 to over one million. This rapid growth was facilitated by the opening up of large export markets on the Continent. In the five years between 1909 and 1913 exports averaged 65 million tons per annum and accounted for about one-quarter of production. In the inter-war period, however, the situation changed dramatically. As European countries improved their own coal industries British mineowners suffered from intense international competition for the first time. Yet as Table 1 suggests, mineowners in Britain, unlike their major rivals, were ill-placed to meet the challenge. In Europe production was concentrated in larger and more efficient mines; by 1938, average annual output of mines in Britain was 122,000 tons as compared to 750,000 tons in Germany. Britain also fell behind in the application of new extraction methods; mechanised coal-cutting accounted for only 55 per cent of output in 1938, compared to 97 per cent in Germany, 98 per cent in Belgium and 88 per cent in France. Productivity growth was also relatively slow, rising by only 7 per cent between 1913 and 1934, while in Germany and Poland it increased by 77 per cent and 63 per cent respectively.

Economic historians of the coal industry have generally discussed its poor relative performance in terms of inadequate

---

This chapter was written by Ben Fine, Kathy O'Donnell and Martha Prevezer.

entrepreneurial (or worker) performance. The poor record of mechanisation and amalgamation is taken either as evidence of the mineowner's reluctance to invest and innovate or as proof of the successful resistance by miners to the introduction of new working practices.[1] Alternatively, the industry's decline is explained by the exhaustion of the best coal seams and a gradual shift to marginal reserves. Declining productivity is thus considered inevitable within an extractive industry.

In this chapter the industry's record of uneven development – specifically, the conditions of relative decline in the inter-war years – is examined in the context of its changing economic and social structure. Particular attention is given to the evolving pattern of industrial relations, the fragmented structure of mineownership and the changing relationship between landowners and mineowners. The character and interplay of these relationships are explored against the background of broader political and economic developments (such as state policy towards the industry and the role of financial institutions). It is argued that elements of this structure were conducive to expansion in much of the period leading up to the First World War; in particular, the relationship between landowners and mineowners facilitated the rapid expansion of mines and high rates of coal extraction. Increasingly, however, major impediments to industrial change and development emerged at the turn of the century. The pattern of mineral ownership, in particular, inhibited the long term planning and design of mines and the diffusion of new production techniques. At the same time, these structural conditions were reflected in, and reinforced by, growing tensions within the industrial relations system. While miners' demands for a unified national wage structure and other terms and conditions increased during this period, mineowners were reluctant to concede these conditions because of marked variations in geological, technical and market conditions. Since we shall argue that a major factor contributing to the diversity of conditions across the industry was the changing relationship between landowners and mineowners, this will provide our point of departure.

Table 1

Comparative Performance of British, Polish and Ruhr Coalfields

	Output per Manshift, Date indicated	cwt 1936	Percentage Increase	Average mine output 000s tons
Poland	23.4 (1927)	36.2	54	750 (1937)
Ruhr	18.6 (1925)	33.7	81	780 (1938)
Britain	20.6 (1927)	23.5	14	122 (1938)

Source: Reid Report, 1945

Landed Property and Mine Development

In 1938 legislation was passed to vest the ownership and control of coal royalties in the hands of a government body, the Coal Commission. This act of nationalisation brought to an end the direct influence of the private landowner on the development of the British coal industry. Although it preceded the act of nationalisation of the mines by eight years, the two nationalisations were in a sense many more years apart. The creation of the National Coal Board in 1947 was undertaken by the post-war Labour government, swept into office by a massive popular vote. The royalties, in contrast, were nationalised by a Conservative government just before the war and in the face of limited opposition from royalty owners whose prime concern was the terms of compensation.[2] This section considers the workings of the private royalty system, its implications for the development of mines and the events which led to the nationalisation of 1938.

The payment of royalties to private individuals was established after the Queen's court case against the Duke of Northumberland in 1568 when all minerals, other than gold and silver, were judged to belong to the landowner in correspondence with surface boundaries.[3] Where landowners worked their own coal there was no need for a royalty to be paid; otherwise some payment for extracting the coal had to be arranged between the landowner and the mineowner. A lease was drawn up between the two parties which specified the terms of the royalty payments and the conditions of mineowners' access to the coal seams. In official statistics royalty payments are usually reported in terms of a payment per ton. But this gives the false impression that this was the basis on which leases were determined. Leases were often based on acreage taking account of seam thickness and other factors. Dead or fixed rents were also levied as a lump sum charge irrespective of the quantity of coal extracted. In addition, royalty payments could vary on a sliding scale with the price of coal. In short, royalty contracts revealed a wide variety of terms, although particular conventions tended to be observed within individual districts. It is important to recognise that the royalty was not the price of the coal in the ground. Nor was it a rental for the lease of the land. It reflected a complex settlement between landowner and mineowner over access to and removal of coal by the latter from the property of the former.

Even though leases were generally negotiated to cover a long period of time, usually between 20 and 40 years, the conditions governing mineowners' access to the coal were not unambiguously predetermined for the length of the lease. Due to varying geological conditions of seams, there was frequent need for renegotiation and settlement between the two parties. Almost any major development within a mine would have effects upon the surface. For example, if the depth of a mine was increased the likelihood of subsidence increased significantly; this in turn restricted other or related activities such as the location of buildings and railway lines. Colliery companies also had to negotiate land for the location of pithead equipment, miners' houses and transport facilities, and these requirements altered as mines expanded. Hence a lease could not specify all future developments within a mine nor predict their effects on land use. As a result, the negotiation, interpretation and possible renegotiation of leases was a complex process in which each party could attempt to pursue a distinct economic interest subject to the general legal framework governing coal royalty contracts.

Such circumstances introduced an element of uncertainty into the long term plans of mineowners. Furthermore, because large capital outlays might be required to sink a mine, mineowners needed to be certain of continuous production over a long period before undertaking such expenditure. But under a royalty system in which mineowners might have to renegotiate with landowners over the terms and conditions of access to the coal seams their long term plans could be frustrated. Moreover, in coming to a settlement within existing leases landowners tended to be favoured by the law of precedent; anything not specified in a contract or by the law was subject to their veto. Faced with these difficulties mineowners had an incentive to pursue other expedients to guarantee production and profitability in the short run. These included extending the length of the working day, reducing miners' wages and forming cartels to raise the selling price of coal.

It follows that the planning and design of mines was determined as much by mineowners' ability to negotiate leases successfully as it was by geological and technical considerations. In other words, the raw materials of the trade were not freely available on the market, as in other sectors, but were locationally specific and tied to a variety of surrounding conditions.[4] Apart from the lack of guarantee of continuous production, it was also possible that additional profits generated by new investment would be appropriated by landowners through higher royalty charges. Where mine and mineral ownership remained separate, the pattern of colliery development – specifically the rate of mechanisation, layout, amalgamation and output growth – was strongly influenced by the terms of the agreements and compromises reached between landowners and mineowners.

These statements can be given more substance by a closer examination of the evolving relations between landowners and mineowners. In the first half of the nineteenth century their character was such that industrial expansion was facilitated. When the mineral deposits of an estate were first developed coal could usually be extracted from a drift mine. The low capital costs associated with this type of mining[5] encouraged landowners to develop their own coal reserves and allowed independent mineowners to negotiate with a single lessor, as long as mines were contained within the boundaries of a single estate. However, once the most easily won coal had been exhausted, pit shafts became essential to gain access to the seams. Although in some cases the additional capital outlay was financed by the landowners themselves, it was more common for them to encourage capitalists to invest in their land. This enabled landowners to share the risk of mining ventures while at the same time facilitating the development of their estates' resources. In other words, landowners and capitalists entered into a relationship of mutual benefit and co-operation. Mineowners provided capital for the development of mines and paid royalties while landowners provided various surface facilities, such as transport services and accommodation for miners.[6] Landowners benefited from an additional source of income while mineowners had access to the coal.

This co-operative relationship was being eroded around the turn of the century, however, as mines began to expand across property boundaries. Tensions and conflicts between landowners and mineowners became common as the latter were required to negotiate conditions of access and royalty payments with several landowners. By 1925 an average of five leases were needed for each mine.[7] As noted above, not only was the process of negotiation extremely complex and time-consuming, but also mineowners had to face the possibility that landowners would attempt to increase their royalty charges as the profitability of mines was improved. The incentives for mineowners to develop new seams or introduce new techniques of production was thus further diminished.

These observations are supported by the deliberations of the Royal Commission set up in 1890 to investigate the impacts of royalties upon the industry. From its comparative study of mineral ownership in other countries the Commission found that the situation in Britain was unique. On the Continent minerals were nationalised at the turn of the nineteenth century because fragmented mineral ownership had impeded the establishment of a coal industry. In the colonies, by contrast, the same law applied as in Britain, but the process of colonisation had in general created a landowning class with large estates, so mineral and land ownership normally coincided. The Commission identified several characteristics of the royalty system in Britain. It discovered the widespread use of fixed rents which meant that even when mineowners did not extract coal they were still obliged to make royalty payments. While these tended to encourage the rapid extraction of coal, mineowners could face severe financial problems if adverse geological conditions prevented the necessary quantity of coal from being mined. Moreover, the payment of a fixed royalty sum often tied a mineowner to a single landowner. Instead of planning the extraction of coal seams on the basis of geological and technical criteria, mineowners would concentrate production within a single property in order to spread the overhead costs of royalty payments.

In addition to claiming royalty payments for the extraction of coal, landowners levied a way-leave royalty upon coal that was transported across their property, either above or below the surface. Thus, even when the coal under one property was entirely exhausted, its underground, shaft and surface facilities may have been essential for the extraction of coal from a neighbouring property. The owner of the exhausted land upon which the shaft was located could charge a way-leave royalty for coal transported underground from the coal-face to the shaft and also charge for coal carried across the surface. The payment could reflect the royalty value of the neighbouring property.

The Commission did not consider these and other problems to be of overwhelming significance. It argued that dificulties arising between landowners and mineowners should be resolved by negotiation and, if necessary, by minor amendment of the law. In our view, the Commission's evidence is significant because it was reporting and recognising that there were considerable obstacles to the expansion of mines across property boundaries just as these were beginning to emerge. It provides support for our thesis that the earlier relationship of co-operation between mineowners and landowners was changing. However, the Commission, pointing to the successful record of the industry, saw no reason to alter the system of private mineral ownership; indeed it put forward arguments to support its continuation. These were essentially Ricardian propositions: royalties, by reflecting differing geological conditions and coal qualities, served to allocate capital efficiently across mines.[8] A change in the system of ownership of mineral rights would thus only transfer income to other economic agents without substantially affecting the conditions of production.[9] Furthermore, it argued that because royalty charges were low relative to the price of coal the effect on the competitiveness of British coal in international markets was negligible.

Despite the Commission's optimism, the problems that it revealed worsened rapidly. Before the First World War a serious and general difficulty concerning liability for subsidence arose. The existing law had been based on the belief that subsidence would only occur immediately above a working. But as the depth of mines increased the effects of subsidence were more widespread. The Howley Park case of 1913 judged that mineowners were responsible to railway companies for all subsidence, thereby reversing the customary practice. It took ten years of complicated negotiations to come to a settlement between the three interested parties (mineowners, landlords and railway companies). So delicate were the interests balanced that legislation for the settlement would not allow for any amendment as it passed through Parliament.

On the Continent, as discussed above, the state took ownership of mineral royalties at the turn of the nineteenth century because of the small size of landholdings relative to mining requirements. In Britain, problems arose with the private ownership of minerals as the industry developed. Compared to the Royal Commission of 1890, the opinions expressed in the inter-war years were based neither on international comparison nor on theory. The system of private ownership of royalties was seen as a practical impediment to the industry's progress. The influential Reid Report of 1945 noted the difference between Britain and Europe in this respect and assumed it to be an obvious disadvantage to the former for the rational organisation of the industry.[10]

The Reid Report's adverse view of the royalty system had become well established through a generation of enquiries. The Scott Report gave official recognition to some of the problems which the Royal Commission had dismissed as unimportant as well as identifying further problems.[11] For example, it was estimated that the practice of leaving coal barriers to demarcate property boundaries had resulted in the accumulated loss of over four thousand million tons of coal, equivalent to more than ten years' output. In 1919 the Sankey Report was unanimous in recommending nationalisation of the royalties.[12] It also favoured nationalisation of the mines, although this decision was only reached after the Chairman sided with the miners' representatives against the mineowners. Even the Samuel Report, which firmly rejected proposals to nationalise the mines as well as arguing that miners' wages should be reduced, recommended nationalisation of the royalties.

The mineowners were, at this time, ambivalent towards private ownership of the royalties. In 1919 they favoured state ownership, but following legislation in 1923, which increased their rights of access to the land, they tempered their opposition to the private landowners. Moreover, the political climate of the early 1920s led to the belief that nationalisation of the royalties could easily herald the further step of nationalisation of the mines.[13] However, during the 1930s there were a number of unfavourable judgements in the courts which proved the earlier legislation, despite amendment in 1926, to be inadequate for the mineowners. With renewed support for nationalisation of the royalties, it was finally accomplished in 1938.

Landed Property and Regional Differences

It is easier to chart opinion and legislation concerning the royalty system than it is to assess its quantitative significance in obstructing the development of the industry. The difficulties between landowners and mineowners did not develop in a regular and uniform fashion. Not only did the timing and nature of the conflict vary, but the way in which disagreements were resolved differed widely across and within coalfields. The impact of the royalty system upon the development of a particular mine depended upon the local pattern of landownership and the scope for renegotiation and compromise between landowners and mineowners as determined by general and individual economic and legal conditions. A highly dispersed ownership of royalties relative to a mine presented practical difficulties of multiple leasing for mineowners, and also raised the possibility that surplus profitability generated by new investment could be appropriated through the payment of way-leave royalties. Conversely, where landownership was highly concentrated and the process of negotiation might be simplified, the power of individual landowners was enhanced by their monopolisation of coal reserves. In either case the system of landed property, by allowing one or more landowners to appropriate the surplus profitability arising from increased individual investment, inhibited the development of mines.

To examine and assess in detail the impediment to the industry posed by the royalty system is beyond the scope of this chapter. Indeed, our analysis suggests that this can only be done by a comparative examination of the fortunes of individual mines and their differing circumstances in which surrounding patterns of landownership would be one important factor. Nevertheless, we can bring forward more general suggestive evidence.

A comparison of royalty levels across the diferent coalfields, for example, shows that they were widely dispersed (see Table 2). In 1925, they ranged from an average of 3.72 pence per ton in the West Midlands region to 7.83 pence per ton in South Wales, and there was wide variation within regions. Table 2 also reveals that, contrary to the reasoning of the 1890 Royal Commission, royalty payments and geological conditions were not necessarily positively correlated. Both South Wales and Scotland yielded the highest royalties per ton, yet although they were at opposite ends of the spectrum of mining conditions it is possible to identify an inverse relationship between geological conditions and royalty payments.

Similarly, there appears to have been little systematic correspondence between the level of royalties and the extent of mechanisation (as measured by the percentage of coal mechanically cut). Again this is illustrated by the cases of Scotland and South Wales; although mechanisation was most advanced in the former and least advanced in the latter coalfield, the royalty payments were of a relatively similar magnitude. It seems as if good geological conditions and a high proportion of mechanisation were alternative sources of high royalties and that otherwise the pattern of royalty payments was randomly determined.[14] A closer examination of the Scottish, Leicestershire and Warwickshire coalfields, however, helps to highlight the factors which influenced royalty payments and the different ways in which private ownership of minerals had an impact upon the development of the mines.

In Scotland geological conditions were poor; the average

Take in Table 2

Table 2

District	Royalties (per ton in old pence) 1925	Average Width of Seam Cut in inches 1924	Percentage of Coal Cut by Machine 1924
Scotland	6.68	39.55	46.4
Northumberland	5.74	41.83	29.7
Durham	6.32	45.26	16.0
South Wales and Monmouthshire	7.83	53.08	5.4
South Yorkshire	4.38	57.07	10.5
West Yorkshire	4.85	43.37	24.2
Nottinghamshire and Derbyshire	3.90	50.97	14.8
West Midlands (Leicestershire, Cannock Chase, Warwickshire, South Staffordshire and South Derbyshire)	3.72	62.33	15.0
Lancashire, Cheshire and North Staffordshire	4.84	52.01	16.7
Average	5.36	49.50	19.5

Source: B. Fine, 'Royalties and the Inter-war Coal Industry', *Birkbeck Discussion Paper*, No. 62.

width of seams was 40 inches in 1924 compared with a national average of 50 inches. They were also deep, faulted and subject to regular flooding.[15] Yet despite these conditions, royalty payments, at just under seven pence per ton in 1925, were among the highest in Britain. To understand why this was the case it is necessary to examine both the pattern of mineral ownership in Scotland and the extent of mechanisation within the mines. The ownership of coal royalties was extremely concentrated in Scotland.[16] While this may have eased the process of negotiation between parties (in 1925, Scottish mineowners typically had to negotiate with only half as many as the British average of five landowners) it almost certainly gave landowners the upper hand in their dealings with mineowners. In addition, an unusually high degree of mechanisation within the Scottish mines – in part a response by mineowners to adverse geological conditions and declining export markets – provided the material context in which high royalty charges could be levied. Under the circumstances, mineowners were ill-placed to resist the demands for higher royalties: given the inferior conditions underground and the more effective production methods of the rival German and Polish industries, mechanisation was a necessary condition of their survival within the industry. But the high royalties and mechanisation were associated with small size of mine compared to the rest of the country, presumably reflecting the interest landowners had in restricting mines to extract coal (and royalties) from their property alone.

In the small Leicestershire coalfield there were twelve major pits in 1938. Each of these was organised around a single estate so that the number of leases per mine in 1925 was on average between two and three. When the royalties were nationalised in 1938, the vast majority of the coal to be worked from each pit was owned in each case either by the mineowner alone or with one other landowner.[17] Mechanisation was well developed in the area, reaching 84 per cent of output by 1938. Here the similarities with Scotland cease; the royalties per ton at just under threepence were half those of Scotland, despite the poor geological and market conditions affecting the latter coalfield. Following nationalisation, there has been little change in the organisation of the Leicestershire coalfield. By 1983, one of the mines had been closed, two had been merged and one other had been merged with a mine in South Derbyshire. Given that there are now less than two hundred pits in Britain, compared with over two thousand in 1938, the structure of the industry in Leicestershire has remained remarkably stable. Arguably mines were not impeded in Leicestershire despite their confinement to major estates for which maximum revenue was generated through high output rather than through high royalties per ton.

The neighbouring coalfield of Warwickshire has some similarities with Leicestershire. For all but two of its fifteen pits, the vast majority of the coal royalties were, in 1938, owned by the mine itself or by a single landlord. Both of the exceptions were associated with a large royalty owner, but each was also surrounded by coal for which the absolute royalty compensation paid upon nationalisation in 1938 was three or four times as much as the other mines. The latter were quite dispersed by royalty ownership. Like Leicestershire, mines were set up in Warwickshire by an association between the mineowners and large estate owners. However, in Warwickshire, following nationalisation, most of these mines have eventually been closed due to exhaustion, so that by 1983 there were only five working pits in the county. Significantly, the two exceptions referred to above have been closed and the large reserves surrounding them have been worked from the Daw Mill pit, newly constructed in 1958 and the first in the country to extract a million tonnes per year and for which there are plans to double capacity. This suggests that the pattern of landownership was an obstacle to the organisation of mine-layout prior to nationalisation when to work this coal would have required multiple leasing and large scale investment.

Similar considerations apply to mechanisation. For most of the mines in Warwickshire, the number of leases in 1925 was low, although slightly higher than in Leicestershire. But there were a few mines with a very large number of leases, two with over forty. Royalties reflect a similar dichotomy, with most being below three pence per ton, but a significant fraction of tonnage yielding five pence. Mechanisation accounted for 69 per cent of output in 1938, higher than the British average, but well below neighbouring Leicestershire. Unfortunately, it cannot be verified on available statistics, but it seems likely that the higher royalties, multiple leases and lower degree of mechanisation might all be associated with the two exceptional mines identified above. The higher royalties would follow from the attempts of many royalty owners to appropriate revenue from the mines. In turn this was a contributory factor determining the low level of mechanisation and the apparent underdevelopment of the mines relative to the potential realised after nationalisation of the mines in 1947.

These examples illustrate the diverse effects of the royalty system in different mining districts. But the impact of the private ownership of minerals upon the overall development of the industry cannot be assessed by simply comparing regional coalfields. The obstacles created by the royalty system in the Warwickshire region were not simply negated by co-operative aspects of the system in other coalfields. Rather the adverse effects of the system in one coalfield had implications for the industry as a whole. By weakening the incentive to invest in specific regions the royalty system tended to erode the coercive forces of competition throughout the industry and hence had a constraining and negative impact on its long-term development.

Although the focus in this section has been on the impact of the royalty system on the development of the industry, its poor performance in the inter-war years cannot be understood in these terms alone. The influence of landed property must be taken together with other factors such as industrial relations, competitive relations among mineowners and government policy, as conditioning and mutually determining the development of the industry.

Industrial Organisation and Industrial Conflict

The expansion of the industry from the mid-nineteenth century until the First World War was dependent upon extending and intensifying hours of work rather than transforming methods of production. Although some mechanisation had occurred before the turn of the century most of this had been concentrated in the construction of shafts, leaving the process of coal extraction largely unchanged. Consequently the development of the industry depended upon the availability of a large class of labourers whose numbers exceeded one million by 1913.

Throughout this period the growth of output was characterised by cyclical movements. There was also an associated distributional cycle in which wages tended to increase with the demand for labour and the price of coal until profitability fell and the process was reversed.[18] Profitability was highly dependent upon the relationship between wages and prices because wages comprised up to 80 per cent of the industry's costs. Negotiations over wages were increasingly conducted at the district level and conflict focused on three main issues. The first was the principle of using a sliding scale for determining wages; the second was concerned with the base from which increases should be calculated and the third the rate at which wages should vary with the price of coal. There was an institutional move toward conciliation boards and arbitration to settle these matters but they operated with varying degrees of success, since they could not permanently resolve the underlying conflict between capital and labour.[19]

Prior to the First World War the predominant method of coal extraction was handgot. Work at the coal-face was divided into three main tasks which were all carried out by hewers. First, the coal had to be undercut, then it had to be ripped from the face either by hand or by the use of explosives, and finally it had to be loaded into tubs which were transported to and from the face by haulage workers. Since the hewers were paid on a piece-rate system based on the volume of coal extracted they were subject to only limited supervision. In the main, this was restricted to ensuring that safety regulations were not completely ignored. In contrast, the haulage workers and the miners who carried out the 'deadwork' tasks such as roof support, the preparation of floors and roads experienced greater direction. The relative autonomy of the hewers was further ensured by the operation of 'butty' systems.[20] This involved the mineowner in subcontracting either whole mines (the 'big butty' system) or sections of the coal-face (the 'little butty' system which survived into the twentieth century). Under this system the subcontractor was a hewer who employed and supervised a group of miners.

Across the coalfields there was considerable variation in the organisation of work. Although this was partly a result of differences in geological conditions it also reflected the outcomes of struggle between mineowners and miners over the way in which work was organised. This is illustrated by Daunton's comparative study of the coalfields in South Wales and the North-East of England.[21] Even though both of these coalfields were leading export districts and subject to similar competitive pressures, there were several major differences in the methods of working. Specifically Daunton identified variations in the organisation of 'deadwork', allocation of work, the pattern of shifts for hewers and hauliers, the method of extraction and the career structure. In the case of shift work, for example, hewers in Wales worked one long shift whereas their northern counterparts worked two short shifts. The haulage workers in Wales had a shift of comparable length to the Welsh hewers but in the North-East the hauliers had to work a much longer shift than their own hewers. In addition, the haulage workers in the north-East were not financially compensated for the longer working day since the wage differential between hewers and hauliers was comparable between the two districts. In the North-East the haulage workers tended to be adolescents who were eventually promoted to the ranks of the hewers and could subsequently benefit from the relatively shorter working day, while in Wales there was little opportunity to progress from haulage work to the position of hewer.

In organisation of 'deadwork' the colliers in South Wales were self-sufficient whereas in the north a separate class of workers was responsible for these tasks. There were also differences in the method of working the coal. Because the workings in the Welsh coalfield were more susceptible to falls there had to be co-ordinated extraction of the coal in order to minimise the portions of the roof that needed support. This encouraged the use of pillar and stall and longwall methods of working.[22] By contrast, the bord and pillar method was predominant in the North-East because of the firmer roof conditions. One final difference between the districts concerned the allocation of places of work within the mine. Since geological conditions could vary greatly within a mine the allocation of workplaces within a seam was important because wages were determined on a piece-rate system. In the North-East this was done by the system of 'cavilling' whereby workplaces were allocated by a lottery. In Wales, the allocation of work was determined by management. Variations in the conditions of work were, in principle, compensated by variations in wages which had to be negotiated between miner and manager or his deputy.

The comparison of South Wales and the North-East has shown that variations in the conditions of work led to a diversity of interests among miners. They were divided not only across districts but also within the same mine as the different shift lengths of the hewers and hauliers in the North-East demonstrates. These diversions within the workforce made it difficult for unity to be established amongst the miners even at the district level. In the nineteenth century, district unions led a precarious existence but by 1889 the majority of the autonomous local unions united to form the

Miners' Federation of Great Britain (MFGB).

The MFGB was a loose-knit organisation which also found difficulty in creating a unified struggle as the controversy over an eight hour Bill illustrates. The Northumberland and Durham District Unions opposed the MFGB's policy of an eight hour day and would not support the call for strike action, and as a result, they were expelled from the MFGB in 1893, having joined only in 1892. As a circular of the Secretary to the Federation revealed, 'the most formidable opponents (of the Bill) are in our own ranks – the miners of Northumberland and Durham.' The dissension of the North-East districts followed from the peculiarity of their workplace organisation. The hewers were already working less than eight hours and had nothing to gain from the legislation. In the North-East haulage workers worked between nine and ten hours a shift. Although as an occupational group the haulage workers would have benefited from a reduction in the working day, the situation for individual hauliers was not so clear. As discussed above, haulage workers in the North-East usually progressed to become hewers and eventually would work a shorter shift. By contrast, miners in the rest of the industry, whether they were hewers or haulage workers, had a common interest in a reduction of hours. Even so the benefit from an eight hour day varied between piece-rate and time-rate workers. A reduction in hours led to a demand from the mineowners for a reduction in wage rates. Piece-rate workers could attempt to offset any such reduction by an increase in the intensity of work. Although they were paid less per ton of coal they could try to maintain their level of earnings by producing greater output. The time-rate workers, who were generally concerned with ancillary tasks such as the sorting and grading of coal, did not have this option. They had to work harder to deal with any increases in coal cut by the hewers.

Despite the workforce's diversity of interests, the MFGB was eventually successful in pressing for an eight hour Bill which was passed in 1908 and implemented in 1910. This achievement represented and consolidated the miners' unity. The Northumberland and Durham district unions rejoined the Federation in 1907-08 and played an active role in the national union. Apart from the issues of wages and hours the miners were also united over other common interests such as safety, health and welfare provisions. These concerns arose because of the appalling conditions of work within the mines. The mineowners showed little or no concern for the life and limb of the miners except in so far as their own property was at risk. In 1918 an average of one miner died every six hours, and every three minutes one suffered an injury.[23] The mineowners only paid minimum compensation in the case of fatalities. For example, in the South Wales coalfield before the First World War, only £18 was paid when a single man with no dependants was killed.[24] By contrast, pit ponies were valued at £40 and much greater care was taken to ensure their safety.

The case of the Davy safety lamp further illustrates the mineowners' disregard for miners' lives.[25] It was claimed that the lamp produced a great improvement in working conditions because its use reduced the likelihood of explosions. In practice, however, its use meant that the mineowners directed miners to workings which had previously been designated as inaccessible because of the high level of methane gas. Following the introduction of the lamp in 1815 there was an *increase* in the number of explosions and deaths. Moreover, although it was known at that time that the problem of methane could be reduced by increasing the ventilation of the mines, the mineowners disregarded this option since it was considerably more expensive than simply adapting the standard miners' lamp.

These are the conditions in which the handgot system developed. From the turn of the century there was an increasing subordination of differences amongst the miners to a common purpose despite the diversity of conditions experienced by the membership. Arnot, the official historian of the miners' union, viewed the development of the MFGB as a struggle for unity. According to his account, the 1893 lock-out ended in victory because the miners achieved their goal with regard to wages; Williams, however, has criticised Arnot for not recognising that it was only a partial victory in that it failed to secure a minimum wage and the setting up of the conciliation boards was not in itself an achievement.[26] In our view district conciliation boards facilitated the development of unions at the local level at the time when the MFGB was in its formative years and divided along many lines. Although the struggles to abolish district wage negotiation in favour of

the North-East, for example, each district had a contrasting mixture of conditions of work (ranging from geological differences to the variations in the shift system), which complicated the suitability of each for mechanised mining.[30] Piecemeal mechanisation in conjunction with depressed market conditions also had the effect of producing unemployment, increasing the downward pressure on wage levels and worsening the conditions of work.

The process of mechanisation led to a deterioration of health and safety conditions in the industry. The introduction of electricity, for example, increased the danger from explosions as sparks were produced which could ignite gas or coal-dust. The noise of the coal-cutting machines made it difficult to hear the movement of the rock strata and falls occurred without any warning, increasing the number of deaths and injuries. The increased volume of coal dust produced by the machines exacerbated the dangers from dust-related diseases such as nystagmus (affecting the eyes) and pneumoconiosis (affecting the lungs). In short, the struggles of the inter-war years remained those of the pre-mechanised era: over the level of wages and the nature of the payment system, the hours of work, and safety, health and welfare. Far from dissolving the basis of these struggles, the gradual introduction of mechanisation intensified them.

Because mechanisation significantly increased the dangers of mining there were pressures, mainly from outside the industry, for the appointment of safety inspectors. Safety concerns, however, often conflicted with the aims of production. This is illustrated by the role of deputies within the management structure. Deputies, drawn from the ranks of the miners, were responsible for safety. After legislation in 1911, the deputies were limited in the work they could undertake. Their duties involved making inspections underground and stopping production if there were dangers from gas, roofing or other factors. But deputies were encouraged to flout the law by both workers (the piece-rate system resulted in miners taking risks) and managers. It was increasingly recognised, however, that the deputies were becoming agents of employers rather than of the miners. Qualities of supervision and control were considered to be of paramount importance and safety itself was of lesser importance. Indeed, it was discovered that many deputies were incapable of carrying out routine tests to detect the presence of gas because nystagmus had led to a deterioration in their eyesight.[31]

After 1911 a new but legally-undefined class of supervisors, the overmen, became established. Their position in the hierarchy of control lay between manager and deputy. It was clearly recognised that they were more concerned with production than with safety. A 1930 survey of 85 per cent of the mines found that there were 2,827 overmen of whom only 754 had certificates of competency, even though there were 2,488 miners holding such certificates.[32] This suggests that overmen were selected for their supervisory rather than for their technical qualities.

There was no major change in safety legislation in the inter-war period despite the introduction of mechanisation. New legislation was postponed until 1951 even though a Royal Commission in 1938 recommended several changes.[33] This Commission noted the conflict between the dictates of safety and of production. It deplored the situation in which these two factors had become embodied in separate individuals, the deputy and the overman, respectively. The proposed solution of reuniting the two functions in a single individual continued to view safety, not as a first call upon the industry, but as something to be set against the needs of production.

The failure of safety legislation to move forward with the technical progress of the industry is in part explained by the diverse forms of organisation of production. In response to miners' demands for improvements, mineowners were unable to concede measures that were acceptable and suitable to the differing work practices that they controlled. Accordingly, they insisted upon a minimum of legislation and a maximum of discretion. Safety legislation had to be suitable for both the smallest mine relying upon the handgot system as well as for the most advanced large-scale machine mining. The effects on the lives of the miners is not difficult to imagine. Between 1911 and 1938, it was necessary for 55 special inquiries to be made into mining disasters. Of these, the one at Gresford Colliery in 1934 stands out precisely because both workers and management colluded in the pursuit of production to flout the letter of an already inadequate law.[34] Nothing could better illustrate the failure of the miners to achieve their common purpose and the failure of the owners to form one.

The General Strike

The key distinguishing feature of the British coal industry during this period was its high degree of fragmentation and unevenness. At the level of individual mines, wide variations of employment were common. In part, those differences reflected variations in geological and market conditions, often reinforced by the uneven effects of the royalty system; also important were the struggles between miners and mineowners, struggles which developed unevenly both within and between regions and also at the level of different work groups. The diversity of work conditions, we have argued, initially posed a major obstacle to the formation of an integrated national union. Nevertheless, miners gradually united around the demands for a national wage structure and general improvements in health and safety provisions. Conversely, employers remained fragmented, unable and unwilling to adopt a permanent, national approach to wage determination and other employment conditions.

The achievement of the miners is all the more remarkable given the political backwardness of the union at the end of the nineteenth century as it was the last major union to sponsor Liberal as well as Labour Party MPs.[35] The 1912 strike and the struggles and successes of the war years helped to consolidate this unity. Furthermore, the demand for nationalisation united the miners since it was universally regarded as an essential precondition for a decent standard of wages and an improvement in working conditions. For some miners, the demand for public ownership represented much more than the means to reorganise their own industry. It was viewed as the first step towards the abolition of capitalism.

The social and economic conditions of the coal industry have to be located within the complexities of British society as it emerged from the First World War. On the political front the Liberal Party was in decline and, although support for the Labour Party was growing, it did not have sufficient parliamentary support to sustain a government in office. The British trade union movement, in terms of organisation and militancy, fell behind the developments within the MFGB.

Although the miners were fighting over basic issues such as wages, hours and safety, the implications of their struggles began to embrace more advanced political issues such as nationalisation. Whilst the miners could count on trade union sympathy over basic economic issues there was no guarantee of support for their political struggles.

The economic circumstances of the coal industry were influenced by the changing fortunes in export markets. Initially, these were extremely turbulent, though subject to substantial decline in the longer run, due to events such as the US coal strike of 1922 and the French occupation of the Ruhr in 1923, each of which temporarily boosted exports. This merely served to delay the day of reckoning for the industry. It has also been argued that the return to the gold standard in 1925 and the subsequent high value of sterling seriously damaged the industry's export prospects by increasing prices on the world market.

This view is associated with a Keynesian perspective. Although Keynes did focus on this aspect,[36] he was also aware of and opposed the material interests of the City which were served by the return to gold. His view was that those holding sterling would benefit from a redistribution of wealth in their favour. However, more generally, the City was concerned with restoring its role in short-run international capital movements. Its ability to do so rested on restricting its commitment to long-term finance to British industry. Consequently, even if the City had been capable of providing the finance and management to restructure the coal industry, its own interests dictated otherwise.[37]

Keynes opposed the return to gold by arguing that money wages would have to be forced down for 'unsheltered' export industries to remain competitive and foresaw the problems of industrial conflict that this would cause. The difficulties associated with the miners in particular loomed large. Contrary to Keynes and others, however, it is doubtful whether the export prospects of the British coal industry would have been greatly enhanced by wage-cuts. Other countries were adopting a variety of measures, including direct and indirect forms of protection, to guarantee their own domestic markets as well as a share in remaining export markets.[38] Reduction in money wages in Britain may well have been self-defeating, merely bringing forth further protective measures from abroad.[39]

Thus, the link between the return to gold and the need for wage-reductions to maintain export competitiveness is extremely tenuous. Consequently, the loss of exports and the necessity for industrial conflict over hours and wages cannot be explained by exchange rate policy. The intensifying struggle between capital and labour had an internal logic of its own which could at most be exacerbated and not caused by the return to gold.

The period after the war was one of political instability at home and abroad, and the coal industry provided a focus for class conflict. The MFGB struggled to overcome the diverse interests of its members and attempted to create a unified organisation. This objective was facilitated by the imposition of government controls during the war years. These involved subsidy payments to the industry which allowed cross-subsidies to take place between districts. Wage increases could thus be granted on a national basis without some districts being forced into bankruptcy. The miners pressed for an extension of these government controls which effectively amounted to a demand for nationalisation of the industry. The basis for the miners' support for public ownership ranged from regarding it as a means 'to get rid of the coalowners' which was an essential precondition for a decent standard of living and a significant improvement in working conditions, to a belief in the need for economic planning.[40] Not surprisingly, the mineowners were opposed to nationalisation of the industry and, given their need for individual autonomy with respect to wages and working conditions, they were also opposed to the existing government controls over the industry. Indeed they pressed for relaxing the controls on the industry at the earliest possible opportunity after the end of the First World War.

The various governments in the immediate post-war years appeared to equivocate between the contradictory demands of the miners and the mineowners. In retrospect, government policy can be largely explained by overall support for private ownership with attempts to appease the miners whenever expedient to do so. For example, when faced with a strike threat in 1919, the government appointed the Sankey

Commission to examine the miners' demands, which included a claim for a 30 per cent wage increase, a six hour day and public ownership of the industry. Although the Commission recommended nationalisation, the government refused to accept it. A similar series of events occurred in the 1920 'datum line' dispute over the basic wage level. Negotiations opened in May of that year and continued throughout the summer until the MFGB proposed strike action on 31 August. This prompted an offer of arbitration from the government, but this did not resolve the dispute. The miners went on strike on 16 October and, largely due to the supportive action by the railway workers, a compromise settlement (which included a productivity agreement) was reached.

In 1921 the government returned control of the industry to the owners five months earlier than originally planned. This relaxation of controls resulted in major conflict because the mineowners pressed for a reduction in wages and a return to wage negotiations and settlements at a district level. The industry spent the first three months in private hands after the war in a state of idleness with a lock-out imposed by the owners. Lloyd George persuaded the other members of the Triple Alliance (the railway and transport workers) to desert the miners and the conflict was resolved in the owners' favour.[41]

The conflict was in many ways a preview of what was to occur in the events leading up to and beyond the General Strike of 1926. By the spring of 1925, the owners pressed again for wage-reductions and also sought to abolish the minimum wage that had emerged out of earlier settlements. An increase in working hours was an additional objective. Again, under the threat of economy-wide industrial action, conflict was postponed,[42] by a nine-month subsidy to cover the period of enquiry of the Samuel Commission that had been hurriedly set up by the government. The Samuel Report was a wide-ranging indictment of the coal industry, calling for schemes of re-organisation but falling short of recommending nationalisation. Significantly, it conceded the need for wage-cuts in the short run whilst arguing against an increase of hours. Neither side of the industry found this acceptable and on 3 May the General Strike began.

On the ninth day the TUC called off the General Strike on the basis of a set of unofficial proposals which the MFGB rejected.[43]

This severely weakened the miners' cause, for once they had lost support from the trade union movement it was impossible to mobilise wider political support. Nevertheless, the miners continued with their own action until they were forced into unconditional surrender six months later. Wages were cut and hours lengthened. More significantly, the defeat shattered the strength of the miners' union and of unionism as a whole as mineowners and other employers undertook widespread victimisation against those who had actively participated in the strike.[44]

The consequences of the General Strike were considerable. Firstly, if the miners had been successful and had defeated the mineowners, nationalisation of the industry would undoubtedly have become the next issue. This would have been a unifying influence not only for the miners but for the labour movement as a whole. Secondly, the defeat of the miners had significance not just for its effect on the strength of the working class but also for its redistribution of power within the capitalist class. The basic division within capital was between the fraction which supported active intervention to reorganise the industry and those who viewed any intervention as undesirable in principle, a possible prelude to full scale public ownership. With the defeat of the miners the latter were able to continue to exploit the backward conditions of the industry – low pay and long hours.

The economic and political relations surrounding the coal industry made the General Strike almost inevitable. The constraints under which capital was organised within the industry ensured that the mineowners could not agree upon nor concede policies of reorganisation as proposed by the Labour Party and progressive sections of the Liberal Party. The defeat of the labour movement, unable to win the immediate struggle, also served to tie the hands of those progressive sections of the ruling class which sought rational reorganisation of the industry. The rationalisation movement, however, reappeared in the 1930s with the ideology of Mondism calling for co-operation between capital and labour to create large-scale and more efficient industries. But its chances of success had already been pre-empted and postponed by the events of the 1920s. State industrial policy in the 1930s was to prove to be a response to the failure of rationalisation rather than its implementation.

Reorganisation and State Intervention

After the miners' defeat in the General Strike the economic structure of the coal industry remained unchanged. In the period between 1926 and 1930, although government tried to encourage voluntary schemes of reorganisation it had little success. State intervention was pushed much further by the Coal Mines Act of 1930. In its first provision, the Act set about organising sales cartels at the level of the districts, allocating output-quotas which would then be distributed to the pits concerned. The motive was to restrict output and competition in order to maintain prices. The administration of the scheme proved extremely difficult because the forces of competition over markets for output were difficult to subdue. Districts proved slow in fixing minimum prices; there was dumping across districts from collapsed export to more stable domestic markets and discounts were offered in the form of higher quality coal and subsidised delivery.[45] By 1936 the scheme had been tightened as far as possible with the threat of government compulsion if the mineowners did not comply willingly.

The second part of the Act of 1930 created the Coal Mines Reorganisation Commission (CMRC), which had the duty of bringing about amalgamation within the industry. It was given powers of compulsion, subject to the judgement of the Court of the Railway and Canal Commission on whether the amalgamations would lower the cost of coal, be in the public interest and accord with the financial interest of those directly concerned. The CMRC, despite violent opposition from the mineowners, was determined to push ahead with schemes for amalgamation.[46] It considered voluntary action preferable but was prepared to use its powers of compulsion. In 1935, however, a test case was heard before the Court whose decision made it clear that the powers of compulsion held by the CMRC were essentially non-existent. The activities of the CMRC were practically suspended. All it could do was to work behind the scenes to press for greater legislative powers. There were not granted in any meaningful way and reorganisation had to wait upon the nationalisation of the industry in 1947.[47]

The dichotomy between these two provisions of the Act has been viewed as an inconsistency. Kirby, for example, has argued that the state-organised cartels, by shielding the industry from internal competitive forces, helped to preserve an outmoded economic structure.[48] His analysis presumes that cartels are in themselves an obstacle to reorganisation since they sustain profitability. But this fails to recognise that even if prices and output are fixed, increased profit can be pursued by cost reduction which may result from amalgamation. As was recognised throughout the period, and, with the advantages of hindsight, by the Reid Report, amalgamations would have allowed for productivity increase through concentrated effort of resources upon the layout, haulage and mechanisation of fewer mines. Although cartel arrangements existed, these did not preclude the possibility of amalgamation and so cannot be seen as an explanation for the failure of the industry to reorganise. On the contrary, cartelisation of markets is often the prelude to and the mechanism for amalgamation in production, as is illustrated by German industry. Furthermore, within the operation of the selling schemes there was potential for reorganisation since transfers of quotas were permitted.[49]

We would argue that the order of causation between the formation of cartels and the failure to amalgamate needs to be reversed. In our examination of relations between landowners and mineowners, the obstructive role played by the private ownership of royalties was revealed, and in particular how it impeded the processes of mechanisation and amalgamation.[50] The mineowners had to pursue crude methods of extracting profit, reducing wages, lengthening the working day and intensifying the work process. This may in part explain their individualism since the economic structure of the industry required it and amalgamations may have stripped them of their 'managerial' skills. There are, however, definite technical and social limits to these forms of exploitation, and the mineowners had to find other ways of maintaining or increasing their profitability. One such device was the formation of cartels since this is a means of increasing profit on the basis of a given level of output. Given the lack of amalgamation and reorganisation, the survival of the industry was contingent on the development of cartels. This argument is supported by the evidence that cartelisation was carried out prior to the 1930 Act which merely served to make the private schemes more effective.

The inevitable effect of the cartels was to increase the price of coal and this affected the industry in two ways. First, it allowed hundreds of small pits to remain at the margins of profitability. The second effect was on the larger colliery concerns – in the 1930s 100 firms produced three-quarters of the industry's output. These companies also had substantial interests in the iron and steel, coking coal and gas industries. Whilst they had diversified into industries where the profits could not so easily be appropriated by the royalty owners, they tended to be coal-related.[51] An increase in the price of coal was of double-edged value to these large colliery concerns. On the one hand it boosted profits from coal production but at the same time it increased the cost of ancillary industries as well as ensuring the survival of the small colliery companies. Clearly there were limits to the value of cartelisation to the large mineowners just as there were to the cruder forms of exploitation. They were merely transitory remedies to tide over the delay in nationalising the royalties in 1938 and the industry in 1946.

Conclusion

Our analysis gives considerable emphasis to the General Strike and its aftermath. The events of 1926 are seen as a major defeat for the British labour movement casting a lasting influence on industrial relations not only within the coal industry but also across the economy as a whole. This is illustrated by the lack of industrial action at a national level by the MFGB until 1935, and more generally by the fall in trade union membership by 50 per cent between 1920 and 1933. The miners' defeat also signalled the end of demands for significant change in the industry. With the concessions of wage cuts and longer hours of work gained by the mineowners they were able to continue exploiting the work force in the same manner as before, without introducing new techniques of production. This analysis runs contrary to the view put forward by Kilpatrick and Lawson,[52] previously analysed in the opening chapter, of the role of the trade unions in the development of the British economy. They argue that the establishment of trade unions prior to the introductin of mass-production techniques has led to the evolution of a decentralised workplace industrial relations system in Britain. In turn this has facilitated the growth of union resistance to changes in staffing levels and production techniques. Applying Kilpatrick and Lawson's thesis to the General Strike it would be argued that the defeat of trade unions would lead to the assertion of capitalist initiative and fundamental changes in production. This clearly did not happen in the coal industry. Moreover, given that the development of the MFGB conforms broadly to Kilpatrick and Lawson's theory of the emergence of trade unions, their analysis is further undermined by the lack of evidence of work-place trade union resistance to mechanisation.

In the relations between capitals, the result of the General Strike represented a substantial defeat for the progressive wing of the capitalist class, the fraction pressing for rationalisation which was later to give rise to the Mondism movement. The results for the coal industry have been discussed. Undoubtedly, the effects of the political weakening of the progressive fraction were not confined to the coal industry. This is of particular importance given the non-interventionist role played by British financial institutions, so that the impetus to rationalising capitalist production in Britain remained extremely weak. The defeat of the miners was to be felt far beyond the confines of their own industry.

Notes

[1] For a standard account of the British coal industry prior to the First World War, see A.J. Taylor, 'Labour Productivity and Technological Innovation in the British Coal Industry, 1850-1914', *Economic History Review*, 1961, Vol. 14 No. 1, pp.48-70 and 'The Coal Industry' in D.H. Aldcroft (ed.) *The Development of British Industry and Foreign Competition 1875-1914: Studies in Industrial Enterprise*, London 1968. For coverage of the period prior to the Second World War, see M.W. Kirby, *The British Coal Industry 1870-1946: A Political and Economic History*, London 1977 and N.K. Buxton, *The Economic Development of the British Coal Industry*, London 1978. See also the Reid Report, 1945, *Report of the Technical Advisory Committee on Coal Mining*, Cmnd.6610.

[2] Ultimately, just over £66 million was paid to nationalise the royalties compared to an original claim for £150 million. To put these figures into perspective, the compensation paid to the former mineowners, following the nationalisation of the industry in 1946, was just over £300 million, and this included payment for some ancillary equipment.

[3] See J. Nef, *The Rise of the British Coal Industry*, 2 Vols., London 1932.

[4] Indeed, for the pure royalty per ton contract, it might be argued that the fixed (future) price and variable conditions of sale contrast with the variable price and more or less known conditions of sale of commodities in general.

For a critique of the notion that a royalty must be considered as either a price or as a rent, see B. Fine, 'Royalties and the Inter-war Coal Industry', *Birkbeck Discussion Paper*, No.62.

[5] This is not to deny the existence of a number of large-scale enterprises at a very early stage. See Nef, op.cit.

[6] Scottish landowners were particularly noted for their involvement in the running of the mines on their estates. See J.T. Ward, 'Landowners and Mining' in J.T. Ward and R.G. Wilson (eds.), *Land and Industry: The Landed Estate and the Industrial Revolution*, Newton Abbot.

[7] See the Samuel Report, 1925, *Report of the Royal Commission on the Coal Industry*, Cmnd.2600.

[8] For a critique of this theory in this context and for the debate over the distinction between royalty and rent, see B. Fine, 1982, 'Landed Property and the Distinction Between Royalty and Rent', *Land Economics*, Vol.58, No.3, pp.338-50. See also the critique by B. Fine, 'Landed Property and the British Coal Industry Prior to World War I', *Birkbeck Discussion Paper*, No.120 of D. McCloskey, 'International Differences in Productivity: Coal and Steel in America and Britain before World War I' in D. McCloskey (ed.), *Essays on a Mature Economy, Britain after 1840*, London 1971, whose assessment of the British coal industry prior to the First World War is based on this theory in its modern version of measuring factor productivity by distributional shares.

[9] For a more detailed account of the Commission's findings, see Fine, 'Landed Property and the Distinction Between Royalty and Rent', loc. cit., pp.338-50.

[10] The Reid Report, op. cit.

[11] Scott had been responsible for the agreement over subsidence. See the Scott Report, 1919, *Ministry of Reconstruction. Third Report of the Acquisition and Valuation of Land for Public Purposes of Rights and Powers in Connection with Mines and Minerals*, Cmnd.361.

[12] Sankey Report, 1919, *Reports of the Royal Commission on the Coal Industry, with Minutes of Evidence and Appendices*, Cmnd.359-361.

[13] The Coal Association, pamphlet, 1920, *The Evidence on Nationalisation of Mineral and Royalties Critically Examined*, for example viewed the nationalisation of the royalties as the 'thin edge of the wedge'.

[14] See Fine, 'Royalties and the Interwar Coal Industry', loc. cit., for more details of the relationship across districts between geological conditions, royalties and mechanisation.

[15] There were also marked differences between the four Scottish districts.

[16] I. Brunskill, B. Fine and M. Prevezer, 'The Ownership of Coal Royalties in Scotland', *Scottish Social and Economic Review*, 1985.

[17] Details of the compensation paid upon nationalisation of the royalties by mine and by landowner have been collected. The data is available upon request from Ben Fine.

[18] See Taylor, 'The Coal Industry', loc. cit., for an earlier assessment of the cycle see R.H. Hooker, 'On the Relation Between Wages and the Numbers Employed in the Coal Mining Industry', *Journal of the Royal Statistical Society*, 1894, Vol.57, pp.627-42.

[19] See R.H. Porter, 'Wage Bargaining under Conciliation Agreements 1860-1914', *Economic History Review*, 1961, Vol.23 No.3, pp.460-75 and 'Wage

Determination by Selling Price Sliding Scales 1870-1913', *Manchester School of Economic and Social Studies*, 1971, Vol.39 No.1, pp.13-21.

[20] See A.J. Taylor, 'The Sub-Contract System in the British Coal Industry', in L.S. Pressnell (ed.), *Studies in the Industrial Revolution Presented to T.S. Ashton*, London 1960. R.E. Goffee, 'The Butty System and the Kent Coalfield', *Bulletin of the Society for the Study of Labour History*, 1977, No.34, pp.41-55 and 1981, 'Incorporation and Conflict: A Case Study of Subcontracting in the Coal Industry', *Sociological Review*, 1981, Vol.29 No.3, pp.435-97 explores the survival of the butty system in the Kent coalfield in the 1930s.

[21] This account of the different methods of mining in South Wales and the North East draws heavily on M.J. Daunton, 'Down the Pit: Work in the Great Northern and South Wales Coalfields, 1870-1914', *Economic History Review*, 1981, Vo.34 No.4, pp.578-97.

[22] The bord and pillar method permitted separate places of work with the roof supported by pillars of coal throughout the working area. Pillar and stall was similar except that the supporting pillars of coal were extracted earlier to minimise the extent of the working area supported. Under the hand got system longwall (advancing) involved an entire face moving forward with, extraction by work teams distributed along its length and the roof being allowed to collapse behind them.

[23] See F. Hodges, *Nationalisation of the Mines*, London 1920.

[24] See B.L. Coombes, *These Poor Hands: The Autobiography of a Miner Working in South Wales*, London 1939, p.61.

[25] For a detailed account of the development and use of the Davy Safety Lamp, see D. Albury and J. Schwartz, *Partial Progress: the Politics of Science and Technology*, London 1982.

[26] See J.E. Williams, 1972, 'The Miners' Lockout of 1893', *Bulletin of the Society for the Study of Labour History*, 1972, No.24, pp.13-6 (and also J.E. Williams, *The Derbyshire Miners: A Study in Industrial and Social History*, London 1962) and R.P. Arnot, *The Miners 1881-1910: A History of the Miners' Federation of Great Britain*, London 1949.

[27] It is a peculiarity of J.E. William's, 'Labour in the Coalfields: A Critical Bibliography', *Bulletin of the Society for the Study of Labour History*, 1962, No.4, pp.24-32 position that he criticises Arnot for writing the MFGB's history without taking explicit account of the coal industry's industrial structure. Yet he forms his own judgements whilst guilty of the same deficiency. In mild defence of Arnot, it might be argued that his focus on the evolution towards union solidarity at a national level is an implicit recognition of the problems of the industrial structure that unionism had to overcome. These considerations militate against the compromise in the debate proposed by B.J. McCormick, *Industrial Relations in the Coal Industry*, London 1979, who draws a false dichotomy between the 'short-run' gains of 1893 and the long-run losses of conciliation.

[28] See *Capital* Vol.I, Chapter X and for a presentation of this argument in the context of the transition from the *laissez-faire* to the monopoly stage of capitalism, see B. Fine and L. Harris, *Rereading 'Capital'*, London 1979, Chapter 7.

[29] This helps to explain the individualism of the mineowners who felt themselves best able to deal with varied work conditions and associated wage

systems without outside interference.

[30] See Daunton, 'Down the Pit', loc.cit.

[31] See the Report of the Royal Commission of 1909.

[32] See the Report of the Mines Department of 1929.

[33] See Safety Commission 1938, *Report of the Royal Commission on Safety in Coal Mines*, Cmnd.5890. It had a summary of recommendations running to 179 paragraphs.

[34] In the disaster 265 men and boys were killed.

[35] For an account of the union's conversion from Liberal to Labour politics, see R. Gregory, *The Miners and British Politics, 1906-14*, Oxford 1968. At the political as at the economic level, the union had to overcome a diversity of interests.

[36] J.M. Keynes, 'The Economic Consequences of Mr Churchill', *Collected Works*, Vol. IX, London 1972.

[37] Similar considerations continued to apply in the thirties after the collapse of the gold standard in 1931 and help to explain the weakness of the banks in promoting industrial restructuring. See M.W. Kirby, 'The Lancashire Cotton Industry in the Interwar Years: A Study in Organisational Change', *Business History*, July 1974, vol.16 No.2 for example, on the cotton industry. A further factor involved in this case is the banks' own conflict between preserving the value of existing assets and devoting additional finances to do so. This scarcely applies in the coal industry because of the low level of capital finance utilised in those enterprises under most serious threat.

[38] Germany, for example, had a guarantee of exports to the extent that war reparations were paid in coal.

[39] This point was made most clearly by A.L. Horner and G.A. Hutt, *Communism and Coal, Part 1: The Economic Situation of Coal Capitalism; Part 2: The Miners and Their Struggle*, London 1928, who observed that the wage cuts and longer hours imposed after the General Strike of 1926 did nothing to improve British exports of coal. They also saw very clearly that, as we shall argue, the political conditions did not exist for schemes of reorganisation to be adopted in Britain along the lines taken by Germany.

[40] K. Coates, *Democracy in the Mines*, Nottingham 1974.

[41] The support from the Triple Alliance fell away on 'Black Friday', 7 April 1921.

[42] The miners were solidly supported on 'Red Friday', 31 July 1925.

[43] The proposals had come from Samuel who returned from holidays in Italy specifically for the purpose of making them. Although the TUC called off the General Strike because of them, these proposals were explicitly unofficial and never gained the acceptance of miners, owners nor government. Once the General Strike was called off, Baldwin was in a position to stand firm and act as if Samuel had remained on holiday.

[44] This is also illustrated by the upsurge of 'Spencerism' or 'company unionism' which became particularly important in certain coalfields.

[45] For a description of the operation of the scheme, its problems and the methods used to deal with them, see the Reports by the Board of Trade of the working of the schemes.

[46] One symptom of this opposition was the frequent questioning of the CMRC's expenses in Parliament and of the salary of its Chairman in

particular. The latter was admittedly particularly high at £7,000 having jumped from £3,000 in his previous post as Permanent-under-Secretary for Mines. See I. Thomas, 'The Coal Mines Reorganisation Commission' in W.A. Robson (ed.), *Public Enterprise: Developments in Social Ownership and Control in Great Britain*, London 1937.

[47] The CMRC and its Chairman, Sir Ernest Gowers, appear to have been a force behind nationalisation of the royalties in 1938. But even here existing leases had to be honoured. At the same time the powers of compulsion for amalgamation were improved, but only slightly.

[48] M.W. Kirby, 1973, 'The Control of Competition in the British Coalmining Industry in the Thirties', *Economic History Review*, Vo.26 No.2, pp.273-84.

[49] In South Wales 7 per cent of quota was transferred in one period at a few pence per ton. Kirby takes for granted, and without explanation, the low level of transfers. This reflects a failure to question whether cartelisation is incompatible with cost reduction. Kirby also presents the most casual evidence to support the view that that state cartel dulled the amalgamation movement from 1930 to 1936 as opposed to the period before its operation from 1926 to 1930. We cannot analyse these deficiencies here in detail.

[50] It is a peculiarity of Kirby's article that he recognises this in his final substantive footnote, having earlier asserted the role played by the selling schemes without having introduced the royalties at all.

[51] A further inducement to vertical integration was the form of wage payments in which workers shared in profits. This created an incentive to transfer profits within a company to its related concerns through a low internal price. It was a source of considerable discontent amongst the miners.

[52] A Kirkpatrick and T. Lawson, 'On the Nature of Industrial Decline in the UK', *Cambridge Journal of Economics*, 1980, No.4, pp.85-102.

IV Conclusion

Chapter 12

Past, Present and Future: The Alternative Economic Strategy

We have written this book in a period when the British economy has experienced a crisis and dislocation whose severity gives it the character of a historic landmark. Although the media, taking their cue from government and from stockbrokers' newsletters, use the language of 'recession', 'slow-down' and 'up-turn', giving it the appearance of normality, there can be no doubt that its reality has been that of a crisis. It has, in other words, been one of those exceptional periods such as the late 1920s and early 1930s, or the years after 1870, when the economy has been severely dislocated and, at the same time, restructured. It has been as if problems fermenting in the economy as it matures reach a point where they can no longer be contained, and the resulting detonation scatters the component parts of the economy for some to fall into place again in a new arrangement.

Britain's crisis has been part of an international one. Since the early days of capitalism the highly integrated character of international trade and production has meant that major economic crises are world-wide. All advanced capitalist countries have been drawn into the crisis of the 1980s, as have the Third World countries where capitalism faces different conditions; the socialist countries, too, have felt its impact and had to respond. Because, however, the history, social structure and political direction of each country is unique, the specific character of the crisis differs from one country to another, so Britain's economic dislocation cannot be reduced to a simple fragment of the international crisis. The difference between the British crisis and the crisis in France, the USA or West

323

Germany has made it necessary to analyse its specifically British origins, especially the peculiarly British character of the state, finance and the labour movement, but the exercise is not purely historical. The need to carry out this study arises from the search for a way forward.

The Alternative Economic Strategy

The economic crisis itself, and the social and political changes associated with it, have made it more possible to pose and work for quite distinct economic strategies; it has forced on to the agenda the question of the policies that can be adopted and the economic strategies that can be pursued by political means. In the dislocation which followed the Second World War there were conflicting options about the character of the economic order to be constructed; choices had to be made and struggles pursued. From the late 1940s to the late 1970s, by contrast, political differences largely revolved around the fine tuning of the economy rather than fundamentally different strategies. Certainly there was concern over fundamental issues (centring particularly on the character of labour relations and the quality of management) and certainly the level of consensus over economic strategy evaporated from the start of the 1970s, but until the recent dislocation it has been a very broad consensus within the limited boundaries of Keynesian policy-making. Indeed, it has been so general that there has appeared to be no economic *strategy* as such, only economic *policies*. But the break up of the post war boom in the 1970s has made reappraisal un-avoidable and created the possibility of conflicts over the way out of the crisis.

Reappraisal began with the boom's first falterings in the mid 1970s. The state dropped the full employment and demand management ideology of Keynesianism (if not its concrete policies) while the labour movement began to formulate a coherent framework for interventionism, conceived as an Alternative Economic Strategy.[1] But the development of new strategies has been uneven. The space left in liberal and right wing policy debates by the decline of Keynesianism was pre-empted by monetarist ideologies which had the great advantage that they were espoused (if not fully implemented) by a Conservative government that came to power on the promise of 'a new way out of the mess'. From this vantage point the radical right strategy has hegemonised policy issues, forcing all other programmes, whether orthodox or socialist, to take it as the starting point. Keynesianism has become a poorly articulated argument for whatever policies were tried and failed in the post-war decades (including incomes policies and a limited expansion of state spending – limited formally by acceptance of the requirement to restrict the money supply). The socialist Alternative Economic Strategy (AES) has, at one level, fared better because in various forms it has been adopted by the Trades Union Congress, the Labour Party and other organisations and so appears to have a real prospect of being implemented when electoral power shifts. But this strength is illusory and does not reflect a real challenge to monetarism, for, despite its formal adoption in block voting, the AES is not deeply rooted in the labour movement's thinking and its logic lies uneasily with many of the ideas current in left-wing movements. In this state of affairs there can be little doubt that, whatever the strategy's formal standing, when the next Labour government is elected it would be difficult for the AES to weather the attacks on it from the right outside and inside the Labour Party. In practice, the likely outcome would be the combination of Keynesian and monetarist policies that Mitterrand delivered to the French electorate which voted for him in the expectation of a socialist programme.

This book's analysis of the origins of the present crisis or, at least, the principal factors underlying its specifically British features, help to put the Alternative Economic Strategy in context and to provide some of the foundations for regarding the AES as the realistic socialist programme for reconstructing Britain's economy and generating a popular economic growth. Understanding the AES's relation to the causes of Britain's crisis is an important basis for developing the strategy (for no strategy can work if it is inflexible and not capable of developing and generating a debate within its own terms) and for rooting it in the real life of the labour movement. It is to be hoped that this will make it easier for Britain to avoid the path France has followed under Mitterrand or, indeed, to avoid the crushing of left wing policies that Labour governments achieved after 1964 and 1974.

The pursuit of the AES, itself, relates directly to one of the historical elements we have identified in previous chapters, the 'weakness' or partial development of the British labour movement. As we have argued, Britain's economic problems can, in some measure, be related to the trade unions' lack of strength on major issues. In many industries they have too readily ceded their potential for influencing production and accumulation by accepting redundancies (with or without productivity deals) and, at the national level, they have failed to develop the political power to influence the direction of the economy. Even in areas where the popular image of British trade unions ascribes great strength to them, wage militancy, we have seen there are grounds for thinking that they have been weak, that if they had been stronger in pressing their claims British capital could have been pushed into developing along high productivity-high wage lines. The Alternative Economic Strategy engages with each of these problems. It is directly concerned with influencing production and accumulation (through planning and public ownership) and its exclusion of incomes policies in a capitalist economy addresses the conditions under which wage bargaining takes place. The involvement of the labour movement in actively appraising, contributing to and working for the AES framework gives it the initiative in strengthening its influence over the economy's direction.

While the pursuit of the AES is an aspect of the labour movement taking a more central role in the economy and overcoming its historical weaknesses in those respects, its content directly addresses the peculiarities we have identified in the roles of the British state, finance and industry – particularly MNCs. This strategy emphasises the role the state would play in planning the direction of new investment and the conditions under which industry and other sectors grow and operate. To achieve this it envisages taking major enterprises into public ownership and otherwise enforcing planning agreements. It also requires significant control over firms' freedom in the spheres of money and trade, for, although these are distinct from production and accumulation, they directly affect them. Thus, controls over foreign investment, over imports and over the foreign exchange markets, are seen as crucial levers to influence the conditions under which factories and enterpsies in Britain operate, as well as being important because movements in the exchange rate have, in several countries (and in Britain) destabilised socialist governments. Such controls would have a strong effect on the City of London, and would shift the role of finance in the economy, but the AES also emphasises the importance of taking the major banks and financial institutions into public ownership. State ownership and resulting changes in operating practices are seen as means of overcoming the problems created by the financial system in Britain's modern economic history and these have been identified in earlier chapters as essentially a blocking role rather than a starving of industry of funds.

The Role of the State

At the heart of the Alternative Economic Strategy, then, is a greatly increased role for the state and a direct involvement in production and the conditions under which investment and growth occur. But the AES conflicts implicitly or explicitly, with arguments and ideas that are widespread and current in socialist circles in Britain, so that to argue for it is to argue against left-wing as well as right-wing criticisms.

The most fundamental point at issue is the role to be ascribed to the state for one strong tendency on the left in the 1980s argues that a strong and interventionist central state is inimical to the construction of democratic socialism. On this view, the new economic and social relations which have to be built to move Britain forward must be 'decentralised', 'local', 'autonomous', or 'small scale' for, although vague, such characteristics are thought to be essential for democratic and co-operative methods of working. This argument has many sources. In part it stems from the history of the welfare state and state industries in Britain, for the right wing's struggle to make the state sector operate according to the same principles as private capital where possible (in the nationalised industries) and to restrict and contain it elsewhere (in welfare and social services) has made the public sector in general neither socialist nor even efficient for capitalism. Its failure to 'deliver the goods' that socialists used to expect from it, combined with undemocratic, bureaucratised ways of working has meant that many on the left see state intervention as more of an obstacle to socialism than a help. Many, nevertheless, have argued for local state intervention, apparently on the rather arbitrary grounds that because it is local it is closer to the people and, hence,more democratic. (More concretely, the argument stems from the fact that, as has been demonstrated by the GLC, Liverpool and other local authorities in the 1980s, the left wing of the Labour Party has found it easier to gain power locally than nationally.)

In this way, these local authorities, and particularly the GLC under Livingstone, have been seen as a symbol of a path to socialism which is an alternative to taking and exercising central state power. Such symbols are offered with very little in the way of supporting analysis. In the case of the GLC's own industrial strategy, in practice the relation between the local and central state has been crucial. This is not simply the right-wing authoritarianism of the Thatcher régime stifling the democratic initiatives of the locality and, in the extreme, trying to abolish the GLC. Rather the London Industrial Strategy (LIS) relies heavily upon central state action to make it possible. For otherwise, there is no basis on which local planning can deal with the run-down of Ford at Dagenham, nor the conditions of homeworkers in the London clothing industry, nor the introduction of Combined Heat and Power/District Heating Schemes, nor preserve and enrich the jobs (heavily concentrated in London) in the (inter)national telecommunications industry as it is confronted by new technology. In a wide range of industrial interventions the Greater London Council's strategy would only be feasible with central support, for the problems of local industry are part of a national and international restructuring.

The problem rarely confronted by the new socialism of 'power to the locality', is the failure to deal with co-ordination at a national level, not merely as a source of administrative efficiency, but as a means of fundamentally challenging the power of capital. With respect to multinationals, for example, the GLC's London Industrial Strategy has been more concerned to organise in a purely defensive support of workers (most notably for Ford and Kodak) and has been incapable of supporting them by offering alternative production scenarios that are realistic or even approachable in terms of its own powers. Moreover, the instrument set up by the GLC to pursue its industrial policies through direct intervention, the Greater

London Enterprise Board (GLEB), bears more than a passing resemblance (not in name alone) to the now defunct National Enterprise Board. In the absence of external political pressure and control, the GLEB – as the NEB previously – will be pressed into the increasing acceptance of commercial criteria and diverted from the pursuit of social objectives, even if it manages to survive.

More disturbing is the opportunism of the right of the labour movement in themselves elevating the significance of new forms of social ownership by which they mean various forms of co-operatives. This is particularly associated with Roy Hattersley (the deputy leader of the Labour Party) whose proposals, in any case, fall far short of and differ from those of the GLC and other local authorities. But the token favour he bestows upon such new forms of social ownership is a political manoeuvre, a sweetener to make the left accept the much sharper picture its darker side presents – a return to contrived reliance upon wage controls and mild reflation and an ill-concealed hostility to state ownership.

But a strongly promoted argument from the left has also been made in support of 'decentralised', 'local' initiatives as an alternative to state ownership, control and national planning. It follows from the assessment that the British people have moved rightward in a fundamental and permanent way and that there is great popular antipathy to the state. The concept of 'Thatcherism' as a fundamental shift in political forces argues that the ideology of 'freedom from state bureaucracy' promoted by the Tories under Margaret Thatcher accords with and has helped to articulate and even create a real movement in popular thought, and that the election results of 1979 and 1983 demonstrate that, in line with this, people reject a strong economic role for the state. It has even been argued that the 1983 election produced a majority vote rejecting the Alternative Economic Strategy, although in fact the Tories were far from having a popular majority. It is illegitimate to interpret general election results as delivering a verdict on a single issue, and the truth of the matter is that the AES did not figure prominently in the election debates. Certainly there has been a growing dissatisfaction with nationalised industries and welfare services, but it is a dissatisfaction with the failure of the state to deliver the benefits those sectors could provide. Rather than being opposed to state provision as such, there is resentment against hospitals that have long waiting lists, schools that have large classes and poor results, and trains that are erratic. Those are failures which, in Britain's post-war history, resulted from large business's political pressure, aided by the operation of the financial markets, ensuring that investment and development in nationalised industries and the welfare state were limited and distorted. Thus, the election of Thatcher, far from demonstrating a fundamental rejection of an economically powerful state, shows an antipathy toward a state that has been economically constrained, misdirected and pushed into impotence, and it suggests that there is a powerful case to be made for a state that breaks with that past and takes a leading role in the economy.

The critiques of the state's role and character in post-war Britain on the grounds that it has been too capitalistic and repressive should not lead to an automatic rejection of a strong role for the central state in building a socialist economic strategy. Such a rejection involves assuming that because it was so, it would always be so, and that argument can only be sustained by adopting a very ahistorical approach and assuming that the features of the welfare state and state economic policy in post-war Britain represent essential features of the capitalist state which are inescapable whatever the party in power and whatever the state of class conflict. It involves building a very pessimistic view of some essence of the capitalist state on the (rather more flexible but nevertheless pessimistic) functionalism of Marxist writings on the state that followed Poulantzas and Miliband.[2] The alternative is to relate the theory of the state to the specific historical circumstances of post-war Britain and examine the manner in which the balance of forces between the classes determined the form of the state's operations. In fact, the outcome largely resulted from the labour movement's failure to move beyond its post-war gains to press for socialist principles in the operation of the nationalised industries or welfare state or even to defend its gains against right-wing attacks. Thus, the experience of the last forty years does not indicate that the state is intrinsically and inevitably an obstacle to socialist economic strategies (even if we ignore the very real material gains the welfare state has brought) but, instead, that if the central machinery of the state is to implement an Alternative Economic Strategy it has to be a continuing object of politics for the labour movement and other socialist forces.

In our view, the issue is whether it is possible to develop an economic strategy to move forward from the crisis without an extensive economic role for the central state. In the day-to-day operation of the British economy market forces have a strong and pervasive impact. Through market operations, finance and capital are moved around and competition in the market, or manipulation of markets, are the channels through which the most productive enterprises obtain their profit and the less productive are eliminated. The growth of multinational corporations internalises some transactions that would otherwise pass between enterprises through the market, but these corporations have also generated new and greatly enlarged markets in goods, money, finance and labour.

One implication of the dominance of market forces is that 'decentralised', 'local' initiatives are generally unable to sustain any different method of operating from those of existing firms. Left-wing strategies in the 1980s have given prominence to the establishment of co-operatives, sometimes *faute de mieux* but frequently as a socialist alternative to state ownership. The latter strategy has been promulgated, too, by Roy Hattersley in attempting to re-define 'public ownership' away from its old emphasis on nationalisation. Unlike Roy Hattersley, however, the left has no excuse for turning a blind eye to the power of capital in forcing its way through the operation of market forces. For co-operatives and similar ventures have to compete for sales and finance in the market and, since they can only survive if they match other firms' efficiency, they are pushed toward capitalist methods of management and operation. Similarly, if non-union plants are important in an industry, firms which honour union agreements on wages and conditions are at a competitive disadvantage and attempts by local authorities, for example, to require union recognition or union participation in management face insuperable difficulties. Because of this, the success on a large scale of co-operatives and other types of enterprises observing socialist principles requires a strong central state, able to interrupt or replace market forces in some areas or, in other words, to create a space by using taxes and subsidies, the allocation of finance, and controls over markets to protect a sector from such competitive forces. For example, if the ending of sweatshops and underpaid homework were to be a serious objective in the clothing industry, and workers' involvement in running such industry were to be achieved, the industry would require protection from foreign competition and only the central machinery of the state could give that through import controls, tariffs or subsidies. Local authorities may provide some assistance in the form of subsidies but without an overall state policy such efforts are necessarily limited.

Apart from the need for the state to create a space within market forces for new types of enterprises, the British economy, whether capitalist or socialist (a point to which we return later), requires the state to take a strategic planning role in order to achieve an integrated, sustainable growth consistent with high employment and living standards as well as modernisation of production methods. In earlier chapters we have examined how the absence of such planning (partly blocked by the City, partly neglected by the labour movement) has been important in the development of the economic crisis.

Industry and commerce have, over a long period since the Second World War, failed to modernise methods of production and build an integrated, balanced economic base. Their response to competitive pressure has been to attempt to maintain profits by keeping real wages low by international standards and the state's response was to encourage that strategy. In the face of international economic crisis and the changing international division of labour, such a policy could no longer offer any defence and the outcome has been more severe dislocation and unemployment in Britain than elsewhere. These characteristics developed in a régime under which market forces were increasingly dominant as wartime controls over capital, foreign exchange, foreign trade, and eventually, over portfolio investment abroad were abolished. It is significant, however, that the rule of market forces meant the increasing domination of multinational corporations and financial institutions operating in the market environment. And the state's encouragement of market forces covered a wide front including the establishment of criteria for nationalised industries which make them simulate private firms in their relation to the market.

That way of organising the economy has proved worse than failure. The initiative seized by Margaret Thatcher's administration in putting forward a 'solution' after 1979 turns on the claim that the way out of the crisis is to strengthen the operation of market forces and the competition they bring. The problem, seen from that viewpoint, is that the state (and trade unions) have blocked and prevented the operation of market forces (although the strength with which the Tory government has proclaimed its determination to roll back the state is not matched by its actions). From our perspective the problem has been that, as the earlier chapters have illustrated, the state has not taken the initiative in directing the economy but has, instead, allowed market forces and the multinationals that operate freely within them, to dominate. The state has had a presence in those markets and has used taxes, subsidies and financial policies to influence their outcome but it has done so in piecemeal, non-strategic ways in all respects (except for a consistent policy of influencing distribution to sustain post-tax profits) and has accepted and promoted the outcome of market forces.

The Alternative Economic Strategy, therefore, is a strategy of breaking that pattern. It is a substantial shift away from domination by market forces and by the enterprises (multinational corporations and financial institutions) that acquire great power in that context. Such a shift can only be undertaken by a state with a powerful central machinery. It requires intervention in and controls over the operation of the markets that have a crucial concentrated role in the economy (such as foreign exchange markets and credit markets) and it requires state ownership of major sectors to enable them to operate according to the principles of that interventionist, planned system. This strategy can only break effectively with the past if it operates according to a plan. And, as we have seen, state ownership and intervention are not automatically socialist but may reinforce capitalist principles of operation. For both these reasons, the Alternative Economic Strategy can only be considered socialist if the state machinery it requires is under socialist control and socialist pressure (which was absent or defeated in the context of the Attlee government's economic strategy).

The AES and Socialism

Implicit or explicit objections to the role the Alternative Economic Strategy would give to the state are the main obstacle to the development of strong and deeply rooted socialist pressure for such a real break from the present economic problems and their origins. Although these objections are rooted in Britain's circumstances and experience we think that, for the reasons we have outlined they are misplaced. Nevertheless, several other criticisms related to that overriding misconception of the AES's role, have also had some currency among socialists. Each in its own way argues that it is not a *socialist* strategy, either because it is merely a modified Keynesian strategy seeking to restore the type of policies used to manage capitalism in the long post-war boom, or because it is an abrogation of international solidarity or because it directly supports the interests of one section of capital, small or medium-sized national firms. Most strong is the criticism that the AES is not truly socialist because it does nothing for the economic and social position of women. Let us look at each of these in turn, leaving the last mentioned criticism to the end because of its breadth and signifcance.

First, critics have argued that the AES does not envisage a real break with the past as it simply envisages a form of Keynesianism (albeit rather hotted up). On this view the AES is essentially a strategy for expanding demand for goods and services in order to achieve growth of output and employment. This interpretation sees the AES proposal to expand state spending as its central feature and considers that the policies for controlling imports, foreign exchange, credit and capital markets are introduced only in order to back up that policy. Import controls, in particular, are interpreted as being wholly negative and as having entered the AES in order to ensure that one of the problems associated with earlier Keynesianism, high growth of imports when aggregate demand is expanded, does not occur. If this were the main content and purpose of the AES it would be rightly criticised, for it would fail to address Britain's underlying problem of the distorted and inadequate organisation of production induced by the economy's structural peculiarities. But as we have indicated, the focus of the AES is different. Its role is to take control of economic development by giving the state a role which interrupts, moderates and in part replaces the free operation of market forces. With controls over market forces in crucial areas and with state ownership of major enterprises the AES is intended to enable the development of investment, production and change according to a planned strategy.

That interpretation of the AES as a Keynesian programme is associated with a further criticism from the left. Seeing import controls as an attempt to reduce imports in order to protect the balance of payments while the economy is reflated, several writers have argued that they are designed, in effect, to export unemployment. Thus,they are seen as a product of nationalism and an attempt to increase jobs in Britain at the expense of workers in Japan, Hong Kong, South Korea, Italy and the other countries from which Britain imports. Again, this is to misunderstand the role of such controls in the AES, for they are envisaged there as one element in a set of policies to control market forces and increase the role of planning. Thus, instead of being designed purely to reduce imports they are intended to be a basis for planning foreign trade so that its direction, volume and growth are in accordance with the planned direction of economic growth as a whole. Moreover, an objection to import controls and planned trade on the grounds that they affect workers abroad should, logically,lead to a renunciation of any policies which affect trade, including traditional policies of attempting to set the exchange rate, for the exchange rate is one of the most powerful influences on foreign trade. But that would imply that it is better to allow trade and the jobs associated with it to be determined by the foreign exchange market and the banks and speculators that inhabit its demand and supply curves rather than have trade under the influence of an elected government.

Finally, socialist attitudes to the Alternative Economic Strategy have to contend with the problem of whether it is designed to manage capitalism better or to create a socialist alternative. Critics, for example, see import controls, envisaged as negative and protectionist, as a policy demanded by some business interests (medium and small national firms) to protect their market and profits. The problem is that most policies and strategies when outlined in general terms, even the general idea of planning itself, can have either a socialist or non-socialist direction. For example, the extensive intervention and planning that the state has practised in countries such as Japan and South Korea, have a strong anti-socialist direction and were designed and operated to foster capitalist development; the long-standing state ownership of major industrial firms and banks in France has, similarly, been an element in a capitalist 'economic miracle'. The specific content and direction of a programme can only be considered in the context of the political situation within which it is being implemented. The socialist aims of the Alternative Economic Strategy can only be envisaged in relation to the political strength of left wing parties, the labour movement and other socialist forces in Britain.

Socialist-Feminist Perspectives

Among these other forces are socialist feminists within the women's movement, but several have argued that the Alternative Economic Strategy is fundamentally flawed because it does not strengthen the social and economic position of women. In its strong form this view would imply that the women's liberation movement should have nothing to do with this strategy because its content is fundamentally opposed to women's interests and needs, whereas our interpretation is that the AES is a broad and far from rigid strategy whose progressive character depends on socialist feminists and other socialist forces engaging with it and promoting it. What is the basis of the view that the AES is fundamentally flawed regarding socialist women's interests?

One problem is that most of the Alternative Economic Strategy is framed in gender neutral terms, thus it implicitly condones rather than combats the oppression of women since their position in society is far from neutral. Some of the specific policies within the AES are relatively advantageous to women, for example minimum wage policies and the expansion of welfare services. But it is the strategic focus of the AES that is more at stake; instead of attempting the impossible aim of gender neutrality it should explicitly recognise the special position of women and confront the specific forms of economic oppression experienced by women in Britain (which themselves relate to the special character of the British economy). It should address the conditions under which women are employed in 'traditional' service industries (such as catering), in 'advanced technology' service posts (such as computer operators) and in certain manufacturing sectors. In all of these, women's employment has been relatively expanding in the 1970s under conditions which involve different problems from those faced in, say, the 1940s and 50s, by the expansion of employment for male engineers. And it should address the conditions under which women relate to the state through welfare services such as health and child care, social security provisions such as supplementary benefit and the tax system, for, again, women's position is different from men's.

There can be no doubt that the Alternative Economic Strategy must address these issues directly and explicitly. Its detailed policies must include equal pay for jobs of comparable worth, controls over the organisation of homework and its rates of pay, the same rights for part-time as for full-time workers, full maternity rights and more. Such policies for workers who are women will benefit the labour movement as a whole. Similarly, broad policies which improve women's position in the welfare state bring wider benefits. Thus, in one sense, it is misleading to conceive of them as 'women's demands'.

Nevertheless, some socialist feminists are unwilling to support the AES because they see it as comprising men's demands, and it is believed that the AES is a strategy whose pursuit and implementation is male dominated. Unions are to have a central role under the Alternative Economic Strategy; according to this argument they are bastions of male power that serve the interests of male union members in opposition to those of women. A major example, it is sometimes argued, is that supporters of the AES have opposed incomes policies (wage controls) whereas some socialist feminists argue that incomes policies have helped raise women's relative pay. Thus, opposition to incomes policies is seen as a self-interested action by male trade unionists. In fact, there is no evidence that women's pay has benefited in periods of wage controls, rather the evidence favours the opposite conclusion if any. And, of course, the idea that unions are incapable of mobilising on issues which, whatever their wider benefits, are of central concern to women has to contend with the TUC-sponsored march for abortion rights, the unions' (unsuccessful) demands for improvements in the 'social wage' in the mid-1970s, the highly political mobilisation in support of women trade unionists at Grunwick and similar actions.

Feminist criticisms of the Alternative Economic Strategy relate to the others. Interpreting it as essentially Keynesian, some feminists consider that it is aimed only at job creation and that the jobs it is aimed at are male full-time jobs like those supposedly created in the post-war boom. And they reject the role it foresees for the central state, seeing it as both possible and desirable to rely on local, autonomous initiatives. We consider both those lines of argument misplaced for the reasons we have outlined.

The Alternative Economic Strategy is a broad programme. The manner in which it becomes a detailed reality depends on the commitment it gets from socialists and their commitment to shaping it in design and practice. There is an urgent need for more socialist feminists to work in and with parties and trade unions toward that end. Similarly, there is a pressing need for an extended commitment by black people and others to ensure that the socialist direction taken by the AES does remedy their special isolation and oppression within the economy. There can be no doubt that the particular group of workers suffering most severely from Britain's economic crisis and its aftermath has been black workers and especially young black workers (or unemployed potential workers). If the AES is to win such support and commitment to shaping it, it has to be seen that in the absence of such a strategy the peculiarities of the British economy have generated the current mess. This book has tried to show that.

The Way Forward

The fact that we are discussing the Alternative Economic Strategy in the context of a book which analyses the historic roots of Britain's problem as a capitalist economy is an illustration of the need for care in determining the political direction of the AES. Critics can point to the fact that we have argued that Britain's peculiarities have weakened industrial capital operating in Britain and worsened the impact of the international crisis on it, and that we consider the AES to be a strategy for overcoming those peculiarities and problems and may judge that our strategy is therefore conceived only as a plan to manage capitalism better. Such a judgement, however, would be wrong. We root the arguments for the AES in our analysis of previous problems because no socialist strategy can fail to take account of the circumstances it inherits or fail to address existing problems. The socialist direction of the AES will depend upon socialist political strength rather than a design which treats the economic history of Britain as a blank sheet.

Notes

[1] See London CSE Group, 'The Alternative Economic Strategy and the British Labour Movement', *Capital and Class*, No. 8, and, by a group with the same name but with different members, *The Alternative Economic Strategy: A Response by the labour Movement to the Economic Crisis*, London 1980.

[2] N. Poulantzas, 'The Problem of the Capitalist State', *New Left Review*, No. 58; R. Miliband, *The State and Capitalist Society*, London 1969. B. Jessop, *The Capitalist State*, Oxford 1982, gives an excellent summary of subsequent developments in the theory of the capitalist state.

Index

Africa, 114
Alternative Economic Strategy, 48, 120, 323-39; and socialist-feminism, 336-8; and black people, 338
American Motors, 259
Anderson, P., 62-6, 71, 75
Arnot, R.P., 302
Atomic Energy Authority, 203, 221-3, 228-9, 231
Atomic Energy (McMahon) Act, 218
'Atoms for Peace', 218
Attlee government, 30, 333

Babcock International, 206-7
Bank amalgamation movement, 124-7
Bank of England, 39, 42, 56-62, 69-71, 77, 138
'Bank Rate', 61
Banks, 122-42
Barclays Bank, 124, 135
Belgium, 25-6, 212, 266, 285
Benn, Tony, 230
Bernal, J.D., 251
BICC, 283-4
'Big Five' banks, 126
'Big Four' banks, 134-5
Bina, C., 81, 85
Blackett, P.M.S., 251
Blair, J., 81, 88
BMW, 258
Bradley, P.G., 114
Brazil, 16, 26, 220, 260-1, 267
Bretton Woods system, 57
British Aerospace, 161, 247-8, 250
British Airways, 161

British Broadcasting Corporation, 151
British Gas Corporation, 161-2
British Leyland, 18, 158-9, 259, 265, 268-73
British Motor Holdings, 269
British National Oil Corporation, 160-1
British Petroleum, 84, 161
British Rail, 151, 154, 162, 164
British Shipbuilders, 248
British Steel Corporation, 151, 159-60, 257
British Technology Group, 158
British Telecommunications, 162, 278
British Telecommunications industry, 20
Bupp, I.C., 211
Burn, D., 228
Burrows, J.C., 85
'Butty' system, 299

Callaghan, James, 16, 57, 71
Cambridge Economic Policy Group, 33
Canada, 90, 92, 96, 107, 118, 213-4, 218-9, 260
Caribbean, 90
Car industry, 257-73; and new technology, 261-4
Carr, Robert, 185
Cartelisation, 82, 84, 86-7, 171, 195, 250, 312-3
Central Electricity Generating Board, 185, 193, 203, 215, 221-31
China, 284

Chrysler, 118, 265, 272
Churchill, Winston, 170
Citröen, 265
City of London, 11-12, 14, 28, 38-47, 55-79, 122-3, 125, 134, 137-9, 250, 269, 308, 327, 332
Clegg, H.A., 175
Coakley, Jerry, 136
Coal Commission, 287
Coal industry, 167-97, 285-315
Coal Mines Act (1930), 312-3
Coal Mines Reorganisation Committee, 171, 312
Commission of the European Communities, 93, 192
Confederation of British Industry, 78
Cotton textile industry: America, 21; Lancashire, 21
Cruise missiles, 244
Curhan, J.P., 116

Dalton, Hugh, 61
Daly, Lawrence, 184
Datsun, 258
Daunton, M.J., 299
Defence Industries Council, 249
De Gaulle, Charles, 229
De-industrialisation, 21-7, 38, 43, 324
Demand management, 15-6, 29
Demarcation, 32
Devaluation, 59, 67
Domenrich, T.A., 85
Dreadnought, 216
Dunning, J., 24, 90, 102, 109

'Eclectic theory', 102, 105
Edwardes, Michael, 271
Eisenhower, D.L., 218
Electricity Council, 161
Electronics, 275-84
English Revolution, 63
Eurodif, 219-20
Eurodollars, 65, 67-8, 139
European Economic Community, 10, 28
Exchange controls, 59, 67
Exxon, 84

Ferranti, 18, 248, 278
Fiat, 262-3
Fleck Report, 174
Fleet Strret, 30
Foot, Robert, 171
Ford, 258, 261, 263, 265-6, 269, 328
Ford, Henry, 261-2
France, 22-5, 29, 43, 45, 89, 92, 116, 119, 122, 135, 141, 238, 275, 285, 323, 325; and nuclear power, 205, 211-2, 214, 218, 220-1, 229-30; car industry, 265-6, 268
Freeman, Chris, 238
Friedman, Milton and Rose, 13
Fujitron, 278

Gadaffi, Colonel, 87
GEC, 18, 23-5, 206-7, 209-10, 212-3, 215-7, 247-8
GEC-Marconi, 247
General Motors, 259, 261-4, 267
General Strike, 1926, 34, 307-12, 314-5
Germany, West, 13, 16, 22-3, 25, 27-8, 41, 43, 45, 89-90, 92, 95-97, 99, 101, 113, 119-20, 122, 129, 131, 135, 141, 237-9, 242, 275, 285, 296, 313, 323; and nuclear power, 205, 211-2, 220, 228-30; car industry, 260, 266-8
Glyn, A., 32
Gold-standard, 55, 64, 308
Gormley, Joe, 188
Greater London Council, 328-9
Greater London Enterprise Board, 329
Griffin, Tony, 35
Grunwick, 338
Gulf Oil, 84

Haldane, J.B.S., 251
Harrison, J., 32
Harvard Multinational Enterprise Project, 93
Hattersley, Roy, 329
Hawkers, 250
Hawkins, R.B., 113
Healey, Denis, 16, 57
Heath, Edward, 15

Henderson, D., 228
Herbert Committee on the Electricity Industry, 154
Heseltine, Michael, 249
Hinton, J., 222
Hirsch, F., 67
Hodges, M., 118
Hoffman-La Roche, 118
Hogben, L., 251
Holland, Stuart, 119
Honda, 259
Hong Kong, 335
Hoverlloyd, 162

IBM, 277-8, 280-81
ICL, 277-8, 281
India, 26, 43, 219
Industrial Relations Act (1971), 185
Industrial Relations Court, 185
Industrial Reorganisation Corporation, 18, 269
Information Technology, 275-84
Information Technology Year, 20
Ingham, G., 41, 63, 65, 68, 72
INMOS, 279-80
International Competitiveness in Electronics, 280-1
International credit system, 45
International Electrical Association, 215
International Monetary Fund, 10, 28, 71
Iran, 87
Italy, 16, 22-3, 25, 29, 119, 141, 205, 212, 265-6, 335
Japan, 13, 16, 23, 25, 27-8, 32, 43, 45, 61, 90-92, 95-7, 99, 101, 119-20, 122, 131, 135, 141, 237-9, 241, 243, 335; and nuclear power, 205, 211-2, 217; car industry, 259-61, 265-6, 268; and Information Technology, 275-6, 278-9
Jenkins, Roy, 59, 67
Joseph, Sir Keith, 14
Joyce, P.L., 109

Katrak, H., 243
Kent, 178, 180, 182, 195

Keynesianism, 148, 235, 250, 324-5, 334, 338; Keynesian principles, 14, 64; Keynesians, 55, 67, 73-4, 308
Kilpatrick, A., 33-7, 314-5
Kirby, M.W., 312
Kokxhoorn, N., 81
Komanoff, C., 226

Labour militancy, 29-37, 41
Labour Party, 30, 45, 170, 188, 252, 307, 311, 325, 328-9
Latin America, 85, 90, 114
Laissez-faire, 148-9, 161
Lawson, T., 33-7, 314-5
Lawther, William, 182
Lazonick, W., 35
Leicestershire coalfield, 296-7
Lend-lease, 43
Levene, Peter, 249
Levy, H., 251
Liberal Party, 307, 311
Libya, 87
Livingstone, Ken, 328
Lloyd George, David, 310
Lloyds Bank, 124
London Clearing Banks, 141
London Industrial Strategy, 328
London Suppliers Group, 220
Longstreth, F., 65
Lucas, 273

MacDonald, Ramsay, 12, 55, 57
Maddock, Sir Ieuen, 239, 242-3
Mandatory Import Programme, 85
Manhattan Project, 217-8
Manpower Services Commission, 18
Marshall, Walter, 205, 215
Marshall Aid, 57
Marx, Karl, 101, 245, 303-4; Marxist approach, 245; Marxist theory, 36, 152, 330
Maurer, H., 216
Mercury, 162
Mexico, 260-1, 264
Middle East, 84-5
Midland Bank, 124
Miliband, Ralph, 330
'Military Industrial Complex', 204

Miners' Federation of Great Britain, 301-3, 307, 309-10, 314-5
Mining Research and Development Establishment, 282-4
Ministry of Defence, 246-7, 249-50
Ministry of Technology, 280
Mintz, N., 113
Mirow, K., 216
Mitterrand, F., 325
Mobil, 84
Mondism, 311, 315
Monetarism, 9, 65, 324-5
Motorola, 278, 280
Multinational corporations, 10, 12, 14, 21, 27-9, 34, 47-8, 81-120, 139, 242, 247, 326, 331-2; and nuclear power, 203-10, 214, 216-8, 229, 231; and arms industry, 247-51; and car industry, 265-8, 272; and Information Technology, 282-4

Nairn, T., 62-6, 71-2, 75
National Buses, 164
National Coal Board, 151, 154, 162, 167-8, 171-6, 178-81, 183-5, 187, 190-6, 223, 226, 282-4, 287
National Economic Development Office, 17, 19-20, 242-3, 272, 275, 279
National Enterprise Board, 18, 157-8, 280
National Freight Corporation, 164
National Health Service, 118
Nationalisation, 17-8, 44, 47-8, 57, 61, 87, 113-6, 195, 330-1; nationalised industries, 147-65, 167-72
National Nuclear Corporation, 209, 217
'National Plan', 17-8
National Power Loading Agreement, 180-1, 183, 187
National Provincial Bank, 124, 126
National Research Development Corporation, 158
National Union of Mineworkers, 171, 176, 180, 182, 184-5, 187-8, 195-6
National Westminster Bank, 124
Nautilus, 216

Needham, J., 251
Netherlands, 25-6, 92
'New Imperialism', 72
New Left Review, 72
New Right, 14-5
New Technology, 19-21, 35, 38, 128
'New Unionism', 34
New York, 35, 45, 67, 78, 136
Nissan, 263
North Atlantic Treaty Organisation, 236-7
Northern Engineering Industries, 206-7, 215-6
North Sea oil, 88-9
Nuclear power, 47, 81, 203-31

OECD, 90, 238, 243, 245
Oil industry, 81-9
'Operation Robot', 60, 68
Organisation of Petroleum Exporting Countries, 87-8

Panic, M., 109
Papadopoulos, R., 225
Pavitt, K., 242
Peugeot, 263, 265
Plan for Coal, 30
Plessey, 278
Poland, 285, 287, 296
Post Office, 151, 164
Potter, W.C., 211
Poulantzas, N., 330
Pratten, C., 23
Privatisation, 18
Production and Productivity Bulletin, 190, 192
Provissiero, M., 113

Racal, 247-9
Reid Commission, 171; Report, 292, 313
Renault, 258-9, 263, 268
Roe, A.V., 250
Rolls Royce, 18, 158, 248; and Associates Ltd., 216-7
Royal Commissions: on royalties and the coal industry (1890), 290-2, 294; on mining safety (1938), 306
Royal Dockyards, 246

Royal Ordnance Factories, 246, 248
Rubinstein, W.D., 72
Ruhr, 287; French occupation of, 308
Russia, 83
Ruder Report, 270-2

Sampson, A., 81
Samuel Report, 293, 310; and Commission, 310
Sankey Report, 292; and Commission, 309-10
Saunders, C., 242
Scargill, Arthur, 184
Schumacher, E., 173
Science and the Nation, 252
Scott Report, 292
Scottish coalfield, 133, 178, 182, 195, 294-6
Sealink, 162
Sedgemore, B., 215, 227
Servan-Schreiber, J.J., 119
'Seven Sisters', 84, 86
Shell, 84
Shonfield, A., 67
STC, 278
Siemens, 20
Singh, Ajit, 25
Sizewell, 213-7, 225-7, 230
Socal, 84
'Social Contract', 30, 187
Socialist economies, 46
Society of British Aircraft Constructors, 250
Soete, L., 243
South Africa, 284
South East Asia, 101
South Korea, 16, 26, 261, 335
South Wales coalfield, 182, 184, 195, 294, 299-300, 303-4
Soviet Union, 118, 218-9
Spain, 16, 212, 265-6
Standard Oil, 82
State credit, 46
State debt, 42-4
Sterling Area, 45, 65, 67, 78
Sterling crises, 74
Stopford, J.M., 106, 111-2
Stout, D., 24, 36
Sweden, 25-6, 96, 212, 238, 260, 266

Switzerland, 92, 141, 205, 211-2, 238

Taiwan, 16, 26
Talbot, 265-7, 272
Texaco, 84
Texas Instruments, 278
Thatcher, M., 16, 56, 328-30; Thatcher governments, 9, 12, 14, 18, 20, 58-9, 147, 247, 333; Thatcherism, 18, 147, 329
'Third World', 16, 43, 46, 213, 264-5, 323
Toyota, 258, 263
Trident missiles, 237, 244

United Nations, 117
United Scientific Holdings, 249
United States of America, 22-3, 25-8, 43, 46, 64, 81-2, 84-92, 95-118, 132, 139-40, 236-7, 243, 323; and nuclear power, 204-5, 211-2, 214, 217-21, 228; car industry, 260-61, 265-7; and Information Technology, 275-6, 278-9, 281-2

Vaupel, J.W., 116
Vauxhall, 265-7
Vernon, R., 101-2, 105
Volkswagen, 259, 263, 268
Volvo, 265-7

Warwickshire coalfield, 296-7
Weinstock, A., Lord, 215
Welfare State, 12, 30
Western Electric, 278
Westinghouse, 212-4, 216
Westland, 248
Westminster Bank, 124
Whitehall, 62, 77
White Paper on Employment (1940), 14
Wilberforce Enquiry, 186
Williams, M.L., 114, 302
Williamson, H.F. *et al.*, 81
Wilson, Harold, 171; Wilson governments, 55, 57, 59, 64
Wilson Committee, 135

Yorkshire coalfield, 182, 184, 195